THIS IS OUR SCHOOL!

This Is Our School!

Race and Community Resistance to School Reform

Hava Rachel Gordon

NEW YORK UNIVERSITY PRESS

New York

NEW YORK UNIVERSITY PRESS
New York
www.nyupress.org

References to Internet websites (URLs) were accurate at the time of writing. Neither the author nor New York University Press is responsible for URLs that may have expired or changed since the manuscript was prepared.

Library of Congress Cataloging-in-Publication Data
Names: Gordon, Hava Rachel, 1974–   author.
Title: This is our school! : race and community resistance to school reform /
Hava Rachel Gordon.
Description: New York : NYU Press, [2021] | Includes bibliographical references and index.
Identifiers: LCCN 2020029786 (print) | LCCN 2020029787 (ebook) |
ISBN 9781479848317 (cloth) | ISBN 9781479890057 (paperback) |
ISBN 9781479843633 (ebook other) | ISBN 9781479811403 (ebook)
Subjects: LCSH: Educational equalization—United States. | Educational change—
United States. | Education—Aims and objectives—United States. | Community and
school—United States.
Classification: LCC LC213.2 .G68 2021 (print) | LCC LC213.2 (ebook) | DDC
379.2/60973—dc23
LC record available at https://lccn.loc.gov/2020029786
LC ebook record available at https://lccn.loc.gov/2020029787

New York University Press books are printed on acid-free paper, and their binding materials are chosen for strength and durability. We strive to use environmentally responsible suppliers and materials to the greatest extent possible in publishing our books.

Manufactured in the United States of America

10 9 8 7 6 5 4 3 2 1

Also available as an ebook

This book is dedicated to my late husband, Jason Oliver McKain. Jason was a movement organizer, and his fighting spirit and sharp wit are all over this project. He was our giant-slayer. We keep you alive in our memories, Jason, and we love you forever and always.

CONTENTS

Introduction

In the spring of 2018, news audiences across the United States were riveted by a succession of teachers' strikes that rocked the country. After a surprisingly successful teachers' strike in West Virginia compelled the state government to raise teachers' wages, teachers union mobilizations in several other red states began to follow suit. In Oklahoma, Arizona, and several other states, teachers turned up en masse to their state capitols demanding not only raises and better job benefits, but also more state investment in public schooling. At the dawn of 2019, other teachers' strikes in blue states followed. This resistance is significant, and comes on the heels of nearly three decades of state divestment in education and the rise of the modern era of school reform. Although this collective teacher resistance has been stunning, and has demonstrated the vast opposition to neoliberal cuts to public education and the workers who toil within it, it is not the only form of resistance against decades of neoliberal assaults on public education. Just as these strikes were gaining momentum, communities across the country have been mobilizing to opt out of standardized testing, oust police from schools, reform suspension policies, expand access to healthy foods in schools, and agitate for more school funding, among other educational justice goals. These mobilizations—especially as they unfold in a single US city, Denver, Colorado—are the subject of this book.

Denver was the first school district outside the South to undergo court-ordered desegregation in 1973. In the decades that have followed this mandated desegregation, the movement to reform, privatize, and corporatize public schooling has radically reshaped the landscape of public education in Denver. School reform experimentation in Colorado's largest school district has earned accolades from national reform organizations and think tanks, while also resulting in the resegregation of public schools and one of the starkest class and racial disparities in student achievement in the nation.[1] The context for school reform in

1

Denver Public Schools (DPS) is also a total redesign of the city itself: over the last two decades, Denver has become a hot spot for urban development and population growth. The city has become a much more expensive place to live and work. The local construction industry has raced to build luxury condos as the city strategizes to attract and accommodate the influx of wealthy young professionals in healthcare and technology industries. Meanwhile, DPS serves just under 100,000 students, 65 percent of whom qualify for free and reduced lunch. Just over half of DPS students are Latinx, 13 percent are Black, and nearly one-quarter of DPS students are White. The school system has become a centerpiece for elite urban "revitalization" and development, and a battleground for urban livability and racial and economic justice from below.

The modern era of neoliberal school reform began with the report "A Nation at Risk" and was solidified in the George W. Bush administration's No Child Left Behind Act (NCLB).[2] NCLB brought neoliberal reform to the center of education policy, and provided the impetus for accountability standards to become the carrot and stick in the game of educational improvement. In turn, these reforms have prompted community mobilizations and resistances that extend beyond the teachers' strikes of 2018–2019. Studying neoliberal school reform through the lens of social movements allows us to gain a bottom-up rather than a top-down perspective, a perspective that can critically analyze how resistance, like that which we witnessed in the teachers' strikes, bubbles up from the lived experiences of people whose lives and fates (whether they be teachers, students, or neighborhood residents) are tied to schools. Rather than focusing on neoliberal education reform from a macro-level policy perspective, a bottom-up perspective allows us to understand how neoliberal reform is carried out in specific places and through specific political alliances. These specificities help to explain why school reform, though ruled by neoliberal ideology, looks different across various contexts as soon as it contends with grassroots movements. This perspective also allows us to better understand how neoliberal education reform impacts different groups of people across race- and class-divided neighborhoods.

Furthermore, grassroots movement victories—whether they make headlines or receive scant media attention—also reveal the extent to which community organizing can meaningfully steer neoliberal reform toward community ends. As importantly, by understanding the setbacks of these movements we have an opportunity to understand why and how community organizing *fails* to reclaim public institutions from neoliberal forces. The major focus of this book is not just on singular movements as they take on the behemoth of neoliberal reform, but also on the relationships *between* different sectors of the educational justice movement, or what scholars term "intra-movement" dynamics.[3]

This book gives special attention to how racial and class inequalities shape these dynamics. As the late sociologist Colin Barker reminded us, "The 'class struggle' occurs not only *between* movements and their antagonists, but also *within* them: their ideas, forms of organization and repertoires of contention are all within their opponents' 'strategic sights.'"[4] Intra-movement class and race struggles, as they play out in local coalition politics, provide us with clues as to why public opinion favors strong neighborhood schools over school choice, for example, and yet complicated systems of choice still reign in cities like Denver.[5] The gap between public opinion and actual neoliberal education policy is only partially explained by the overwhelming strength of the elite neoliberal reform movement. The other key factors in explaining this gap are the intra-movement dynamics that shape visions for educational justice from below. The way movement organizers determine how *and with whom* they fight for their visions of educational justice also determines the direction that school reform takes in specific urban contexts.

In the popular press, the current battle over school reform appears to be polarized between two clear camps. On the one hand, there are the "innovative" reformers who shake up school districts through charter school expansion, school closures, and experimental systems of tying teacher pay to student test scores. They remake city school boards or obliterate them altogether; replace veteran teachers with Teach for America teachers who are well-educated but not credentialed; and claim to work in the best interests of children who have long been failed by the public education system.[6] On the other hand, there are the teachers unions that rally against their eroding power, wages, and job security, and defend their profession against the market assault on education. At times, this popular media coverage shifts to other community struggles over school reform, especially when these struggles are connected to teachers' mobilizations. For example, in Chicago the 2012 Chicago teachers union strikes emerged as a result of the powerful coalition between anti-reform teachers (Caucus of Rank and File Educators, or CORE) and racial justice community organizations.[7] In these moments of labor-community alliance, a few media outlets gave us glimpses into the racialized nature of school reform struggles. For the most part, however, these racialized dimensions are vastly underreported. In Chicago, most of the teachers and community mobilizations were co-organized by African American and Latinx low-income residents who launched an explicitly antiracist agenda against a school reform movement they publicly framed as White supremacist and corporatist. Some media picked this up, though many outlets did not.[8]

In the wake of the 2018 teachers' strikes, however, major news outlets mostly emphasized the struggle of teachers fighting for their jobs in an era of political attacks on public sector workers.[9] The media emphasis on these battles for education primarily frames the movement against school reform as one that is fundamentally about labor rights. This framing, in turn, fuels reform advocates' critiques of teachers' resistance as merely about self-interest. The reform movement uses this to counter that reformers are the ones fighting for *children*, especially low-income Black and Latinx children, who have long been relegated to substandard education. They stand against the teachers unions, who they argue represent self-interested adults rather than children's rights to better educations.[10]

While teachers' strikes are undoubtedly a leading edge of resistance to neoliberal reform, labor is *not* necessarily the major force that resists an elitist and corporatist school reform movement in specific locations where market-driven reform is negotiated and contested. At the time of the landmark teacher walkouts and strikes in Wisconsin in 2011, Chicago in 2012, and the various state teachers' strikes across the United States in May 2018, African American, Latinx, and White progressive community collectives across cities in the United States have been organizing to protest the closure of their neighborhood schools, transform punitive discipline policies, opt out of standardized testing, prevent co-locations of charter schools inside their neighborhood schools, institute community-responsive school board members and school leaders in their districts, promote culturally responsive curricula and nutritious food in schools, and advocate for more school nurses, social workers, and counselors instead of school resource officers. Many of these smaller-scale, community battles rarely make the nightly news, yet they fundamentally shape the local battlegrounds of school reform. They even bolster the successes of teacher mobilizations, as in the case of the Chicago teachers union strike and the 2019 Los Angeles teachers union strike.[11]

In this book, I will argue that contrary to what is portrayed in the mainstream media, resistance to neoliberal education reform is much more varied and more localized than teachers unions and communities of color on one hand, and pro-market reformer elites on the other. *One aim of this book is to document and analyze the various struggles of collectives that resist market-driven reform in order to outline the diversity of these movements.* It is a diversity that is often left out of mainstream media coverage, yet these grassroots struggles drive urban school reform politics in specific cities. Various activists resist school choice, school closures, privatization, and other neoliberal reforms, and their struggles advance important critiques of and visions for schooling that move beyond those articulated and demanded by striking teachers. I use Denver as an example of this localized urban context of movement struggle over school reform policies and practices in order to demonstrate the many community battles over school reform—and the mark these battles make—upon one single, rapidly changing city.

Another aim of this book is to evaluate the relative success and failure of these movements in reshaping local education policy and reclaiming public education. Who wins and who loses in the battle to shape public education? What is the impact of these resistance movements? How hegemonic *is* the national market-driven reform movement? Which elements of neoliberal reform are more resistant to community pushback, and which are expansive enough to incorporate community demands? The key to answering these questions lies in understanding the potential for local resistance movements to band together and join into powerful coalitions. As education scholar Pauline Lipman has demonstrated, the Chicago teachers' strikes of 2012 were emboldened and supported by a successful coalition of labor and local neighborhood and community justice organizations.[12] In this book I will argue that despite the widespread resistance to market-driven school reform, and despite the potential for local movements to harness neoliberal school reform to community ends,[13] movement discourses, strategies, ideologies, and frames often fall along the same racial and class lines that also divide diverse communities in gentrifying cities. These racial and class tensions, coupled with the institutionalization of grassroots movements, often prevent the kinds of powerful cross-racial and cross-class alliances that could more effectively counter neoliberal agendas. Ultimately, grassroots movements in specific cities *do* matter in determining the shape of education reform in specific locales. Sometimes they even matter *more* than teachers' labor struggles, especially in cities where labor has not effectively coalesced with community organizations, and especially during the long stretches between teachers' strikes and labor movement abeyance. But because movement coalitions fracture or simply never materialize, their victories are limited. This is why the elite neoliberal reform movement can maintain hegemony in urban school reform hot spots like Denver *despite* the presence of a broad and diverse community resistance.

At the same time, the reform movement is actually advanced by reform advocates who form tenuous coalitions with other community activists around specific reform goals.[14] These coalitions help to move reform forward, despite widespread popular resistance. In this book I spotlight Denver in order to highlight these partnerships, tensions, and ruptures between movements. Rather than representing a polarized standoff between elite reformers on one hand and teachers on the other, Denver's case reveals that local elite reform movements can operate by simultaneously marginalizing some community activists and welcoming others. Although this complex landscape of alliance means that some community activists can effectively force neoliberal policy to adopt progressive stances for educational justice, this also poses significant challenges for broader social movement coalitions to effectively counter the hegemony—and more specifically the *racial dispossession associated with gentrification*—that is brought on by neoliberal urban policy and practice. In this sense, Denver provides the perfect case study for understanding the extent to which grassroots organizing can counter neoliberal pressures, and under what social conditions it falls short.

A Focus on Movement Coalitions

Although it is vital to understand the national context of neoliberal education reform and its rise to preeminence (further described in chapter 1), critical scholars often miss the importance of local mobilizations that animate the lived realities of neoliberal education reform in the urban context. In ignoring these mobilizations, we miss a host of crucial questions about how neoliberal education reform is articulated, contested, and implemented in specific cities. These questions include the following: *Who* are the local movers and shakers of reform who champion educational privatization? Where do they come from, and how did they enter the movement? What is their racial consciousness, and how do they think about racial justice, their own privilege, and most importantly, the children they are trying to "save"? What explains their outreach to select low-income community collectives, as well as their relative insulation from other communities' critiques? And how do we make sense of the sometimes surprising reformer-community partnerships that propel specific neoliberal education reform initiatives forward? How much do the agents of neoliberal reform need community buy-in, and how do they secure it?

At the same time, we also need to understand more about the potential for grassroots movements to shape the direction of reform from the ground up. What are the possibilities for social justice movements to expand the neoliberal imagination? How do different constituencies view educational *justice* in relation to education *reform*? What does the neighborhood school mean to rapidly changing Black and Latinx community networks, and what does it mean to the mostly White gentry with young children who are usurping the public institutions and spaces in these neighborhoods? What is the potential for these movements to coalesce, and how does racial and class power and privilege drive a wedge in these coalitions? There is also the latent power in formal community justice organizations, especially in major cities like Denver with strong social movement histories. In contrast to more loosely organized neighborhood collectives, what potential does the institutionalized movement context hold for grassroots activists to gain a seat at the table with elite reformers and meaningfully participate in school reform conversations? Importantly, how does their nonprofit status also constrain these players in their efforts to more forcefully bring racial and educational justice issues into reformer visions for urgent reform?

This book builds on existing studies of how resistance movements emerge to counter the negative impacts of neoliberal reform.[15] These existing studies teach us that although neoliberal ideologies are hegemonic in education policy and urban development, this hegemony is never total, nor is it uncontested. Indeed, the force of resistance movements may very well slow or buffer the impact of neoliberal reform on even the most marginalized communities. However, we must seek to understand what stands in the way of even greater victories for these movements. How can such a broad tapestry of resistance exist, yet still fail to mitigate the forces of neoliberalism? Of course, part of this answer lies in the elite power of the neoliberal reform movement. Certainly there are money and political power behind this movement, and these essential elite forces cannot be understated. But the other part of this answer requires a more complex and critical assessment of resistance movements themselves, not only to critically assess their weaknesses, but also to better understand what these weaknesses reveal about the political landscape on which they organize and the historical moment in which they develop.

In this book I argue that it is only by examining the local mobilizations over school reform—and specifically how these manifest in coalition politics—that we can determine why and how neoliberal education policy takes hold in specific places, in specific forms, and at specific moments. Neoliberal education reform does not passively rain down from above; it is pushed by an organized movement of elite reform advocates, and is resisted by both newly emerging neighborhood groups and established community organizations that spring from older, localized legacies of resistance. Although the reform movement is anchored in big business and big money,[16] it is also moved forward by committed advocates on the ground, and at times, through movement coalitions. These coalitions push for educational changes that could be potentially progressive and transformative, but so often end up serving exclusionary visions that result in racial displacement and dispossession. Instead of simply looking at one movement as it hits the ground (e.g., how reform advocates organize on the ground to push forward reform), or one movement as it resists reform (e.g., those who are most displaced by reform), we must understand the local landscape of organizing to determine to what extent grassroots movements can challenge neoliberalism, and where and why they fall short. The secret to this success or failure is how effectively resistance movements coalesce and cultivate shared power by joining forces against neoliberalism and the continued racism and classism on which it relies.[17] In an era in which White supremacist education policy masquerades as race-neutral and even antiracist, coalitions of resistance that are at their very roots antiracist and multiracial hold great potential to successfully unveil school reform's neoliberal mechanisms of inequality and advance more just visions for antiracist and equitable schooling. But in which instances do these movements coalesce? And what explains their failure to coalesce? As I will show, multiple movements in the same city simultaneously attempt to influence the pace and shape of school reform. These movements stand in relation not only to the hegemony of neoliberal reform, but also to each other. These movements *matter*, and sometimes they claim victory over certain elements of the neoliberal paradigm. Yet despite their shared resistance to neoliberal school reform, these movements also reflect the same racial and class divides that characterize the larger urban politics in which they live and in which their children learn. These racial and class tensions, coupled with the institutionalization of grassroots movements (also shaped by neoliberal forces), often prevent the kinds of powerful cross-racial and cross-class alliances that could more effectively counter neoliberal agendas.

Chapter Overview

Chapter 1, "The National Context: Neoliberal Education Reform, Race, and Resistance," outlines the national and local contexts of school reform. I demystify the term "neoliberalism" in order to unpack *which* facets of neoliberalism, as these hit local communities, conspire against racial justice and inspire collective mobilization around educational issues. I pay particular attention to the role of race and racism in neoliberal education reform as these play out in the rise of standardized testing; charter school expansion; systems of urban school choice; gentrification, residential displacement, and dispossession; as well as the racial rhetoric of neoliberal reform and its implications for justice, diversity, and inclusion. After outlining these specific racialized facets of neoliberal school reform, I turn to the particularities of Denver as a compelling case study of reform and resistance.

Chapter 2, "The Reformers: Race, Privilege, and Saving Children from Disaster," begins this examination of local school reform activism by focusing on the reform advocates who are responsible for bringing "reform" into being in Denver. These are the local movers and shakers of urban school reform, the self-described "reformers." Rather than viewing reform as a faceless market-driven force that shapes education policy from above, I illustrate reform as it is lived through the passion, outrage, and privilege of the local advocates who align themselves with this national (and often elite) movement. They are journalists, principals, school board members, district representatives, foundation officers, consultants, and representatives of national nonprofit organizations. They strive to forge relationships with other activists in the city in order to push forward reforms and effectively frame educational justice issues to the public. In this chapter, I argue that it is vital to understand local reformers' racial consciousness and their perceptions of community and parental value in order to understand the racialized dimensions of neoliberal urban school reform. Drawing on the narratives of these reformers, I illustrate the guiding principles of their movement; their racial consciousness and the ways they actively translate market reforms into social justice and civil rights rhetoric; and their reliance on double standards as the policies they champion work to escalate racial and class segregation in the name of urgently saving low-income youth of color from broken schools (and presumably "broken" families). In this chapter, I highlight the ways reform advocates assign value to other community activists as either worthy allies in the pursuit of radical reforms or unworthy and illegitimate defenders of the status quo. I demonstrate how this partial valuation of some community activists over others accelerates Black and Latinx community dispossession, even as it opens a door for forging broader coalitions with other educational justice activists in the city.

Chapter 3, "The Dispossessed: Neighborhood Activists Beating Back Gentrification," examines the devastating impact of neoliberal education reform experimentation in African American and Latinx communities in Denver, those who are the most marginalized and delegitimized in the reformer imagination. In this chapter, I outline the ways these communities experience reform experiments in tandem with gentrification. This chapter explores how school reform, as a racial project[18] and a settler colonialist project, operates as a lived experience for Black and Latinx low-income residents. This chapter also details the ways these communities mobilize to fight neoliberal school reform in their neighborhoods, as well as the steps reformers take to delegitimize their oppositional movements and marginalize their voices in school reform debates. I give special attention to school choice, new discipline policies, and duplicitous reformer engagement processes as the most significant dimensions of neoliberal education reform that impact these community members and inspire their resistance. I then discuss how their fight for comprehensive neighborhood schools stands as the antidote to the community fragmentation and gentrification that school reform facilitates. This chapter highlights three community organizations that rise up to take back neighborhood schools and fight dispossession: the African American Parent Project (AAPP), the Community Education Collective (CEC), and Democrats for Educational Justice (DEJ). These non-institutionalized organizations—which operate without clear meeting spaces or 501(c)3 status—engineer new modes of information sharing, attempt to take back community institutions beyond the school, and organize to harness the power of the vote. This chapter evaluates their non-institutionalized resistance within the larger context of gentrification and in a city in which media outlets, foundations, and other local institutions overwhelmingly align with the corporate reform movement.

Like chapter 3, chapter 4, "Fragile Alliances: Cross-Racial Solidarity and Conflict in Community Claims to the Neighborhood School," examines non-institutionalized local networks of neighborhood activists who are fighting for comprehensive neighborhood schools and against neoliberal school choice. In contrast to the previous chapter, however, this chapter examines the fight for neighborhood schools among the more affluent gentry who settle into traditional Latinx neighborhoods on the other side of town, and who are usurping public institutions and staking their claim to the neighborhood schools. Although traditionally the beneficiaries of choice and privatization, these neighborhood activists rally for diverse schools and take risks to give up some of their educational advantage for the sake of creating vibrant neighborhood institutions that work for *all* families. Despite their oppositional stance to corporate reform and their cherished value of community diversity, I argue that ironically the risks they take to commit their energies, resources, and children to low-performing neighborhood schools are undergirded by unexamined racial and class privilege that in the end alienate Latinx allies and contribute to their movement demobilization. This chapter also explores the role of racial and class privilege in producing limited social movement successes for these activists, successes that are not enjoyed by the Black and Latinx neighborhood schools activists portrayed in chapter 2 who express many of the same criticisms of neoliberal education reform and the same community calls for neighborhood schools.

Chapter 5, "No Permanent Enemies, No Permanent Allies: The Politics of Reformer-Community Nonprofit Partnerships," compares the strategies, successes, and setbacks of the non-institutionalized neighborhood networks detailed in the previous chapters with those of the activists who leverage their work from inside formal nonprofit community justice organizations. These formal organizations, rooted in local racial justice legacies and straining under the weight of neoliberal pressures, interface with elite reformers and forge tenuous alliances with them around specific reform initiatives. Like reformers, these organizations see this as an unusually open historical moment to make changes to a school system long plagued by racial and class inequalities. Propelled by their own autonomous racial justice agendas, these nonprofit organizations are able to organize broader networks of activists from across the city to push reformers to include new discipline policies, more equitable school funding and transportation policies, and a more just stance toward a growing immigrant student population in their calls to radically reform schools. Using the leverage of the funded nonprofit, these activists challenge the color-blind rhetoric of the neoliberal reform movement and propel powerful reformers to privilege racial justice issues in local and state reforms in ways that their non-institutionalized counterparts cannot. Especially for those who are the most marginalized and objectified in neoliberal reform rhetoric—the youth of color who are the very objects of reformers' "rescue" efforts—the nonprofit context provides a route to political power for youth who would otherwise be shut out of school reform debates. However, reformers find these alliances very valuable to their own efforts to gain community buy-in, and soon these alliances become constraining for the nonprofit activists who walk the fine line between partnering with reformers and holding them accountable. In order to keep their seat at the reformers' table, these activists struggle with tamping down their racial justice messages and their critiques of neoliberal reform.

In the conclusion, I bring together the various strands of theorizing throughout these chapters in order to illustrate the potential impact of local social movement organizing on urban school reform. I elucidate the common role that race and class privilege and power play in the elite reformer movement and the gentrifier movement that opposes it. I also highlight the ways the neoliberal nonprofit context and institutionalization of social movements enables activists to stretch the neoliberal imagination, while also forcing these activists to push more radical educational justice visions to the "backstage" of their organizations. I then move on to analyze the significance of the working-class African American and Latinx fight against school choice, school closure, and reform experimentation, and what this means for neighborhood mobilization against neoliberal school reform as a tool for gentrification. In this conclusion I also offer an analysis of the ways racial and class inequities, as well as the neoliberal forces that give rise to new forms of these inequities, determine the constellation of movement alliances in the city and shape the direction of school reform politics. While these neoliberal forces in part determine school reform and the resistance to it, they do not wholly determine this story. I conclude the book with lessons learned about how broad but fragmented resistances can more effectively combine into deeper antiracist and economically just coalitions that hold the power to take back schools and neighborhoods from elite market forces.

1

The National Context

Neoliberal Education Reform, Race, and Resistance

The critical literature on neoliberal education reform is vast. In this chapter, I highlight those reform trends in particular that have inspired community resistance and mass mobilization in urban reform hot spots like Denver. Certainly, not every facet of neoliberal education reform elicits grassroots resistance. For example, the abstract notion that neoliberal education reform turns citizens into educational consumers does not necessarily inspire mass resistance, even though critical scholars might highlight the dangers of this larger shift toward educational consumerism in society. Rather, it is *how* this shift from citizen to consumer manifests in people's everyday lives that determines the rise of social action. Relatedly, the reform advocates I portray in this book who push reform forward do not identify themselves as "neoliberals," nor do they use the language of "neoliberalism," even though neoliberalism cannot advance without their advocacy of market reforms.

At the same time, although this book is focused on the local context of neoliberal reform and community resistance, the case of Denver is not completely localized. The various ways people experience and contend with the forces of neoliberalism are nested in larger national (and even international) forces. This section demystifies the relationship between neoliberal school reform and racism by foregrounding critical race perspectives on school reform; maps the larger national trends that have shaped the direction of reform in Denver; and traces reform's disproportionate impact on communities of color.

Modern Education Reform and Resistance: From No Child Left Behind to Betsy DeVos

After the desegregation efforts following *Brown v. Board of Education*— the cornerstone Supreme Court ruling of the civil rights movement that established that "separate" is inherently unequal—the 1970s, 1980s, and 1990s began to see a rollback of desegregation mandates and a retrenchment of educational inequity. Writer Jonathan Kozol's classic book *Savage Inequalities* documented these lived class and race inequalities in several major US cities. His book stood as a shameful reminder that one of the iconic Supreme Court cases of the civil rights era had been, in just a few short decades, eviscerated by the persistent currents of racism that led not only to a national racial resegregation of our public school system, but also to the continuing segregation of neighborhoods across the major cities in the United States.

At the turn of the millennium and in the context of a globalizing economy, national policy became hyper-focused on education as a route to maintaining global dominance in the face of deindustrialization and the formidable specter of emerging superpower economies like China. No Child Left Behind (NCLB), which was signed into law in 2002, increased the role of the federal government in holding schools accountable for student performance. If states did not comply with the law, they risked losing Title I money. NCLB required states to bring all students to a level of proficiency by 2013–2014, though it gave states the latitude to decide what "proficiency" should mean.[1] States were required to test students annually and provide data to the federal government, including specific data on English language learners, special education students, students of color, and low-income students. If schools did not make adequate yearly progress (AYP) for two years in a row, they could be subject to severe sanctions such as closure, turnaround, and loss of funds. NCLB was as much an attempt to recapture US dominance on the global stage as it was an attempt to provide quality education to every child.[2] It opened the floodgates for a national reliance on standardized testing that despite its rhetoric about "accountability" and "equity" remains a key project in what education scholar Wayne Au calls "neoliberal multiculturalism." According to Au, standardized testing, as a facet of neoliberal multiculturalism, masks the existence of continuing systemic racial inequalities in education by masquerading as an objective measure of learning that will bring equity to all children and families. It deploys civil rights rhetoric even as testing's consequences disproportionately impact low-income students, students of color, English language learners, and special education students most severely.[3] NCLB and the development of standardized testing deserve special discussion in the modern history of education reform in the United States, since this was the bedrock for a host of neoliberal reforms in education to follow. Bush's NCLB Act galvanized bipartisan support for school reform and drew together various interests in the pursuit of national educational improvement.

For developers and city planners, education reform became a key ingredient of city improvement and "urban renewal," and the movement for school accountability escaped the bounds of education and became part and parcel of the larger movement to revitalize crumbling and neglected urban cores.[4] The administration of Barack Obama continued to put education reform at the center of national policy, appointing Arne Duncan as the head of the Department of Education. With this appointment, Obama brought to the national stage Duncan's brand of educational improvement in Chicago, a city that now stands as a national model for the reform movement. The Chicago model of reform has been widely criticized for closing schools, allowing business elites to take control over the city's housing and education systems, and displacing poor students and families of color.[5] In the Trump era, some of the basic elements of the reformist agenda intensified under education secretary Betsy DeVos. DeVos aimed to expand school choice and voucher programs, as well as private schooling, religious schooling, and virtual schooling. She famously referred to traditional public schooling as "a dead end," echoing the reform movement's criticism of the public sector as "broken" and even "irreparable," and therefore in desperate need of market solutions.

The continuity of market-based reform across the pendulum swings of Republican and Democratic presidential administrations—from Bush to Obama to Trump—signals that the rise of school reform over the last few decades has become a tool for urban development, national development, and capital accumulation in ways that transcend party lines. As education policy expert David Hursh notes, this continuity in support for neoliberal school reform across political parties represents a deeper societal shift at the turn of the millennium, from one that reflects a view of social institutions as deliberately democratic, to one that reflects a view of social institutions as markets rather than public goods.[6] In this same vein, education scholar Michael Apple argues that neoliberalism is now *the* hegemonic ideology pervasive throughout educational policies and practices.[7] This era of education reform is marked by a collusion of land developers, private companies, urban revivalists, major foundations, hedge fund managers, and policy makers. Perhaps there is no better figurehead that represents this collusion than Betsy DeVos. She is the secretary of education who has never attended public schools and has never sent her own children to public schools, nor has she ever been trained as a teacher or held an administrative position in a school. And yet it is her very "outsider" status as a billionaire charter schools advocate that makes her qualified to shake up a presumably bureaucratic and broken educational system.

Although education reformer figureheads like Arne Duncan have vociferously spoken out against DeVos in particular as Trump's choice for education secretary, the Obama-era version of education reform represented by Duncan also retained at its core a welcoming of such affluent outsiders into its highest ranks. The figure of the educational outsider suggests a vision of educational improvement that is delivered by successful market executives rather than education professionals, let alone the very communities who are served by public schooling. The entrance of the successful market executive who innovates a public school system just as one can innovate new products or services in the market is at the heart of this new era of education reform, and represents the creep of the market into the public sector. The impact of the marketization of education has precipitated huge shifts within education, and has prompted broad community mobilization that includes, but extends far beyond, teacher resistance. These mobilizations have tackled the various elements of neoliberal education reform described in this chapter.

Standardized Testing and Accountability

The No Child Left Behind Act signed by George W. Bush stipulated that states develop uniform standards of educational performance as measured by standardized tests. This followed on the heels of Ronald Reagan's support for ending desegregation in the 1980s.[8] Its very beginnings stem from a concern about global competitiveness. Like the earlier "Nation at Risk" report, NCLB argued that public education should be geared toward global competitiveness and job readiness. This bent toward educational economic efficiency is one of the ways public goods like education have been transformed from cornerstones of democratic process and inclusion into mechanisms for national competitiveness. Although discussions of national supremacy are often presented as race-neutral, critical race scholars point out that such discussions, especially in a context of neoliberal globalization, veil a nationalist discourse that is anchored in White supremacy.[9] In this sense, despite calls for better education for *all* US children, NCLB's nationalist vision was a vast departure from the civil rights era's various fights for educational equity, racial justice, and self-determination and community liberation.

NCLB's push to "hold schools accountable" through standardized testing not only provided a path for education to midwife a new era of national competitiveness, it also fortified neoliberalism's emphasis on education as market competition. For neoliberal advocates of NCLB, turning schools into market commodities required a quantifiable rating system to stimulate competition in the educational marketplace.[10] According to this neoliberal ideology, a uniform standard could be created for a new class of education consumers, who would then use their consumer mobility in order to stimulate market innovation and competition. This rationale argued that market innovation and competition would eventually improve educational products. NCLB was the first significant piece of national policy that transformed education into a market product and commodity, and students and their families into educational consumers. According to journalist Nikole Hannah-Jones, this was also the first piece of major legislation to signal the national turn *against* the civil rights-era fight for integration. NCLB imagined that educational equity could be better served by accountability and testing than racial integration.[11] This was no surprise, as NCLB came on the heels of decades of White resistance to civil rights-era desegregation policies in cities across the United States, and a return to school segregation after levels of school integration reached their peak in 1988.

While some school reform critics decry the making of public education into a market, and characterize the accompanying shift from educational citizenship to educational consumption as a general weakening of democracy and a hallmark of neoliberalism,[12] critical race scholars argue that this neoliberal shift also carries specific consequences disproportionately shouldered by communities of color. NCLB and the neoliberal ideology it espoused posited that market consumption could be an equalizing, color-blind force. By providing "objective" data to education consumers, accountability standards could make transparent substandard education and compel poorly functioning schools to improve or face replacement or closure.[13] The market, in effect, would wash out long-standing racial inequalities deepened by the rollback of post–civil rights desegregation laws.

As Hursh and Au have argued, despite the early (and continued) attempts of neoliberal advocates to promote accountability standards as the new frontier of racial equity, high-stakes testing has instead exacerbated racial inequality.[14] Au places recent high-stakes testing as one historical moment in a longer history of educational testing designed to differentiate the national population by race and class.[15] Like the decades of standardized testing before it, NCLB and its flood of standardized tests have professed to test objectively, but hide a White middle-class bias that favors a specific type of cultural capital at odds with those possessed by most low-income communities of color.[16] In this sense, contemporary standardized testing, even that which is well intentioned, cannot be abstracted from a longer racist legacy of standardized testing in the United States. This testing has long functioned as a sorting mechanism for test takers, and unevenly distributes resources and opportunities to different communities based on testing outcomes.[17] Standardized testing, as an educational sorting mechanism, has placed low-income communities and communities of color at a disadvantage.

Education historian and policy analyst Diane Ravitch argues that standardized testing also reflects a deep distrust of teachers' knowledge, expertise, and professionalism, since teachers do not have meaningful opportunities to design tests according to what they actually teach in the classroom.[18] Parents and members of students' broader communities also lack opportunities to weigh in on the content areas of these tests, which instead are developed by major educational for-profit consulting companies.[19] The participation of private companies that stand to reap a profit in the remaking of public education—such as those that together comprise the growing testing industry—is another hallmark of education reform in the neoliberal era.

While critics have long warned of the middle-class biases inherent in standardized testing, NCLB exacerbated this class and racial disadvantage in testing by tying these tests to high-stakes consequences. Testing has always played a role in differentiating the lives of students of color and low-income students, but *high-stakes* testing determines the fates of entire schools, neighborhoods, and teachers. Schools that don't make adequate yearly progress (AYP) face closure, turnaround, and a loss of federal funding. Because standardized tests are more likely a measure of class and racial advantage than objective knowledge, test scores are correlated to class status and levels of racial segregation.[20] This means that lower test scores are typically clustered in underfunded schools where students are already struggling. Thus, underfunded schools serving low-income communities of color are more severely impacted by high-stakes standardized testing. Schools that are shuttered or radically redesigned as a result of high-stakes testing are most often in high-needs neighborhoods.

While reform advocates assert that students are failed by failing schools, and therefore failing schools must be shuttered and replaced, school closures have had a devastating impact on segregated communities. Pauline Lipman, for example, has documented the impact of closures of schools in poor Black neighborhoods in Chicago. This major epicenter of reform was held up as a model of national education reform, and was imported into the Obama administration with the appointment of Arne Duncan—former CEO of Chicago Public Schools—as national education secretary.[21] Although the ideological promise of school closures is that students will be funneled into "better" market choices if their current school is not making adequate yearly progress, the research demonstrates that students from shuttered schools transfer into similarly low-performing schools. Testing, by itself, does not guarantee specific outcomes that will improve the education of low-income students of color.[22] Transportation is not guaranteed when a neighborhood school closes and students need to find another school outside their immediate neighborhood. School districts do not guarantee a seat for these displaced students in a significantly higher-performing school, nor do they guarantee that the receiving school will not be shuttered. Significantly, when a school is closed, teachers lose their jobs. In some cases these teachers are of color and have ties to the community, or know the community outside school. Many have developed caring relationships in ways that Teach for America teachers, who are placed in high-needs schools for a short time, cannot.[23] The displacement of children of color is coupled with the displacement of community-based teachers when a neighborhood school is slated for closure.

Beyond the racialized impacts of school closures, high-stakes testing also narrows the curriculum in already under-resourced schools. As education scholars Eve Tuck and Julie Gorlewski write, "As measures of learning become increasingly standardized, what it means to be an educated person contracts."[24] Arts, physical education, recess, and other essential activities for kids are often cut out of the curriculum when standardized test scores—which assess a very narrow slice of content— determine the fates of teachers, students, and the very schools in which they labor and learn. This narrowing of curriculum is also a hallmark of the economics of neoliberal education reform, a reflection of years of state divestment in education and the growing scarcity of educational resources. Parent-teacher associations (PTAs) in wealthier communities can raise capital to pay for those aspects of the curriculum that are cut from state budgets, including music, arts, and language programs. In already under-resourced and racially segregated schools, PTA programs are less able to fill these gaps caused by state divestment and driven by testing mandates. As a result, low-income students of color are more likely than their White counterparts to receive a test-driven curriculum administrated by non-credentialed instructors rather than by highly trained and experienced professional teachers.

The school closures, teacher layoffs, and student displacement associated with high-stakes testing constitutes the "dispossession" in what geographer David Harvey calls "accumulation by dispossession." The subsequent charterization of the public school system, another hallmark of neoliberal education reform, constitutes the "accumulation" side of the equation: the transfer of community resources and public goods into private hands.

Charter Expansion

Advocates of corporate school reform have long held up New Orleans as a model for national reform, so education policy scholar Kristen Buras's lessons and critiques of post-Katrina reform are instructive for understanding the aims of school reform advocates in cities across the nation.[25] In the immediate wake of Hurricane Katrina, the majority of New Orleans city schools were transformed into charter schools. New Orleans now has the largest proportion of charter schools in any major city in the United States, and the majority of New Orleans students attend independently run charter schools. Journalist Naomi Klein argued that the charterization of New Orleans schools is a prime example of economist Milton Friedman's "shock doctrine" philosophy. Friedman proposed that radical market takeovers of public systems like schools are typically unpopular, and must happen in the wake of a crisis, real or perceived.[26] It is no accident that massive charterization has taken place in the wake of large-scale disasters such as Hurricane Katrina and more recently, Hurricane Maria in Puerto Rico.[27]

Buras examines the role that standardized testing played in the charterization of New Orleans schools. The threshold or "cut point" for school failure and school closure was, in the immediate days that followed Katrina's destruction of the city, set *higher* so that more schools were eligible for closure. Schools that were not deemed "failing" before the hurricane were deemed failing after the disaster, and therefore eligible for charter takeover. Counter to reform advocates' claims that test scores operate to "hold schools accountable" and ensure educational equity for students no matter what their race or socioeconomic status, Buras reports that after schools were taken over by charter companies in New Orleans, the standards and benchmarks for school failure were subsequently *lowered* again, and charters have since been able to operate even with outcomes that score *below* pre-Katrina levels.[28] The story of standardized testing and charterization in New Orleans highlights the moving targets that are accountability standards. The case study of New Orleans demonstrates that accountability and standards, though presented as primary and neutral instruments for educational equity, can shift capriciously in the service of privatization and accumulation. Indeed, in the decades since NCLB, standardized testing has shifted and changed from year to year across the country and various states.

Although some charter schools *do* outperform traditional public schools, and despite pro-charter films like *Waiting for Superman* and *The Lottery*, most charters *do not* outperform traditional public schools. Charters began in the early 1980s as laboratories for innovation aimed at improving traditional public schooling, but later became corporatized models pit *against* traditional public schools.[29] Charters are often run by or subcontracted to educational management organizations (EMOs) that are either private or nonprofit. However, Au notes that just because an EMO is nonprofit, it does not mean that the EMO does not stand to gain wealth from educational disaster and takeover.[30] Certainly, charter school operators make significant salaries; their nonprofit status simply means that they are governed by a board of directors. Although they may be held to the same state standards as traditional public schools, charter schools can operate outside of union contracts, and have more control over their curriculum. One of the most controversial aspects of charter schools is that as market-driven experiments, they market to the public and try to boost their test scores and success profile by selectively admitting specific kinds of students. Charters are much less likely to admit English language learners (ELL) and students with disabilities, while traditional public neighborhood schools must accept the students in a given enrollment zone.[31] Furthermore, charter schools tend to specialize in specific content areas like science or sports and offer narrow curricula; thus they can admit students based on these areas of specialization.[32] As a result, even if these charters are geared toward low-income populations, critics charge that they siphon the families from the higher end of the reduced and free lunch spectrum, leaving the poorest students—those who typically score the lowest on high-stakes standardized tests—to further concentrate in the traditional, under-resourced schools that are so often slated for closure or redesign.

Buras and other scholars have also noted the correlation between charters and the strict disciplinary school cultures that they cultivate inside their schools. Some charters, such as the "no excuses" schools, rely on rigid militaristic and disciplinary cultures for their low-income admits.[33] Although "no excuses" is the charter movement's progressive discursive message to the public that poverty is "no excuse" for low-income students of color *not* to achieve, Garth Stahl notes that in practice the "no excuses" message is a disciplinary mechanism for both students and teachers inside charter schools that hold students and teachers to high standards and enact severe consequences, like teacher firings or "coaching students out" (a euphemism for counseling lower-achieving students to find a different school) if students do not perform well on standardized tests. A host of critical scholars have examined the ways these cultures of discipline institutionalize racism and classism and teach limiting cultural skills that are actually antithetical to college success.[34] In some of these charter schools, students experience joyless educational environments designed according to the same "broken windows" theory used to police low-income communities. Aesthetics of the school (such as lighting and classroom smells) and the behavior of students (including strict school uniforms) are meticulously policed for any small sign of "decay" or disorder that might invite bigger problems down the road.[35] Indeed, charters tend to have high attrition rates even if they boast better graduation rates in their marketing.[36] Charters with militaristic cultures are not the type of educational environments that ready students for the critical thinking that will be demanded of them in higher education. Thus, critical race scholars question how well these schools prepare low-income students of color for college. Additionally, charters are more likely than traditional public schools to have higher teacher turnover and burnout, and rely on non-credentialed teachers who have less teacher training. In his ethnography of working at a high-performing "no excuses" charter school, for example, Stahl observed that the school he worked in actively sought teachers educated at Ivy League schools who did *not* study education, since their charter management organization (CMO) believed that teachers' exposure to standard educational theory would contribute to the "soft bigotry of low expectations" and clash with their "no excuses" philosophy.[37] Thus, trained teachers professionalized in higher education teaching programs are often *not* selected to work at these schools.

Toward the early to mid-1990s, charter school advocates argued that charter schools can and should function as innovative laboratories that cultivate new models of teaching and learning, which can then be imported into failing schools. The push for charters has now morphed as education reform enters another decade in the new millennium. Reform advocates no longer argue that the primary function of charter schools is to innovate new educational models that can be used to resuscitate traditional public schools. As charters proliferate, they become permanent fixtures in the educational market. They overwhelmingly serve segregated and isolated populations of low-income students of color, and contribute to increasing racial and class segregation within city school systems.[38] In contrast to this dominant charter school model, however, there is also a smaller subset of "prestige" charter schools that are becoming attractive options for affluent families in gentrifying neighborhoods. Unlike the majority of charter schools, which cater to low-income families, prestige charter schools share the following characteristics: they are founded by advantaged community members; they have high levels of affluent parental involvement; they are guided by niche themes (such as language immersion); and they center social and emotional growth—rather than raw test scores—as their educational mission. They resemble private schools and actually compete with private schools for the same families. In gentrifying neighborhoods they are becoming "publicly funded private-feeling options" for affluent parents who do not want to opt for private schooling or choice their children out of their neighborhoods.[39] Despite its elite status, this smaller subset of prestige charter schools, like its "no excuses" counterpart, also contributes to increasing race and class segregation in the urban school system.

Finally, the charterization of the public school system has extended well beyond charter schools. Since charterization accompanies a portfolio management model, new models of charter-like, autonomous public schools have proliferated around the country.[40] Even if these are not charters per se, these autonomous schools have more flexibility to dictate their curricular foci and governance, hire and fire teachers, and circumvent teachers unions. The proliferation of charters and their counterparts has served to create an educational landscape that is challenging for even the savviest consumer to decipher. I will discuss this more in the next section on school choice.

School Choice

In the contemporary era of neoliberal reform, the educational marketplace is awash in various school models governed by different regulations (union versus non-union) and subject to different forms of funding (public taxes and private philanthropy) and governance (central school districts, educational management organizations, boards of directors, etc.). Reform advocates argue that the growth of market choice is not only beneficial for the general cultivation of better educational environments and outcomes, it is also consistent with a civil rights agenda that seeks to release low-income students of color from their failing and underperforming neighborhood schools. The neoliberal push for school choice emerged from the ashes of the national push to integrate schools and the subsequent White flight to suburbs across the country. This White resistance and White flight over the decades after *Brown v. Board of Education* resulted in a rollback of desegregation policies and a growing resegregation of schools. School choice has actually worked to *accelerate* this resegregation of schools already fostered by the dismantling of desegregation laws toward the end of the twentieth century.[41] Indeed, America's schools are even *more* segregated now than are their surrounding neighborhoods.[42]

In the current era of neoliberal reform, racial segregation is rarely framed by reform advocates as the primary educational injustice, even though generations ago the fight for integrated schools and other public spaces rested on a progressive civil rights ethic that viewed state-sponsored separate-but-equal policies as fundamentally *unequal*. This fundamental progressive insight has been jettisoned by contemporary reform advocates, who argue that *substandard education*, segregated or not, is the *real* root of racial injustice. In their view, market choice can liberate students from having only one choice: a failing neighborhood school. Choice, in fact, can open up new hope for those who have been disadvantaged by the neighborhood school system.

While the ideology of choice maintains that racial justice and equity can be realized through market liberation, critics of school choice note that "choice" is rarely ever free. Because many school choice schemas still give priority to neighborhood residents, affluent urban communities still have access to their highly resourced, high-scoring, and affluent neighborhood schools. Low-income students outside these catchment areas do not have reasonable access to these schools if these prioritized seats are already taken. In this sense, although school choice does expand the geographic zones in which children go to school, it rarely disrupts the kinds of connections between property values and school resources that Kozol vividly illustrated several decades ago in *Savage Inequalities*. In fact, in an era of school choice, land developers are even *more* invested in school reform processes, since educational quality—as a lever for urban revitalization—helps to determine home values in a given area.[43] The neoliberal era's system of publicly ranking schools, which is informed by standardized test scores and is designed to give educational consumers quantifiable criteria on which to judge school quality, also helps to assign value to specific neighborhoods, thereby increasing property values. The "freedom" positioned in the rhetorical use of "choice" is much like the faux freedom enshrined in larger neoliberal agendas like free trade.[44]

Civil rights-era desegregation policies aimed to redistribute resources and bodies by racially integrating schools. Soon to follow was an exodus of White city dwellers to the suburbs across the nation, an effort on the part of the educationally advantaged to undermine these policies and escape integration. This was part of a larger White rebellion against desegregation, which eventually culminated in a national abandonment of integration as a cornerstone of racial equity. Since then, urban revivalists, policy makers, and educational administrators have focused on strategies to bring back suburban Whites and their resources to the urban core.[45] School choice aids in this goal, as it allows White newcomers to settle in city neighborhoods and choose from a range of schools in these geographic zones, without relegating themselves to a single neighborhood school. These White commitments to the neighborhood school—especially in gentrified neighborhoods—can end up further segregating specific White neighborhood schools from other schools that are predominantly populated by students of color in the same neighborhood.[46]

In short, instead of liberating underserved communities, it can be argued that choice overwhelmingly consolidates privilege among those who are already educationally advantaged by pooling affluent community resources into specific urban schools and subsequently increasing property values. Beyond the role that school choice plays in the resegregation of schools and neighborhoods, the choice process has long been criticized for perpetuating racial inequalities. As education scholars Stephen Ball and Carol Vincent have persuasively argued, the choice process depends on obtaining "hot knowledge" through a social grapevine, a savvy approach to networking with other parents and institutions in ways that maximize the advantages of choice. Wealthier and more advantaged populations tend to rely on grapevine knowledge as an extension of their broader class-based consumption, and an attempt to distinguish "good" educational products from less desirable educational products. Although in theory standardized test scores and the "objective" rankings that arise from these should even out the playing field and

provide families with the same metrics from which to judge school quality as they make their choices, Ball and Vincent's research demonstrates
that, depending on their class status, families utilize different sources of
information that move beyond official rankings.[47]

This is also compounded by race; low-income Black families tend
to choose their neighborhood schools over other choices outside their
neighborhoods, even if they express serious criticisms of their neighborhood schools.[48] And finally, the proliferation of so many types of
schools means that "choice" is nearly indecipherable to most people. It
takes work, for even the most advantaged, to understand the meaningful differences between traditional-neighborhood, charter, innovation,
or magnet schools. For low-income communities of color with fewer
temporal or financial resources to investigate different public school options, the choice process that relies on the "savvy" consumer is inherently biased toward those with more resources. Indeed, the term "savvy"
obscures the resources one must already possess in order to make such
an important decision.

An obvious barrier to making the choice process equitable is transportation. For new White arrivals to the city, choice holds the promise
of living in one neighborhood but "choicing" in to a higher-performing
school outside that neighborhood. This opportunity, however, depends
on private transportation. Most choice policies in major cities have been
enacted without putting into place equitable systems of transportation,
so that a "choice" too far from home or work may be in reality no choice
at all. School closures—which are outcomes of standardized testing,
ranking, and consumer choice—exacerbate the problems of transportation in low-income communities. When these communities are more
likely than their more affluent counterparts to have their traditional
neighborhood schools shuttered as a result of high-stakes testing and
"accountability," their families are forced to find educational choices
further away from where they live. Writer Erin Einhorn documents the
severe case of "education deserts" in Detroit, for example, in which low-
income Black parents and their children must travel hours by bus in
the morning and evening just to find schooling for their children. The
arduous treks made by these families to keep their children in school do
not represent the promised liberation of choice; these are geographical
burdens that are disproportionately carried by those who have long been

maligned by the public education system, have the least resources to leverage in the market landscape of choice, and have the most to lose.[49]

Neoliberal Reform, Gentrification, and Dispossession

Although neoliberal reform rhetoric is saturated with images of saving struggling students from decades of educational disaster and righting the wrongs of racial injustice that have produced poor educational outcomes for Black and Brown children, in practice neoliberal education reform is a central piece of urban redevelopment—the elite remaking of the global city. Education policy scholar Kenneth Saltman, for example, traces the ways that education reform amounts to a privatization of the educational market by bringing in testing companies, educational management organizations, and philanthropies into the corporate rush to solve educational problems.[50] Beyond this, however, the marketization of education is also nested in the elite takeover and privatization of the city itself.[51]

Standardized testing and school choice create differentiated learning opportunities that function to mark certain areas of the city as "failing" or "blighted" and in need of significant capital investment and "renewal." Lipman argues that this very process publicly devalues specific urban neighborhoods in order to bring White capital investment to the urban core.[52] It is the "disaster capitalism" that can only be pushed through in the wake of a crisis, real or perceived.[53] When high-stakes testing is used to publicly rank high-performing and low-performing schools, and is joined with reformist rhetoric of educational disaster and urgency, shockingly poor test scores provide the crisis that legitimizes the remaking of entire sectors of the city. At the same time, a small tier of high-performing public school choices receives the majority of a district's investment in order to secure educational advantage in gentrifying or solidly middle-class neighborhoods and to draw or keep White capital.[54] The participation of real estate developers in school reform processes signals the extent to which educational market choice preserves and even accelerates the decades-old relationship between property values and schools.[55]

Education scholars such as Thomas Pedroni and Pauline Lipman have illustrated how austerity has also guided school and urban reform processes in cities like Detroit and Chicago. In Detroit, for example, new education reforms undertaken by the Detroit public schools emergency financial manager worked in concert with the mayor's office to close and consolidate schools in conjunction with the closure of public services like bus lines, firefighting stations, and police stations in specific parts of the city.[56] In fact, Pedroni reports that the shuttering of city services to predominantly African American neighborhoods was *guided* by the plans for school closures.[57] In neoliberal urban restructuring, tracts of land are identified for development through closure, displacement, and containment of specific populations, usually low-income communities of color. Therefore community displacement is endemic to both school reform and the processes of urban revitalization that hinge on this reform. Lipman's work on Chicago in particular underscores how school reform, as a centerpiece of neoliberal urban revitalization, is used not just for local or national capital accumulation, but also for global development. In cities like Chicago, school reform in conjunction with housing reform attempts to remake the city core into an anchor of global investment and capital, effectively turning large urban centers into what sociologist and globalization scholar Saskia Sassen terms "global cities," where global technologies, infrastructure, and investment are concentrated into global power centers.[58] Even in the case of Detroit, a city not normally identified as a "global city" like Chicago, education and real estate reform are designed to lure the predominantly White, upwardly mobile knowledge workers of the creative class, produced by a stratifying globalizing economy.[59] The International Monetary Fund (IMF), which prescribes the neoliberal vision of national global development, includes these same mechanisms of local education and urban reform: state divestment and austerity, land reform, community displacement, a weakening of local forms of democratic governance, and an influx of external capital in order to open up public goods and public spaces for private investment. Just as the IMF's coercive neoliberal development mandates have inspired global resistance, so too have these same neoliberal mechanisms tied to urban development and education reform inspired community uprisings on a local level. In this sense, urban education reform, though rhetorically about saving children, is deeply implicated in the broader processes of globalization.

This critical frame of globalization can help us to see how deeply racialized these processes of capital accumulation are, as leveraged through urban development and education reform. Critical scholars of neoliberal globalization view modern neoliberalism as neocolonialism, in the sense that free-market ideologies promote "development" through privatization and export-oriented production in order to entice wealthier nations (often, though not always, the same nations that were formerly colonial powers) and their global elite to invest in countries bled dry by centuries of colonization.[60] In this same sense, we can see neocolonialism and settler colonialism as driving forces behind urban school reform. As Tuck and Gorlewski underscore, settler colonialism is a specific manifestation of colonization marked by the appropriation of land for settlement. Both neocolonialism and settler colonialism are characterized by the removal and displacement of communities of color. These communities are themselves shaped by histories of colonization, exploitation, and enslavement.[61] In order to assign real estate value to a neighborhood occupied by low-income communities of color, development executives and policy makers must scrub clean certain neighborhoods of their racial connotations like "dangerous," "blighted," or "underdeveloped," first, by labeling these communities as such, and then by creatively destroying these communities with the justification drawn from these racialized labels.[62] School closures are a key part of racially remaking an area, displacing communities of color, and renewing tracts of urban lands.

As Pedroni argues, schools are particularly potent holders of community histories. In the quest to remake cities, schools cannot simply be rehabilitated for the current inhabitants. Rehabilitation will not suffice to racially scrub "clean" an area of the discursive racial imagery that has long contributed to property devaluation. Disaster and crisis must be invoked and institutions closed in order to achieve the blank slate that will attract investment and make it safe to Whiten formerly "no-go" urban areas. Adding insult to injury, Pedroni argues that in the case of Detroit—as in many cities—the cultural "cool" of the displaced community in a newly gentrifying neighborhood is marketed to hipster settlers, even as the community of origin was perceived as the threat to land value, renewal, and development. In this way, public institutions like schools that hold historical memories and even community culture itself are expropriated for capital accumulation.[63] From the perspective of low-income Black and Brown communities, urban renewal—and the school reform at its core—is a process of dispossession and displacement.

On one hand race is potently translated into euphemisms like "school failure," "violence," and "decay" in order to legitimize the takeover and remaking of predominantly Black and Latinx neighborhoods that are slated for investment and renewal.[64] But on the other hand, "race" is deftly veiled by market discourse. The rush to save children from educational disaster and remake public schooling into a market neglects the roots of this disaster as well as the most recent precipitators of racial inequality in the post-desegregation era. Nowhere in this public outcry around school failure do reform discourses point to the impact of resegregation, growing racial income inequality, and state divestment in low-income schools, much less the longer history of public schooling, segregation, and inequality that preceded these trends. In this sense, the very real impact of "race" (and most importantly, racial inequality) is erased in public discourses about educational failure. Racist histories (just like colonial histories in free-market global development discourses) are rendered invisible in the public zest to bring equity, via school choice and accountability, to students who have long been denied a quality education. Thus, contemporary neoliberal discourses around school reform deny the histories of racial segregation and the political and economic crises that have shaped cities in the making of urban public school inequities.[65] At the same time, not only do they discursively devalue specific neighborhoods and schools, publicized standardized test scores shame and devalue Black and Latinx kids, their families, and their teachers too.[66]

Critical education scholars argue that this shaming, dispossession, and veiling of racist histories in the remaking of the city constitute state-sponsored racial violence.[67] Market education reform is not simply about creating a market of choice within an educational district; it is both discursively and fundamentally about place making and remaking. It is about the devaluation and revaluation of urban land in the resegregation of cities and the Whitening of public spaces. Despite market rhetoric, school closures are not simply functional tools to root out educational failure and make way for new models of educational improvement. They are part and parcel of a process to devalue and revalue entire neighborhoods marked for revitalization and displacement, while erasing and denying decades of urban racial and economic injustice in the making of educational crises. As urban studies scholar Ryan Good writes, "The story of a community's relationship with a local school over generations has the capacity to root that community in space and to legitimize their claims to that neighborhood. The school closures that frequently accompany the expansion of charter and magnet school sectors should be understood as part of an erosion of those claims."[68] In short, there is a place-based dimension to the politics of urban school reform. Market reforms in urban school systems fundamentally shape broader processes of place making and community belonging in a neighborhood. School reform has been, in practice, inextricably bound to the larger forces of urban revitalization that appropriate land from low-income people of color.

Neoliberal Reform and Racial Rhetoric: Justice, Diversity, and Inclusion

Although many critical scholars argue that at its core the neoliberal era of reform is neocolonial and racist, these neocolonial and racist threads are often veiled by color-blind and even overt antiracist language. Like the rhetorical appropriation of "free" that helps to accelerate capital accumulation and corporate-led globalization by promoting radical corporate interventions as liberating for oppressed and colonized peoples, the rhetorical use of civil rights and antiracist language helps to market controversial reforms that so often accelerate disadvantage among the already disadvantaged.

This appropriation began with NCLB. George W. Bush's education secretary fervently argued that "accountability" ushered in by high-stakes testing would deliver underserved populations from what Bush termed "the soft bigotry of low expectations."[69] Wayne Au terms this neoliberal push for standardized testing "meritocracy 2.0," which positions equity through accountability and choice as the ultimate antiracist individualism. In this way, old ideologies of meritocracy are recast as antiracist and multicultural in corporate education reform.[70]

As education policy scholar Janelle Scott has pointed out, reformers have used antiracist and civil rights rhetoric to reimagine and rewrite the civil rights past by, for example, positioning Rosa Parks herself as a charter schools advocate. Scott argues that reformers' appropriation of civil rights language distills the most individualist threads of actual civil rights-era battles for educational equity in ways that are fundamentally anti-collectivist. As she notes, these do not map on to actual community civil rights struggles:

> Lost in this elite rendering of civil rights is the fact that Rosa Parks and Martin Luther King Jr., typically the signifiers of the Civil Rights Movement in popular understandings, were nested in robust social networks calling for radical redistribution of opportunity in education, yes, but also in terms of broader social policy. They worked alongside and belonged to communities that had a long history of social struggle. . . . Far from being entrepreneurial, market aficionados, each was engaged in collective action aimed at helping the United States live up to its democratic promises by equalizing opportunity and remedying generations of structural inequality.[71]

Critical education scholars like Scott and others highlight the extent to which corporate interests champion marketization and privatization through public images and messages that resonate with multiculturalism, diversity, civil rights, and antiracism. An egregious example is Betsy DeVos's claim that historically Black colleges and universities (HBCUs) were "pioneers" of school choice. According to Kevin Clay, this rhetorical maneuver functioned as a denial of the state violence against Black people that led to the creation of HBCUs and a denial of contemporary school choice and reform as racist. It stands as an example of what Clay calls "Black resilience neoliberalism," which Clay defines as "both the normalization and the valorization of exercising human capital in relation to 'overcoming' or enduring structural racism, both of which obscure or ignore Black suffering."[72] Scott also underscores that grassroots activists of color who engage in collectivist civil rights struggles against corporate-led reform seldom gain traction in these struggles, especially given elites' co-optation of racial justice rhetoric and their resources. She writes, "In this curious educational reform climate, the new reformers in many ways obviate the historical struggles, voices, and participation of traditional civil rights and grassroots organizations, as well as the expertise and insights of education professors, teachers, and principals of color while embracing language that communicates aspirations for social justice."[73] The neoliberal push for school reform has used civil rights and antiracist discourses to champion standardized testing, charter school expansion, school closures, school choice, and corporate and philanthropic partnerships for education reform.

A critical perspective would insist that we remain suspicious of policy agendas that speak the language of racial justice, especially when they are formulated and promoted by elites who are predominantly White, who have little history working with and within the very communities of color that will bear the brunt of marketization's radical reform, and who themselves and their children have never attended public schools. Though the discourse is laden with progressive antiracism, the reform movement is overwhelmingly White, wealthy, and male.[74] Buras, for example, writes about the paternalism of the elites who descended on New Orleans and charterized the city school system in the wake of Katrina. Lipman also points to the White paternalism of the elite who push through radical reforms in Chicago. Given that neoliberal reform imagines the public sector operating more like a competitive market, it is no wonder that the corporate discourse of diversity, which emphasizes "selective inclusion" into the upper echelons of the ruling class, imports so easily into the fight to remake public schools into new educational markets.[75] There is a revolving door between corporate America, Wall Street, and elite education reform circles, and with this revolving door come new multicultural corporate logics and discursive strategies. As sociologist Ellen Berrey argues, it is often the language of "diversity" that actually masks the consolidation of racial and class power in institutions like higher education and the corporate boardroom:

> The corporate managers, community leaders, and other decision makers who champion diversity have redefined racial progress for the post–civil rights era, from a legal fight for equal rights to a celebration of cultural difference as competitive advantage. . . . It claims the moral high ground, disavowing racism and discrimination. . . . It does not necessitate that leaders address racial inequalities throughout the organization or housing market. . . . Much discourse on diversity leaves advocates without a language for talking about inequality.[76]

Sociologist Pamela Quiroz pinpoints how selective enrollment schools "manage" diversity as part of the new urbanism.[77] This movement to renovate and revitalize urban spaces by displacing poor and working-class communities of color ironically relies on a pronounced marketing of diversity, since the lure of diversity and inclusion is vital to the modern Whitening of urban spaces in a "post-racial" era. Quiroz points to the careful management of mixed-income housing, schooling, and other diversity projects in the urban core as projects of the new urbanism, since these projects must convincingly market inclusion and diversity while still marketing public spaces and institutions as "safe" and inviting for White inhabitants. Quiroz writes,

> The question remains whether in the environment of markets and ex-
> treme individualism, programs . . . are designed to address the needs of
> under-represented groups or simply filter enough individuals into the
> system to assure those with access to that system, that they are indeed in
> an integrated environment—in other words, to have just enough contact
> but not too much?[78]

The marketing of diversity, inclusion, and even racial justice as part of the new urbanism is at odds with the reality that specific urban spaces grow ever more White as a result of these very racial projects that are marketed to a (White) resourced public as "inclusive."

Although the reform movement is overwhelmingly White, wealthy, and male, political scientists like Adolf Reed Jr. and Cedric Johnson also point to the participation of the Black professional class in these projects, which has aided and abetted the broader neoliberal project of housing and school privatization across the United States. The partici-pation of the Black elite represents a class interest convergence between White and Black politicians that has fueled the commonsense notion that both low-income public housing and public schooling are breeding grounds for depravity and mediocrity; they are systems that require rad-ical reform. For example, Reed underscores this interest convergence, congealed in hegemonic ideology about the pathology of these public institutions, as he analyzes the futile struggle of the Black working-class and poor to stem the tide of public housing destruction in post-Katrina New Orleans. He writes, "Activists' inability even to slow down demo-lition reflects how thoroughly hegemonic underclass ideology has be-come. The commonsense 'knowledge' that low-income public housing is a breeding ground for a pathological underclass sufficiently perme-ates everyday black middle and working-class understanding that it can override and reinterpret contrary personal experience."[79] It is important to remember that Black and Latinx political elites have also positioned neoliberal privatization as solutions to racial injustice, especially since the 1970s.

The Black political regime first arose in the post–World War II United States as a challenge to White-dominated urban political regimes. As Johnson notes, "The result was a form of ethnic empowerment that eventually enabled black constituencies to wrest control from White ethnic-dominated governments in many cities, but which also averted a working class-centered politics by institutionalizing the view that racial identity and political constituency were synonymous."[80] This histori-cal development has given rise to a common perception that there is a unitary "Black community" with monolithic interests based on racial identity, which has allowed a Black political elite to promote neolib-eral solutions to social and political problems in the name of antira-cism. Contemporary Black political elites like Cory Booker, Ray Nagin, and Adrian Fenty have demonstrated even more of a commitment than their predecessors to market-oriented policies that compound working-class and poor Black dispossession. This problem is not reducible to these Black political figures being "sellouts" or simply uncaring. Rather, Johnson argues, this development reflects the complex historical de-mobilization of the movements of the 1960s, and the rise of Black elite governance in helping to shape the growing consensus over neoliberal restructuring since the 1970s. This consensus has emerged through in-creasing alignment between the Black professional-managerial class and the Democratic Party, private foundations, and corporations.[81]

Janelle Scott argues that the co-optation of civil rights language in corporate-led reform transforms the revered collective struggle for ra-cial equity into a contemporary individualist quest for excellence and mobility, and fundamentally stands at odds with authentic working-class and poor community struggles for racial justice.[82] However, I would argue that in very limited ways, the elite reformer rhetoric around racial equity, radical change, and accountability resonates with *some* institu-tionalized community movements around specific racial justice cam-paigns that in the end help to produce strange bedfellows in local fights for educational justice. There is a discursive middle ground where the new urbanism's racially progressive rhetoric pries open a space for some community racial justice activists to advocate for authentic and collective racial justice initiatives as part of these education reform processes. At the same time, these episodic partnerships are often used to further delegitimize other community activists—especially those who are not located in nonprofit settings—who are contesting school reform as a major tool that furthers gentrification, dispossession, and community displacement. In this sense, the appropriation of civil rights discourse is not only about marketing educational privatization to the general public, it is also about seeking community buy-in by linking arms with authentic civil rights struggles that emerge from longer histories of advocacy around educational justice. As reform experimentation in communities of color deepens and leaves a lasting resentment, community buy-in via coalitions with select movement organizations becomes even more important to the continued advancement of marketization in the wake of extended reform failure.

These core elements of neoliberal school reform, including standardized testing and accountability and the proliferation of charter schools and expanded systems of school choice, have all inspired community mobilization and action. For example, a burgeoning national "opt-out" movement has grown among relatively advantaged populations and low-income populations alike. For more affluent families, the growth of standardized testing and the corporatization of public schooling have threatened to hollow out what would otherwise be high-quality college-preparatory public school education.[83] For low-income students of color, standardized testing narrows the curriculum and increases educational instability by carrying the threat of school closure. It contributes to a climate of surveillance that publicly disciplines schools and low-income Brown and Black children themselves, who are marked as "failing."[84] In New York in 2015, a statewide opt-out movement resulted in 70 percent of students in some areas—predominantly those that are low-income Black and Latinx—opting out of high-stakes testing.[85] High school students and parents have mobilized to claim a voice in evaluating their schools, widening the criteria (beyond standardized test outcomes) that can hold schools accountable and determine educational quality. Other community mobilizations include the push for healthy food and state-subsidized breakfasts and lunches in schools, and the expansion of other forms of human security like healthcare in schools. Still others attempt to counter charter schools' push-out and cultures of militaristic discipline by fighting against expulsions and suspensions and organizing for restorative justice programs in schools. In many cities, communities have organized for more comprehensive transportation programs, so that the ideological promise of "choice" is not stymied by a lack of transportation. Some of these community projects have resulted in partnerships between city bus systems and school districts to provide discounted or free bus passes to public school students, or specific transportation systems in regions within a city. Finally, in Chicago, community mobilizations fought to return the city to a democratically elected school board after mayoral takeover.[86] These community-driven projects attempt to carve inroads into the marketization of public education, transforming antiracist and civil rights rhetoric into substantive social change.

The Local Context: Reform and Resistance in Denver

Local examinations of school reform highlight the commonalities of national trends, but also draw attention to the context-specific manifestations of reform. These are rooted in local histories and reveal local political configurations that do not map onto other contexts easily. Lipman's in-depth examination of school reform politics in Chicago, for example, draws out the threads of corporate elites' racist displacement of African American communities and dispossession, especially in the elite project of making Chicago into a global city. Meanwhile, Pedroni's heartwrenching account of neoliberal reform in Detroit argues that Detroit's model is more like those imposed in Iraq, Chile, or post-Katrina New Orleans: a radical testing ground for Milton Friedman's shock therapy and an extreme imposition of free-market economics through a swift and deep downsizing of public infrastructure.[87] Although Denver has certainly adopted many of the hallmarks of neoliberal reform named in the previous sections, Denver's case is somewhat different than Chicago, Detroit, and elsewhere. Like Chicago, Philadelphia, New Orleans, Washington, DC, and other cities, Denver has been hailed as a model for national reform.[88] Unlike Washington, DC, Philadelphia, and Chicago, however, Denver has not instituted mayoral control over the district's school system. Throughout Denver's recent reform history, the elected school board has remained. Although Denver's reform-oriented district has taken a decidedly pro-charter school stance, Denver's superintendent, Tom Boasberg, who left office in 2018 after nearly a decade at the helm of the Denver Public School system, had also pushed charters for more open access for children with disabilities, had publicly advocated more protections for immigrant children, and had advocated for increased school funding for the district. As of 2018, he approved a one-year moratorium on school closures.[89]

These and other progressive inroads into neoliberal policy reveal more than just the superintendent's individual brand of leadership and benevolence. They reveal the extent to which several different social movements in Denver have succeeded in pushing the district to adopt these policies as part and parcel of reform. Indeed, Betsy DeVos singled Denver out in a speech about reform, alleging that Denver wasn't aggressive *enough* in providing real choice in education because it did not support private school vouchers. That Denver is simultaneously held up as a national model for reform and criticized by even more extreme reformists reflects the strange mix of neoliberal and progressive threads that run throughout its brand of educational change, and the mark made by both elites and grassroots activists in the fights for better public schooling.

In this section, I will outline Denver's particular history of school reform as it has evolved with new urbanism, as well as Denver's unique movement history that has shaped some of the political pushback to the havoc that neoliberalism can wreak. I argue that although Denver's particular brand of neoliberal reform—as it has evolved with Denver's movement history—is fundamentally local, it does provide a window through which to observe why some forms of community activism succeed in steering neoliberal policy toward community ends, while others do not. Denver's model evinces a certain openness to community activism, even as it participates in accumulation through dispossession. The aim of this book is to explore what this openness accomplishes, and for whom; what this signifies about the ability of communities to mobilize and undermine elements of neoliberalism's White supremacy; and which community visions and potential urban futures are sacrificed in the process.

In the national history of segregation, desegregation, and urban school reform, Denver was significant long before it emerged as a national model for neoliberal reform. The Supreme Court ruling *Keyes v. School District 1* in 1973 made Denver Public Schools (DPS) the first district outside the South to undergo court-ordered desegregation through forced busing. The ruling, which was focused on the Park Hill neighborhood, found that DPS was maintaining essentially two separate and fundamentally unequal school systems: one well-resourced school system for White families, and one poorly resourced and poorly run for the city's Black and Latinx families. The Supreme Court ruling resulted in the institution of a unique mandated busing system that integrated White, Black, and Latinx families in some of Denver's biggest neighborhood schools. Although these often resulted in tracked schools in which White students were disproportionately placed in Advanced Placement tracks and Black and Latinx students were concentrated in vocational tracks, many argued that the schools benefitted from White affluence and resources.[90] In the wake of the Supreme Court ruling, however, White families began to leave for Denver's newly emerging suburbs in order to escape racially integrated schools. In 1968, for example, DPS could count sixty-eight thousand White families. Three decades later, only about eighteen thousand White families remained. Civil rights-era desegregation policies across the United States resulted in the highest rates of racial integration across schools by the late 1980s. However, after years of White pushback and resistance to desegregation, by the mid- to late 1990s these policies were dismantled. In 1995 new Denver legislation argued that three decades after *Keyes*, the city and school district did not resemble the same segregated city of the late 1960s, and thus busing could be discontinued. The exodus of White families from the Denver Public School system prompted city planners and school district officials to strategize ways to bring back affluent families to the city's schools.

By this time, NCLB came on the heels of these urban planning discussions and brought the full force of national policy behind local plans for urban revival. The goal was to reverse decades of White flight to the suburbs and increase the concentration of White affluence in urban centers. High-stakes testing provided the metrics for school districts and city planners to identify parts of cityscapes that must be torn down, closed down, and made anew. The remaking of urban neighborhoods in the name of educational improvement first manifested in educational experiments on the West and East Coasts of the United States, and then in larger cities like Chicago and Milwaukee.[91]

By 2005, Denver was attracting the attention of one of the signature major philanthropists that has funded reform throughout the country in an attempt to restructure a major city high school.[92] This high school, Central High, had long been the heart of a neighborhood that Beat writer Jack Kerouac referred to as the "Harlem of the West."[93] The neighborhood had long been the heart of Denver's Black community, both because redlining sustained explicit and official racial segregation since the beginning of the twentieth century, and also because major jazz greats, Black poets and writers, and other Black artists would come to this neighborhood to perform throughout the 1930s, 1940s, and 1950s. The neighborhood held the city's concentration of jazz clubs and drew audiences from across the city and across racial lines. By 1950, Blacks comprised 43 percent of the neighborhood's population. Later, the neighborhood mix shifted, especially in the wake of the 1964 Civil Rights Act. Blacks began to leave the neighborhood and settle in other nearby Denver neighborhoods. Latinx people began to move to the area in the late 1960s and 1970s. By 1980 Latinx and Black residents together comprised 80 percent of the neighborhood's population.

Between 2000 and 2010, the beginning years of Denver's most intense urban renewal, the racial majority in this neighborhood flipped to White at 68 percent, with Latinx and Black residents evenly split as the remainder of the population. A light rail line placed in the heart of the neighborhood in the mid-1990s connected the city's downtown core to this neighborhood and the White suburbs bordering the other end of Denver, spatially opening the neighborhood to other parts of the city and to the Whites who had fled to the suburbs a generation before. Even so, by 2012, Denver's city council designated the neighborhood as officially "blighted," a designation that opened up the land for "renewal" by the Denver Urban Renewal Association (DURA). DURA argued that the designation would give access to tax-increment financing and a path to revitalize the neighborhood through new development projects. Many residents, however, passionately argued that the designation would subject their properties to eminent domain over a twenty-five-year period, leaving them with unease that their properties could be seized at any time. This is a prime example of the ways city governments collude with land developers to first publicly and officially degrade and devalue neighborhoods in order to justify their revitalization.

Throughout decades of change in the neighborhood, but before the turn of the millennium, Central High had helped to produce a local economic base for this community. The school trained beauticians, auto mechanics, and other blue-collar workers who subsequently settled in the area and served the community, providing some economic consistency through the population changes of the late twentieth century. The 1973 *Keyes* Supreme Court ruling set in motion integration through busing, so that White students from more affluent nearby neighborhoods were bused in to Central. When in the mid-1990s busing was ended and *Keyes* was effectively dismantled, the White flight from Central and the declining student population, coupled with low standardized test scores, set the stage for Central High's closure in 2006. This was happening in concert with state divestment in school districts across Colorado. Like the neighborhood's future designation of "blight" that was to follow Central High's controversial closure, Central High's makeover began with the designation of a "failing school" that needed urgent and radical development. Soon, Central's rebranding was buttressed by national foundation money to support a controversial small schools experiment that was shut down only a year after it began. Although the experiment was in essence a failure, it signaled the arrival of the neoliberal reform movement in Denver and put the city on the national reform radar. The Central High experiment will be explored in greater detail in the next two chapters.

The aftermath of Central's closing and subsequent experimentation also gave birth to various incarnations of Black and Latinx mobilizations in the neighborhood that organized to halt this national reform movement and the takeover of their neighborhood and their most sacred institution. When the district announced that it would close Central, parents, teachers, and students walked out in protest. They confronted the school board at meetings, picketed DPS headquarters, and called on their local representatives to halt the decision. Despite the community outcry, the shuttering of Central and its experimental re-creation proceeded. However, in the years since Central's initial closure in 2006, neighborhood Black and Latinx residents have been organizing in various capacities against reform and the larger forces of gentrification. These mobilizations will receive more attention in chapter 3.

In 2008 the reform push in Colorado gained momentum through the efforts of the Black political regime, when Terrance Carroll, former speaker of Colorado's House of Representatives, and Peter Groff, former Colorado State Senate president—both the first African Americans to hold these respective posts in Colorado—cosponsored Senate Bill 130, otherwise known as the Innovation Schools Act. This bill allowed the creation of innovation schools, quasi-charter schools run by the district but not overseen by an independent charter company. They are free to hire and fire teachers at will, set their own hours, choose their own textbooks, and operate outside union contracts. Innovation schools are eligible for waivers from district or state teacher employment, salary, or evaluation regulations. They are also exempt from some teacher trainings, tend to hire new teachers or teachers with little experience, and sustain higher teacher turnover, as charter schools do.[94] Senate Bill 130 represented a historical progression of political legislation in Denver—supported by the new incarnation of the Black urban regime—that signaled what Johnson terms "a multicultural, corporate-centered growth coalition."[95] This coalition in Denver had been spurred by Wellington Webb's support for free trade–style economic growth and neoliberal restructuring from 1991 to 2003, when he served three terms as Denver's first Black mayor.

Two years before the Denver City Council declared Central's neighborhood "blighted," the Colorado Senate passed Senate Bill 191 in 2010, also known as the Teacher Effectiveness Bill. This legislation ties teacher pay to students' academic growth, as measured on standardized tests. This legislation was another pivotal reform moment that garnered the praise of reformers nationally. Coupled with the district's promotion of a portfolio-style collection of schools, including a vast array of charters and innovation schools, by 2016 Denver rose to the top ranks of the most promising cities for school reform.[96]

While the teachers union opposed the bill, arguing that it would capriciously purge good teachers from DPS, some community-based Latinx organizations—whose origins descended from the Chicano student movement of the late 1960s—backed the bill. Denver is one of the central birthplaces of the Chicano student movement, and boasts a long history of educational justice activism. It is the site of the legendary Crusade for Justice, which formed in the mid-1960s. Led by iconic Chicano movement leader Rodolfo "Corky" Gonzales (a graduate of Central High), Denver's Crusade for Justice organized anti-war demonstrations, movements against police violence, and high school student strikes. One of the largest student strikes was the West High School walkout (also known as the "blowout") in 1969, in which Mexican American students called for an end to racial discrimination in their classrooms and a demand for bilingual education and courses in Chicano history and arts. The Crusade for Justice also organized major Chicano youth liberation conferences that drew Chicano activists from across southwestern states. These conferences provided a forum to map out important directions for community self-determination and political power. These conferences and the Crusade also gave rise to several formal political organizations and nonprofit community-based organizations. Many of these organizations are rooted in neighborhoods across the river from Central High, further out on the western, northwestern, northern, and southwestern edges of the city. These neighborhoods, like the neighborhood around Central High, have also transitioned to majority-White since the turn of the millennium. Rising rents, housing prices, new light rail transportation, and the larger trends associated with gentrification have pushed lower-income Latinx families—many of whom have lived in these neighborhoods for generations—out into nearby suburbs and further from the city's core. The White gentry who have moved into these neighborhoods have sometimes surprised reformers with their own brand of resistance to neoliberal reform. Their struggles to decide the fate of their schools and neighborhoods, and their struggles to form cross-racial coalitions with the Latinx families who share their schools are explored further in chapter 4.

Educational justice has always been a central anchor of Denver's Chicano civil rights movement, and the reform movement's messages about racial equity in proposed legislation such as the Teacher Effectiveness Bill signaled a movement toward ensuring that teachers and schools are held accountable for student learning outcomes. Reformer legislation to compel accountability resonated with some Latinx-based nonprofit organizations and provided an opening for these groups to demand equity in education and an end to discriminatory teaching practices and the larger patterns of educational discrimination that lead to the racialized school-to-prison pipeline.[97] That some select Denver Chicano and immigrant social justice organizations view the reform moment as an opportunity to redress a longer pattern of educational injustice in the school system underscores the neoliberal moment as an opening of political opportunity not just for market advocates, but also for progressive social movement organizations. These movement organizations, and their alliances with reformers, are the subject of chapter 5.

By 2016, the conservative Brookings Institution rated Denver number 1 in the country for school choice. Moving into the 2020s, there are more charter and innovation schools in the Denver Public Schools system than there are traditional neighborhood public schools. Prior to the school board elections in late 2019, the Denver school board has oscillated from 4–3 majority reform, to 7–0 majority reform, to 5–2 majority reform in its seven-seat composition over the last decade. The continued dominance of a majority-reform board has reflected the continuing influence of the national reform movement and its wealth in these local school board politics.[98]

These fluctuations in school board composition also serve as a reminder that the hegemony of Denver's pro-reform movement has never been total, nor without contestation. They have demonstrated the continuing power of the dissenting electorate that manifests in the minority voices in these board decisions. As of the writing of this book, the backlash against market-based school reform in Denver, as it is in other cities, is gaining traction. Certainly, the Denver teachers' strike that made national headlines in the beginning of 2019—the first strike called by the Denver Classroom Teachers Association (DCTA) since 1994—stands as a clear rebellion against the corporate reform movement that has produced lower wages for teachers and high teacher turnover in the district. The Denver teachers' strike of early 2019 also galvanized a growing movement to "flip the board."[99] In November 2019, city voters seated three new teachers union–backed candidates on the school board, reversing the decade-long majority reform board in a new 5–2 majority union-backed board.

It remains to be seen whether this backlash will be enough to radically usher in a new era that is markedly different from the reform era. Boasberg ended his tenure as DPS superintendent, and has been replaced by

Susana Cordova, the sole finalist in a national search. Cordova, a long-time DPS insider, seems poised to continue the reforms that Boasberg and his predecessor Michael Bennet (former superintendent turned senator turned presidential candidate) instituted. The newly elected Colorado governor, Jared Polis, has assembled his education team. Backed by and aligned with the school reform movement (and himself a charter schools advocate), his team includes the director of the Colorado Democrats for Education Reform (DFER). This inclusion of DFER's director on Polis's statewide education team is a clear statement in itself, since in the spring of 2018 delegates at the Colorado Democratic State Assembly called on DFER to remove "Democrat" from its name. This was a bold rejection of reform privatization and school segregation associated with the reform movement. And yet, as divisive as reform is in party politics, the reformer movement still has a strong hold over both the school district and state politics. None of the newly elected DPS board members have yet committed to ending Denver's long-running school choice experiment or halting the expansion of new charter schools.[100]

Over a decade of reform experimentation in Denver has produced mixed results. Boasberg and other reform advocates have lauded Denver's reform policies for increasing graduation rates of Black and Latinx students in particular. At the same time, Denver's achievement gap between White students and students of color and between affluent students and poor and working-class students is one of the highest in the nation. Teacher turnover in DPS is much higher than the state average due to the rising cost of living in Denver and the ProComp pay system, and the size of DPS administration is much larger than the state average. The bloating of the district administration, the instability of teacher pay and turnover, and the widening achievement gap and school segregation that accompanies it can be understood as some of the unsavory outcomes of neoliberal reform. The larger backdrop for these city politics is also the shortfall in state funding: Colorado funds education $2,000 per student below the national average. This is partly a result of the Colorado Taxpayer Bill of Rights (TABOR), which was passed in 1992 and prohibits the state from raising taxes unless first approved by voters. TABOR also stipulates that any state surplus must be returned to taxpayers instead of going to state services like education. This taxpayer revolt is consistent with a global pattern of national and state divestment in public goods that so often characterizes the neoliberal historical moment.

Even though the recent Denver teachers' strike and mounting condemnation of DPS schools' racial achievement gaps have prompted a local and national conversation about the shortfalls of more than a decade of corporate reform experimentation in Denver, neoliberal reform still continues to maintain hegemony in this city. The chapters that follow demonstrate how fissures between educational justice movements ultimately blunt their power to meaningfully coalesce and resist this particular brand of reform.

The role of the Denver teachers union deserves special mention in this story of community struggles over urban school reform. The 2019 Denver teachers' strike thrust Denver teachers to the national forefront of resistance to reform, and signaled a collective and visible turn against the tide of elite reform in Denver and across the state. However, during the course of the research documented in this book (2008–2013), the Denver Classroom Teachers Association (DCTA) was remarkably compliant regarding—and even complicit in—the great DPS reform experiment over the first two decades of the new millennium. Although the DCTA opposed Senate Bill 191 (Teacher Effectiveness Bill), which tied teacher pay to students' academic growth on standardized tests, the DCTA actively lobbied for what turned out to be the direct target of its later strike in 2019, the ProComp system. This was documented in a 2005 *New York Times* article, "Working with the Enemy," in which Douglas McGray reported the unusual collusion between the DCTA and free-market reform advocates. Denver's ProComp is a complicated pay-for-performance system that provides onetime incentives for raising student test scores, teaching in hard-to-fill areas like math or special education, and teaching in high-poverty schools. Although originally the DCTA embraced the merit-based ProComp pay system as a meaningful way for teachers to receive raises, by 2019 the DCTA argued that this bonus structure was highly variable, failed to stabilize the skyrocketing teacher turnover rate of 25 percent in the district, and failed to retain teachers or provide a livable wage. Furthermore, there was very little evidence to suggest that the ProComp system actually resulted in closing the achievement gaps between White students and students of color, or between middle-class and low-income students. The union argued instead for an increase in base pay and a return to a predictable pay schedule for all teachers. This is something that most teachers unions had been demanding in 2005.

Denver's 2019 teachers' strike was undoubtedly part of the larger wave of teachers' strikes in both red and blue states in recent years, but it was largely focused on Denver's ProComp system for teacher pay. This stands in contrast to the 2019 Los Angeles teachers' strike, which included a broader range of issues such as caps on charter school growth and increased funding for mental health school services, in addition to salary increases. Teachers' strikes continue to make headlines and together can be seen as one indication of a national backlash against neoliberal school reform. However, the variations in their battles, both in what they demand and what they win, are direct reflections of the coalitions they build years before teachers ever take to the streets. In the Los Angeles case, as in the Chicago case, a progressive caucus of the teachers union had been actively organizing with community groups in a model of "bargaining for the common good" instead of just the union's membership.[101] This is why immigrant rights and housing justice were also issues that the United Teachers Los Angeles (UTLA) brought to the bargaining table.

In the Denver case, the turn toward union progressivism has been relatively new. As former teacher and education writer Eric Blanc observed about the recent Denver strike, "Given the DCTA's longstanding deference to Democratic politicians, it's a sign of the times that Denver's strike is happening at all. . . . Denver's action is taking place under the aegis of the union's old guard, which until recently was reticent to confront the district, let alone organize a work stoppage."[102] The 2019 strikes have signaled a new progressive orientation and worker militancy within the DCTA, but this is in its infancy. The DCTA's shift to "bargaining for the common good" will require more time and more direction from its newly emerging progressive caucus. The relative absence of the role of the DCTA in the chapters that follow is not an oversight; in the first few decades of Denver's reform experiment, the DCTA was simply not invested in forging substantive coalitions with any of the local movement networks detailed in these chapters. As an organization, it was relatively acquiescent during Denver's heyday of reform in the first two decades of the new millennium, and was not the leading edge of resistance to market-based reform experimentation. This is not to say that teachers were *not* active in opposing neoliberal reform experimentation before the Denver teachers' strike of 2019. Rather, the teachers who engaged in this struggle found their voices *outside* the union. Some veteran teachers of color, for example—who faced displacement by impending school closures or turnarounds—discovered moments of alliance with the non-institutionalized neighborhood groups featured in chapters 3 and 4. As the DCTA transitions toward "bargaining for the common good," the lessons drawn from this book can help this growing labor movement transform multiple community struggles for racial justice and urban sustainability into legitimate educational justice issues worth fighting for in the streets and at the bargaining table.

Since the end of court-ordered busing in the mid-1990s and into the first two decades of the new millennium, Denver has become a more expensive, sought-after city with a growing reputation for urban style. School reform has been a major mechanism for remaking this city into a desirable place for affluent young professionals—what urban studies theorist Richard Florida terms the "creative class"—to live and work.[103] It has enabled elites to restructure the city and its most cherished neighborhood institutions. In doing so, elites have also been complicit in the dispossession of Latinx and Black community schools, businesses, parks, and homes in the same ways they have in other gentrifying cities across the nation. As in other cities remade anew by neoliberal reform, Denver's brand of school reform has at its center a school choice system governed by standard rankings to ensure accountability and aid the savvy educational consumer. Denver's brand of reform has also heavily relied on the expansion of charter schools and other quasi-charter models. At the same time, the reform process in Denver has not taken place in an elite vacuum. Rather, it represents a fusion of some progressive social movement initiatives with neoliberal impulses, and a clash of other progressive social movement initiatives with reformer goals. In this sense, Denver is a perfect case study to understand how, and to what extent, grassroots community movements can either shift the balance of power and help to determine the future of neighborhood schools, or remain isolated in their battles to lay claim to their community institutions. This is a critical moment not only for Denver, but for a nation engaged in a decades-long experiment with neoliberal privatization. The legitimacy of this sweeping reform movement is beginning to unravel, and the future of neoliberal education reform is unclear. In cities like Denver, teachers' strikes and school board electoral victories for union-backed candidates stand as a sharp indictment of the failures of decades of reform experimentation. However, we cannot predict the future of education reform or the outcome of this growing revolt against educational privatization without first analyzing the coalition politics of the city-level movement networks that shaped Denver's reform story.

2

The Reformers

Race, Privilege, and Saving Children from Disaster

Decades ago, Central High was a popular high school in the heart of the historic African American community in Denver. The school, in a slice of the city long known as the "Harlem of the West," was historically racially diverse. It is one of Denver's oldest schools, having existed since the late 1800s, and was one of the first schools to educate African Americans. The school produced some of the city's major Black leaders, including Wellington Webb. Legendary Chicano activist Rodolfo "Corky" Gonzales also graduated from Central High. As part of desegregation efforts of the 1970s, court-ordered busing ensured that a majority-White student body from outside the neighborhood was bused in to Central. The school offered a variety of courses and boasted a talented football team that seemed to draw the diverse student body together. This was especially important in a racially diverse school that had been heavily tracked; the school provided an advanced track that funneled many of the White students into top colleges, and a vocational track that provided hands-on automotive and cosmetology training for the Black neighborhood students. Many Central High grads trained in the school's vocational programs went on to open their own businesses in the neighborhood, and these anchors in the neighborhood became testimonies to the school's success and function in the community.

In 1995 a federal court ended mandated busing. Middle-class Whites no longer had to attend Central High in order to fulfill desegregation regulations, and some left for other high-performing schools in their own neighborhoods nearby. Funding dried up and budget cuts decimated staff and courses. As one former Central High teacher noted, "We tried, but we had nothing to offer the students." Test scores and attendance rates precipitously dropped, and despite massive community outcry the school was closed just after the turn of the new millennium.

Funded by a generous grant from a prominent national foundation, the single high school was transformed into three small schools and was re-opened the following year. The small schools experiment quickly turned into a disaster. The three principals of the three distinct schools battled over common school resources like the gym, classroom spaces, and other school territory. Students were barred from entering certain sections of the shared building. Hundreds of students could not be accounted for in the transition from a neighborhood comprehensive high school into the new charter-like experiment. The school was closed again just one year later. In 2007 the school was opened again as an innovation school, a particular institutional classification that enables school leaders to more easily control their school budgets and have more flexibility over their teacher contracts. As a result, teachers at Central High are hired with year-to-year contracts and little job security. Even more controversial to the community was that innovation status allowed the school to engage in "managed enrollment." This meant that the school could selectively accept a few students to start the first incoming class and allowed the principal to more carefully construct a new school culture. This effec-tively left most of the neighborhood kids without access to what was formerly their neighborhood school. Critics charged that the district es-sentially denied Denver's Black community a viable neighborhood high school.

Since 2007 teacher and principal turnover has been high at Central, and student test scores and attendance have remained low. Every new principal at Central has advocated a new educational model. One model emphasized college preparation for all, while a later model centered ex-peditionary learning at the core of its educational approach. Each of these models have only lasted a year or two before the district ordered a change of leadership in the name of fixing persistently low test scores. To critics of the recent spate of serial reforms at Central High, the school has become a guinea pig for education reform. After nearly two decades of reform at Central High, student achievement, by any measure, re-mains dismal. As profound as the low student achievement, however, is the eroded trust between the community that Central High serves and the central school district. While the school still serves a majority-Black and Latinx student base, the neighborhood around the school has transformed from a majority-Black and Latinx neighborhood in the

1990s to a majority-White neighborhood in the 2000s. The changing demographics of this neighborhood continues to put Central High in the sights of local politicians and urban developers who view the future of this school as inextricably linked to the future of this neighborhood's and city's "renewal."

The small schools experiment was the first of a succession of experiments brought about by a cadre of self-identified "reformers," a loose network of mostly White middle- to upper-class professionals spanning local foundations, media outlets, think tanks, education watchdog groups, and even the centralized school district. Some are networked with national reform organizations such as DFER (Democrats for Education Reform) and pro-reform organizations such as the Bill and Melinda Gates Foundation.[1] It was this experiment at Central High that signaled that the reformer movement had taken root in Denver. This was not just a district-managed closure and redesign. The experiment brought in big foundation money and extra-local advisors who advocated a small schools model that had first been instituted in bigger coastal cities. The Central High saga also established Denver as one major epicenter of a growing national reform movement, and major media outlets as far away as New York watched closely as these experiments unfolded.

Although it is widely recognized as a "movement," there is surprisingly little written about the *advocates* who drive this movement, beyond their role as instruments of neoliberal policy. In much of the critical literature, education reform is often portrayed as a process driven by neoliberal policy directions that passively flow down from social elites to low-income schools and communities. In other critical studies, the reform agents, when they are explicitly named, are presented as hostile to community partnerships, and as elite bearers of a broader abstract market-driven logic. For example, Pauline Lipman demonstrates how the major mover of Renaissance 2010 in Chicago was a tight-knit network of corporate, financial, and political elites known as the Commercial Club.[2] Similarly, Kenneth Saltman found that a major player in school reform is the philanthropic foundation.[3] Reform advocates' use of *discourse* has been documented in other works, with critics demonstrating how reformers' use of civil rights language operates as a disingenuous ruse to push through market-based reforms.[4]

All of these important critiques have largely focused on neoliberal education reform in terms of education policy and rhetoric (in a macro sense), rather than on the reformers in local communities who move these policies forward.

In various phases of the Central High reforms, the district—in conjunction with foundation representatives and other reformers—convened community forums to discuss possibilities for reforms. Reformers invited some community nonprofit organizations to establish outposts inside the school and act as liaisons to the community. Reformers spoke publicly to the news media and at neighborhood association meetings about the injustices of substandard schooling at Central, citing the need for urgent change. Many of them became familiar faces to the families of students most affected by the reforms. The self-proclaimed reformers in Denver align themselves with racial justice work, place themselves in a historical lineage of civil rights activism, and invite select community partnerships in their quest to reform schools and neighborhoods. In the course of my research I saw these reformers regularly appear at community events hosted by a select group of nonprofit grassroots organizations they invite to work with them. Even as they align with an elite national reform movement that is seemingly disconnected from local communities, local reformers seek common ground with institutionalized grassroots social justice groups that are also organizing for racial justice in the school system. It is important to understand reformers' identities as educational justice advocates and their perceptions of social and educational justice in order to understand their coalition politics. Without an understanding of who these reformers are and what drives their advocacy, we are unable to make sense of their attempts to mobilize localized support for controversial market-based education reforms.

Reformers' advocacy contains openings for partnerships between themselves, their organizations, and the various community-based justice groups who share their concerns. Far from being faceless vessels for a more distant and destructive neoliberal agenda, these reform agents attempt to coalesce with specific community organizations that are also concerned with the fate of public education in this city. Overwhelmingly, they see themselves as representing a profoundly righteous movement for civil rights. As other scholars have noted, elite reformers use civil rights language as policy rhetoric that in the end functions to deny the existence of systemic racism.[5] But they also use this language as a strategic tool to find common ground with local grassroots racial justice activists and build nascent coalitions with groups they see as valuable allies. In cities like Denver where school reform is a contentious and pervasive project, these coalitions matter in making reforms politically palatable. Reformers' coalitions with community groups are all the more important to the project of neoliberal reform in the wake of school reform disasters like Central High's small schools experiment. Reformers seek community partners to legitimize and champion controversial reforms such as school closures, turnarounds, and new charter school models. As one reformer admitted to me, "Honestly, I think we need community groups more than they need us." In essence, they need community coalitions in order to effectively sell the public on the proposal that market-based reforms, even though led by elite and predominantly White educational outsiders, are part and parcel of a long history of civil rights advocacy in education.

At the same time, reform advocates' effort to coalesce with select grassroots organizations in the name of educational justice masks two fundamental processes. First, it masks the degree to which reformers use these partnerships to translate market logic—which is not publicly palatable—into the auspices of an educational equity project, which *is* more publicly palatable. Second, reformers' partnerships with grassroots organizations mask their role in designing the racial exclusion and dispossession that make urban renewal possible. As critical race scholars point out, their racial exclusion and dispossession are systemic, and are perpetuated *despite* reformers' good intentions and identities as civil rights advocates.[6] Reformers' attitude toward social justice involves a host of paradoxes and double standards that in the end constrain their community reach. They are motivated by a desire to see equal access to education for all children, but they refuse to situate educational inequality within larger frameworks of systemic racism. This omission fundamentally limits their ability to meaningfully partner with a wider range of racial justice activists across a broader array of issues, and ultimately limits the scope of their community work. They advocate racial equity but excuse and even promote school segregation; they strive to bring middle-class cultures to newly reformed schools while fervently opposing the actual redistribution of tax monies or middle-class resources to under-resourced schools; and they champion schools to which they openly admit they would never send their own children. Even as they see themselves as passionate civil rights advocates and actively seek out community partnerships, they also promote color-blind market-based staples of reform (such as school choice, educational experimentation, and standardization) as the best and often the *only* routes to racial equity.

Reformers seek community partnerships with certain institutionalized community nonprofits but shun others, especially the Black and Latinx community activists outlined in the next chapter. While I saw reformers show up regularly to community forums when they were hosted by local nonprofit movement organizations, I rarely saw reformers show up to neighborhood African American community events or discussion forums. Once, I sat for an hour at one Black neighborhood forum as Black and Latinx community activists in the loosely organized group Community Education Collective (CEC) waited for a prominent school reformer to show. Although he said he would come talk to the group about a recent district decision to close a local low-performing high school, he never showed. Even as reformers claim to be fierce advocates of racial equity, they often discredit the informal networks of parents and community activists who have demanded to have a voice in school reform, particularly in Black neighborhoods where experimental reforms don't align with community goals. I argue that the paradoxes replete throughout reformer identities, philosophies, and approaches help to explain how and why these reformers reach out to form community partnerships with some groups even as they exclude, alienate, and discredit others.

The local network of reformers described in this chapter represents an array of institutions and interests. This includes representatives of small foundations, some local and some national, as well as think tanks that are affiliated with larger national interest groups. Their members include former principals and leaders of elite private schools, prominent Democrats, alums of the national program Teach for America (which places teaching fellows in low-income schools as teachers), state and city school board members, school-community liaisons employed by the city school district, independent reform consultants, newspaper reporters, and bloggers. Few of these reformers would call themselves "neoliberals," and many might even say they object to the overarching free-market philosophy that underscores school reform. There is not necessarily a guiding text or core book at the center of their ideology. Rather, they see themselves as passionate, motivated, well intentioned, and fundamentally *qualified* to revamp the education system. They are clear about their identity as "reformers" and claim the title eagerly— even as other community activists periodically partnering with these reformers are careful to distance themselves from this contentious label. Their emphasized identity as reformers is not just rhetorical maneuvering; these activists are engaging in activist identity work that represents their perceived centrality in the battle to make educational equity the final frontier of the civil rights movement.[7] Here is another paradox at the heart of their movement: even as reformers stress to the public that they want to work collectively with diverse community groups, their perception of themselves as "real" reformers relegates any coalition partner outside the reform movement as peripheral.

Existing critiques of school reform highlight the ways reform's proposed programs are fueled by neoliberal ideologies that embrace market forces and individual choice, and rely on the increasing privatization of public resources. Yet in focusing on the ideological underpinnings of policy reform, we often lose sight of the ways ideologies animate social actors. Rather than viewing reform as a faceless market-driven force that shapes education policy from above, I argue that these local reform advocates actually "activate" neoliberal policy, which entails the difficult work of organizing agents *outside* the reformer movement to support market reforms. At the nexus of a national elite movement and a local landscape of racial and immigrant justice movements, these reform activists position neoliberal market logic as the ultimate expression of social justice, and use this ideology to guide their coalition building. As Quiroz argues, in the context of urban gentrification, racially inclusionary initiatives (such as the reformer-community alliances described in this chapter) can work to further marginalize specific communities of color. They "are in fact, what often allow us to sustain (and deny) the pernicious effects of racism."[8]

Reaching Out: Reformers as Civil Rights Advocates

I'd say New Orleans is a model for reform. I wish we could just have a hurricane in Denver! But you don't have a tornado or a hurricane every day. For a reformer it was a perfect blank palette, right? You've wiped out the entire infrastructure of a school district or the parish system and all of a sudden there's a whole bunch of kids that still need an education. You have some buildings and you have absolutely no district infrastructure, so it's the perfect place for reformers to start new schools. And that's what they've done, right? It's fascinating. But I think in New Orleans there's a fair amount of consensus about charters being a good mechanism or tool for reform. I'd say that's less the case everywhere else. And certainly less the case in Denver.

—Terry, reformer

Terry, a lifelong sports enthusiast and Ivy League graduate, had worked in public policy before blending his passions for sports and education into a stint leading sports education programs for kids. Terry recalls that he felt personally transformed by the power of sports to change kids' lives, especially those living in poverty and struggling academically in their schools. In Terry's view, sports education, unlike traditional public education, has the power to challenge kids socially and emotionally and to build grit, a kind of individual resilience he sees as necessary for academic achievement.[9] All these qualities, he believes, contribute to students' academic achievement and growth. This formative experience of teaching sports exposed Terry to the troubling gap between the persistent "underachievement" of low-income students of color and their capabilities when given an innovative challenge and unique educational environment. Although not a trained teacher himself, Terry left his position as a leader of sports education programming with what he felt was a call to overhaul public schooling. He began networking with other professionals to start a local education reform think tank. The aim of this think tank is to invite innovative reformers from cities like New Orleans, New York, Chicago, and Washington, DC, to share more about the national push for innovative reform and other cities' educational experiments. The think tank, as it has evolved, champions local experimental approaches to education such as new charter schools, and attempts to forge an education "community" out of the various likeminded local policy makers, investors, entrepreneurs, bloggers, foundation representatives, individual school leaders, and journalists who identify education reform as a pressing social issue. To be clear, they argue that the issue of education reform is as relevant to urban development and renewal as it is to civil rights.

Education reformers from this network tell me often that education reform is "*the* civil rights issue of our time." At community meetings hosted by an immigrant rights community nonprofit, I have seen other reformers publicly draw on their own histories as activists or their parents' histories as civil rights activists to claim affinity with the racial equity work community organizations do. Terry, for example, tells me that he sees himself as a local civil rights activist who represents the kind of national network of reformers like those instrumental in New Orleans and other cities, a movement that is largely White, male, and elite.[10] Several self-identified reformers in Denver tell me that Terry is one of the most influential local reformers and is an unapologetic proponent of charter schools, foundation-infused educational experiments, and aggressive closure and reinvention of low-performing neighborhood schools. As Terry laments in the passage above, there is no magic hurricane to wipe away a dysfunctional public school system in Denver. Without a natural disaster, it takes a think tank and a network of committed activists to accomplish the same radical overhaul of the public school system, one that in Terry's view will finally bring educational justice to the children who have long been denied it.

It is telling that in Terry's description of the school reforms that followed the devastation of New Orleans, he perceives broad-based "consensus" over reform, thereby discounting the landmark Black community organizing against neoliberal reform in that city. In fact, there were many protests aimed to stop school closures, teacher firings, and charter takeovers, but these details are all but invisible in Terry's narrative about New Orleans as a model for radical reform. As critical race and education scholars Adrienne Dixson, Kristen Buras, and Elizabeth Jeffers argue,

The seizing of public education by way of school buildings, jobs, and the curriculum is premised on White supremacist notions that African Americans are unfit not only to govern but also to teach Black children. The entire power structure of public education in New Orleans has been recast to represent the views, beliefs, and desires of a White minority.[11]

As Terry's quote demonstrates, the African American resistance to the reforms in New Orleans is delegitimized to the point of invisibility, and falls in line with this assessment of White dominance in education reform. However, Terry also underscores that in a city like Denver, a lack of "consensus" means that reformers must work harder to mobilize the public to support reforms. Terry's think tank also studies how reformers in other cities have involved community groups in their reform agendas. Paradoxically, in a movement dominated by a White minority, there are conditions under which communities of color become visible as useful and important allies.

One example of this is the Urban Parent Network (UPN) in Denver. This organization largely represents low-income urban White and Latinx parents around the city and across several schools. The UPN's goals have included organizing parents at newly reformed schools, increasing per-pupil funding at low-income schools, and helping to design new transportation systems that enable low-income families to take advantage of choice. One evening, in front of a packed gymnasium at a local school, UPN members (first speaking Spanish and then translating to English) stand on the gymnasium stage next to the seated district superintendent and elected local school board members, and aggressively grill the school representatives with questions and present their demands: "Will you commit to more innovation in the schools?" "Will you pledge to increase the pace of reform in our schools?" The school district representatives on stage, all of whom are vocal advocates of the reform movement, quickly agree to the parents' demands and promise that they will do their best despite the structure of the sluggish bureaucracy within which they must work (and technically oversee). Commenting on the UPN organizers' seemingly brash demands, one reformer says into the microphone, "I think UPN is starting a revolution tonight!" and the audience in the gymnasium loudly applauds. There are several of the city's reformers in the audience as well.

On other occasions, I witness another Denver-based organization, Justice for Our Communities (JOC), hold several public forums—in front of media and a packed room of supporters—to address racial disparities in discipline and academic achievement across the district. Key reform activists, including those representing the school board and the school district, repeatedly show up to these events. Even though these reformers are interrogated in the same way as they are by the UPN in other public forums, they sported the same T-shirts that the JOC youth activists wore, which read in graffiti-style print, "Educate, don't discriminate!" The matching T-shirts would seem to suggest, upon first glance, that reformers and local racial justice activists share the same goals.

In contrast to existing critiques of neoliberal education reform that argue that this elite movement discounts low-income community power entirely, reformers in this study overwhelmingly agree that community involvement in schooling—and to a certain extent in school reform processes—is a worthy goal of the reform movement. Reformers emphasize to me in their interviews that community engagement is essential to raising student achievement, and are encouraged by emerging discussions in school reform circles that recognize the possible links between parent and community engagement and student achievement. Many offer accounts of how specific schools in the city had been successfully "turned around" when parents and community groups have cooperated with innovative school and district leaders. As evident in the meeting with the UPN above, reformers see community activists as informed and successful when they choose for themselves the reforms that most easily align with neoliberal reform goals, namely, school choice and charter school expansion. When they don't, they are quickly seen as ill informed, self-defeating, and even dangerous. One reformer laments the lack of community mobilization to create charter schools: "We need to figure out how to mobilize these [neighborhood] activists to actually work towards what's in their best interest. Unfortunately we don't see the same community passion around promoting charter schools as we've seen around opposing them." Reformers often recognize the value of community participation in reform, and try to figure out how to convert community activists from mobilizing around neighborhood schools to mobilizing around better school *choices*.

"We Can't Wait One More Day": Urgency and Accountability as Shared Coalition Values

Reformers struggle to find community support for their proposed education reforms, but they also want to involve diverse stakeholders in education, insofar as these stakeholders advance the reform philosophy. Many of the reformers I interviewed describe the school reform movement as a democratizing force in the battle to improve schools. In their view, reform allows an entry point for innovative and well-meaning entrepreneurs with management experience and business smarts to save a failing system from the grip of what they see as an out-of-touch collection of education professionals—teachers, administrators, curriculum specialists, and unions—who have for decades mismanaged public education. Central to reformers' visions for educational change and social justice are two values that make the reform movement particularly open to local coalition building: *urgency* and *accountability*.

For reformers, an ethic of urgency is required in order to make meaningful change to a failing school system. As one former private school principal charged with resuscitating a low-performing public school puts it, "This is serious business. We have no time to waste." Likening school reform to high-stakes surgery, this principal, a self-identified reformer, continues,

> Imagine yourself operating on a brain transplant or something like that, some unprecedented surgery, and, you know, it's high-stakes, because you've got this patient on the table and the risks are high and the stakes are high. And then you've got all the people up there, watching the surgery, like in the gallery. The pressure of the patient's life is the stress. But those people observing . . . I think for an experienced surgeon, they're not paying attention to who's watching.

In this analogy, this new principal of a struggling school is an expert surgeon trying to operate on a critically ill patient (the students), with people (the community) watching from the gallery of the observing room. Driven by the importance of the task, he suggests, he is impervious to the audience's presence and concerns. Reformers' language about schooling disaster is filled with this kind of vivid imagery about the dire nature of urban schooling. Metaphors of reformers "saving" struggling students on an incredibly tight timeline are ubiquitous throughout reformer narratives. This language of immediate, radical life-saving reform allows reformers to position the entire public school system as fundamentally and irreparably broken. In this worldview, it is a system that in fact harms children. Almost all reformers I interviewed express a profound dissatisfaction with incremental change and display a heroic impatience for this vision of rapid change. A local foundation representative, who passionately argues that education is "*the* civil rights issue of our time," puts it this way:

> You have to deconstruct the system in order to save it. You have to destroy it in order to fix it. It sort of feels that way. If it felt like we have only been trying to fix the system for three years, or five years, and were making progress, then it would drive us to say this is pretty bad, I think we need to slow down, give this more time. But it's been twenty years, you know. . . . There's been no progress. That just tells me all I need to know. I'm just not very good at being patient to keep up with the generations of kids going through that system, and falling off the cliff.

The discourse of crisis is often used to usher in neoliberal reforms that privatize formerly public goods and circumvent public input and democratic processes.[12] What some have called "disaster capitalism" is alive and well in neoliberal moves to radically alter the public education system.[13] In disaster capitalism, the language of "disaster," "crisis," and "urgency" is used to secure public consent while radical and rapid neoliberal reforms are implemented before local communities have a chance to meaningfully participate in (or block) the process. Throughout the country, severely underfunded schools that have been ignored and divested for decades by wealthier communities are now being heralded as emergencies—disasters that must be fixed immediately. This language is readily available to reformers, who use it to drive the importance of demolishing existing underfunded schools and rebuilding something new.

Many of the racial justice activists in the city's more formal community nonprofit organizations demand immediate reform for urgent educational problems like the racial achievement gap and the dearth of college-ready curricula across the district. Some of these movement organizations, especially those descended from the Chicano student movement, see the current moment of education reform as more open to grassroots pressure than were previous eras. In contrast to past efforts to participate in discussions with impenetrable public school bureaucracies, this historical moment provides an entry point for select institutionalized movement organizations to enter into school reform debates and initiatives, along with the social entrepreneurs of the reformer movement who are also not trained education professionals. As Naomi Klein points out, the rhetoric of "urgency" and "crisis" helps to legitimize elites' unilateral radical changes to education, housing, and other public goods. In reformers' view, efforts to slow down a reform process to study its effects or to deliberate using democratic processes in fact only prolong the crisis, further harming students. For local community organizations, urgency can also represent a moment of "interest convergence" that in practice holds the potential to unify reformers and racial justice activists, at least momentarily, in shared campaigns for educational change.[14] It also demands that those responsible for educational success be held accountable to show improvement.

As education scholar Tatiana Suspitsyna notes, "accountability" has been showcased by government, business, and industry as an absolute good since the turn of the millennium; it "has become engrained in American education and spawned its own culture that places a strong value on transparency, measurement, and evaluation."[15] Although community groups that mobilize around educational justice issues also demand accountability and transparency, Suspitsyna argues that the market-oriented accountability in recent decades of education reform has functioned more as tool of neoliberal managerialism. "Largely because accountability within the dominant new managerialist paradigm seeks to manage rather than erase inequality, it has a limited potential for critical evaluation of and change in the existing praxis of education."[16] This neoliberal notion of accountability filters down to the movement level, as reformers expect grassroots groups to be the primary agents of managerial accountability. Rather than viewing community groups as responsible for crafting the solutions, the reformers in this study who insist that community engagement is important to school reform and student achievement use the language of *accountability* to describe the best role for parents and community groups. They argue that community engagement is vital for holding schools accountable to reformers' agendas. Accountability, at its core, requires a demonstration that students are learning more than they were before. For reformers, this, quite simply, translates into measurable improvements from standardized testing.

From this perspective, reformers imagine that parents could be responsible for monitoring these measures and complaining when kids don't improve. For example, one reformer, the director of a reform-oriented advocacy group, tells me that parents can be "trained' to have an eye for data and the hard test scores:

> Let's take a parent-teacher conference: All right, parents can know, or can be taught, I think, what a good parent-teacher conference is. If a teacher comes in and says, "Your son is great, he's doing well, really well, he's smart," you ought to know there's a problem. I mean every parent can know, "I want to see *data* on my kid's performance." They ought to know about a school's test scores. You know, if their school is producing *x* and the school down the street with the same demographic is producing *y*, they ought to know, I mean they ought to be able to raise hell about that.

Nearly all reformers in this study strongly believe that parents and the community groups representing them should have this kind of empowerment—understanding how to read scores and compare them to those of other schools—and that test scores should be transparent to the public. They believe that parents should be able to see which teachers are adding value to their child's education (as evidenced in test scores), and which are subtracting value (presumably by falling scores). They should have the hard data in their hands. For reformers, this should be the goal of community organizing.

Despite the value these reformers see in educating and empowering parents and community groups to become knowledgeable about educational justice in the context of standardized metrics, the urgency to save children from substandard schooling works to narrow the scope of community engagement in reform. Reformers, like activists in low-income communities of color, demand quick and urgent reform to failing schools. Unlike community activists, however, these reformers consistently value urgent change *over* community participation and negotiation in moments when community participation might be contentious or multifaceted. This would represent a complication that would inevitably slow the process of reform. Because reformers value cooperation over dialogue and debate, the coalitions they seek to build are tenuous.

As reformers recognize the ways they fail to build long-lasting coalitions with communities, the rhetoric of urgency serves to justify this shortcoming. One former state school board member who brokered many school closures around the state emphasizes his appreciation for the important role that community participation can play in reshaping neighborhood schools. However, he pinpoints the fundamental conflicting timelines between community participation and the urgent need for innovation, positioning meaningful community participation as an element that slows school reform. As such, he tempers his appreciation of community input in favor of expediency. Noting this intractable dilemma, he explains, "It's partially this attitude of the school reform movement: 'We have failed these low-income kids for so long, we can't let them fail for one more day and we have to do something about it.' And so what is the balance? What is the balance between helping the kids and getting community involvement? That's the crux of it."

Reformers who defend the urgency of school reforms in the name of "not letting kids fail for one more day" at times see community involvement as being at odds with the larger project of urgently saving kids. Racial justice activists in community nonprofits like the UPN or JOC also value urgency in education reform. Yet for reformers, urgency is invoked as justification for why community participation should be jettisoned if it is contentious and slows down the pace of reform. Similarly, the shared value of accountability narrows the scope of coalition building between the reformer movement and other social justice activists, since for reformers "holding schools accountable" relates only to standardized metrics, and not to other less tangible but equally important dimensions of school success such as equitable discipline and suspension policies and cultural competency, for example.

Deficient Community Allies: The Lack of Parental and Community Expertise

Reformers imagine that community coalition partners share their mandate for urgent reform and have the power to hold school leaders accountable for implementing the reforms they innovate. But they distinguish these "good" community partners—who are typically housed in formal nonprofit organizations and are seen as worthy of partnership—from the "backwards" community activists who band together in less formal settings and demand ownership over their neighborhood schools.

Most reformers recognize that low-income parents experience multiple barriers to participating in their children's education, which include work schedules, lack of education, and language barriers. Rather than working to tackle these barriers, reformers accept these barriers as a given, and see them as a reason why increasing parental and community engagement in children's education is unlikely to be an achievable and "replicable" large-scale school reform goal. As one Teach for America graduate who is currently helping to direct a state reform advocacy organization puts it,

> You have kids from a home where English is not spoken, where the parents, you know, the mother is at home with the little kids and doesn't speak English, the father is working, like, four jobs, and they couldn't even understand the homework, much less help them with calculus at the high school level. I don't know if that offers any replicable solutions there because those parents are going to not be as engaged as, you know, parents who have other opportunities and backgrounds . . . so I guess I do think parent involvement matters tremendously, but I'm not sure it can be done on a widespread scale.

For reformers like this one, schools, not parents, are ultimately responsible for student achievement. In the face of economic, linguistic, and cultural barriers to effective parental engagement, this parental and community engagement is of questionable value. Reformers often speak of low-income parents in terms of deficits: they are admittedly stakeholders, but ones who lack the real expertise necessary to participate in some of the more urgent school reform debates. One representative of a local education reform foundation likens schools to hospitals, and vividly describes the importance of expertise as a qualification for entrance: "It's like the hospital. I mean, you know, medical personnel only beyond this point. You don't just walk in." In many ways, this analogy captures the sentiment of many reformers: there is a time and place for community coalitions, but as important as low-income parents are to those spaces, they cannot compete with the educational expertise of reformers and thus don't belong in their conversations and processes. Another reformer at a foundation that funds reformer-community initiatives describes the important conversations school reform requires for which parents are unqualified to participate:

> You know, there are limitations to what community organizing can accomplish. And this is a field where we have to understand that there is a body of knowledge and an expertise and that at some point you have to let the professionals, who we hope are trained, do their job. And we have to trust them. So you can't have parents mucking around the curriculum. You can't have parents making determinations, for the most part, around what a quality teacher is.

In these perceptions, parents and loose-knit movement groups (such as those profiled in the next chapter) are seen as unqualified and should not be included in reform efforts. In contrast, formally organized community groups that work to speak reformer language, which includes efforts to examine the data from which school reformers draw their conclusions, are seen as legitimate "experts" in the school reform debate and are provided opportunities to participate. Notably, even though reformers see themselves as maverick educational outsiders well positioned to shake up broken school districts, they nevertheless perceive themselves to be "qualified" to design and execute reforms. In their view, actual professionals who hold education degrees and trained teachers are not qualified either; they are responsible for decades of educational failure and represent the status quo. In the reformer lexicon, "innovation" and "experimentation" become core methods of educational improvement, even when they periodically fail. In contrast, the "status quo" and anyone perceived as defending it become potent enemies.

One pro-reform school board member describes why she respects the UPN: "They have worked to create their own capacity, to make sure they have become knowledgeable themselves, so we're having a conversation *on the same level.*" Rather than being seen as an "angry community group," as many parents who are excluded from the process of reform are, this group that supports rapid reform is seen as a valuable collaborator and partner. The UPN's public and aggressive display of holding the district leadership accountable to its promises for reform was ultimately read by reformers as cooperative, and did not conflict with reformers' own goals for swift reform and school choice. UPN activists do not consider reformers inside or outside the school district to be unconditional allies (further explored in chapter 5). Yet all reformers consider the UPN to be an example of a cooperative and not "angry" community group and an important school reform ally.

Illustrating this distinction, one school board member compares the UPN to a neighborhood-based African American network that recently protested another neighborhood school closure. While the UPN is seen as data-driven and supportive of change, this other group is cast as delusional, emotional, and reliant on "nostalgia" in its opposition to change, rendering its members fundamentally unqualified to participate in discussions:

> And there's this other group saying, "The community should decide." Well, you know, there's a whole group of people who are living in the past, and folks whose own experience for success in education was so poor that they couldn't even articulate or have a vision of what successful education ought to look like, you know? It's nostalgia. And nostalgia isn't a strategy for reform.

As the above quote demonstrates, there is a pervasive belief among many reformers that low-income parents' values and visions for quality education should not be trusted. Several reformers housed in local foundations and two who work at a prominent reform advocacy organization used the term "happy talk" to describe low-income parents' perceptions of quality schooling, which they largely perceived parents themselves had not had. One foundation representative describes it this way:

> "Happy talk" is a lot of unsophisticated parents who maybe haven't had a lot of training or background in school reform. They go into their kids' school on a sort of PTA basis and they say, "Oh, this is such and such, my kid's teacher is so nice" and "Oh, my son is so happy and he seems to really enjoy coming to school" and they never get to the question: what is

the school's track record with academic achievement, and what are they doing to change it?

In considering how to move reform forward, they see happy talk as something that holds back progress. Instead, they imagine that training parents to read data would be a better formula for success:

> Let's get past that and let's give parents the tools to know whether the kids are learning in the schools. Johnny is coming home and he's happy but he doesn't have any homework, he doesn't progress, and he isn't reading at grade level. But you think it's a great school because the teachers and principals are nice to you? So, you know, you have to have ownership over that research knowledge in order to make good decisions.

Reformers imagine these efforts to provide "ownership over research knowledge" to be a kind of community empowerment, consistent with their ideals for creating educational equality. They champion this kind of empowerment even as they discount parents' lived experiences with educational institutions. In the reformer imagination, "good" community allies like the UPN are distinguished by their access to expert knowledge and their desire to work within an urgency framework. Instead of opposing reformers, they aggressively advocate for reform in the name of educational equity. "Backwards" community voices value the wrong things and ultimately stand for the status quo. They, not the schools, then, hold their children back. As Janelle Scott writes,

> The current advocacy politics have created a context in which critics of market-based reforms are relegated to being supporters of an indefensible status quo. The result of this rendering is that market advocates, many of whom are White and come from elite backgrounds, are seen as legitimate, the "real reformers," even when their efforts contribute to racially stratified schooling and are silent on other matters of inequality and poverty. And those who raise questions about the directions and effects of their reforms are seen as obstructionist, in the pockets of the teachers unions, as anti–civil rights, and in support of maintaining a racial achievement gap.[17]

It is worth noting that reformers' perceptions of "happy talk" and "nostalgia" are not necessarily representative of what parents actually say or do. As detailed in the next chapter, African American community activists who network across their gentrifying neighborhoods evidence very little "happy talk," and express multiple critiques of their children's schooling even as they fight for the preservation of the neighborhood school model. Yet reformers interpret their calls for neighborhood schools—and their insistence on open, transparent, inclusive, and democratic decision making—as preserving the status quo. Reformers, frustrated by these parents, their community networks, and their refusal to engage data and metrics in discussions, write off African American neighborhood activists as fundamentally against change and therefore deficient change agents who are unqualified for meaningful participation. Parental and community engagement is seen as most valuable, then, when it is fundamentally cooperative with school reformers, and when it embraces their timeline for urgent change. Those who oppose reformers' goals are dismissed as undermining children's well-being. It is partially through this denigration of Black non-institutionalized community activism that reformers position themselves as the "real" reformers.[18]

This reform advocate identity contains a contradictory element. A "real" reformer's genesis is *outside* the formal school system, as opposed to the bureaucratic-heavy career educator, principal, or administrator. Yet compared to "nostalgic" and backwards low-income people of color, the "real" reformers are somehow also more qualified to engineer educational experiments because they come from privileged backgrounds. Compared to these "backwards" community members, "real reformers" are also qualified professionals, though it is not clear *what*, besides racial and class privilege, qualifies them to remake school systems and cities.[19]

Drawing Inward: Resegregation and the Remaking of School Communities

The reformer values of urgency and accountability provide openings for select institutionalized community groups to find interest convergence and stretch the neoliberal imagination. Often, these reformer-community partnerships hold the potential to infuse market-based visions of reform with racial justice goals. However, reform advocates further restrict their coalition building in several ways. As demonstrated in the previous section, reform advocates reach out to institutionalized nonprofits while shunning informally networked community groups (such as the low-income Black neighborhood schools activists profiled in the next chapter). Adolf Reed Jr. provides a potent explanation for elites' preference for institutionalized nonprofit activism: "This translates into a preference for a brokered 'politics as usual' that limits the number and range of claims on the policy agenda. Such a politics preserves the thrust of inherited policy regimes and reinforces existing patterns of systemic advantage by limiting the boundaries of the politically reasonable. . . . Those [NGO] organizations often earn their insider status in the first place by providing a convincing alternative to popular political mobilization."[20] But reformers also reject racial integration as a legitimate racial justice goal, and instead advocate building segregated school communities guided by middle-class values. These visions diverge from both formal and informal racial justice organizations, and limit the extent to which they can build strong and long-lasting coalitions around reform initiatives.

Racial segregation in public schooling has been growing since the 1970s.[21] Despite the enduring gravity of the 1954 US Supreme Court decision in *Brown v. Board of Education*, which concluded that separate is intrinsically unequal, racial integration has *not* been a goal of the reform movement, even though reformers themselves see their work as extending the legacy of civil rights organizing around educational equity. Instead, "choice" has replaced integration in the reformist imagination. According to reform advocates, access to choice de-links poverty-stricken students from their crumbling neighborhood schools. It sets them free, and allows them to search for a better option. Reformers argue that choice prevents one's zip code from determining one's destiny. It is *choice* that delivers equal opportunity, not necessarily racially integrated schools. As one influential reformer journalist explains, racial integration does not necessarily ensure equal opportunity:

> Well, I don't think segregation is the issue. I think it's *opportunity*, and kids who have been deprived access to opportunity, or deprived oppor-

tunity. And segregation does that. You know, we have pretty segregated schools. . . . But I think for the first time, we're making a good-faith effort to prioritize equity, and to prioritize opportunity for our students.

In this reformer's vision, resegregation endangers educational opportunity, but racial integration is not necessarily the only way to ensure this opportunity. Resegregation can be balanced out by the provision of school choice.

What is striking in school reformer narratives is the emphasis on economic integration rather than racial integration. Education scholars have begun to notice that in the last few decades, there has been a rollback in the quest for racial desegregation in education and more emphasis on economic diversity and integration.[22] As Linn Posey-Maddox argues, relying on an influx of middle-class families into the urban school system as a central education reform policy results in exacerbated racial and class inequalities, including school resegregation and the exclusion of low-income families from school decision-making processes.[23] Yet, in my interviews with reformers, there is uniform consensus that economic integration will make schools better and improve education for low-income kids. Indeed, most agree that it is the *key* to improving education for low-income kids. For example, one reformer succinctly describes the intractable challenges presented by poverty: "There are so many layers and complexities, all the challenges, and different competing interests, that there's no way that under the current structure those kids are going to be able to fix themselves." For reformers, low-income kids (and by extension their families and neighborhoods) need what middle-class families have. The solution is to create schools that draw children from different neighborhood and socioeconomic levels that position middle-class families (reformers' use "sophisticated" and "savvy" as euphemisms for class- or race-advantaged) as the squeaky wheels who demand the "right" kind of change. The result that reformers imagine is a kind of trickle-down educational quality that results from this economic integration, since middle-class parents know how to put the "right" kind of pressure on schools to get what they want. As a result, they succeed in bringing in resources to the school that benefit *all* kids. One reformer explains,

It's just basic hard politics stuff, which is if you got savvy sophisticated parents who know how to work the system in the school, they're going to get better stuff for that school than if the school is full of low-income, disconnected parents. So what tends to happen is people advocate for their own kids.

Reformers advocate different strategies to attract middle-class families to schools with socioeconomic diversity. Some reformers see that new charter schools could be engines for revitalizing low-income communities. These schools could double as community centers and job training centers for the adults in the community, could partner with local libraries and recreation centers, and could work synergistically with already existing parks and urban infrastructure. These reformers, who have a broader vision for neighborhood change, see charters as not only creating educational opportunity, but also potentially opening up possibilities to shift whole neighborhoods in order to attract the desired middle-class population to move into those neighborhoods. They imagine that this influx of savvy middle-class residents will ultimately make schools better. Other reformers argue that by simply changing the internal culture of low-income schools, they could also change the image that low-income schools project to outsiders. This would make public schools more attractive to White middle-class families. This is in fact something that new schools are intentionally trying to do. One new principal of a reformed school explains his efforts, contrasting reformers' cultural makeover with what criminologist CalvinJohn Smiley and public health scholar David Fakunle critique as racist "thug" imagery, a term that has been broadly used by mainstream media outlets as a tool for criminalization and "a way to describe Black males who reject or do not rise to the standard of White America."[24]

There is some obvious stuff that we're doing, [making schools into] safer environments, showing that our kids aren't, like, these urban thugs. And also things like uniforms help. But the more we can, like, start to see our kids in the neighborhood looking like students engaged in student activities and, you know, hearing more positives about increasing student attendance, increasing academic achievement, increasing college attendance, improve graduation rates, I think they're going to start to get the vibe. . . . But if they perceive this as an urban ghetto school with, like, a bunch of low-income kids who aren't doing well academically, a lot of discipline problems, of course it's going be off-putting.

Almost all reformers agree that changing the image of low-income schools and courting middle-class students are the ultimate goals. However, most recognize that bringing in a majority middle-class population into the schools would be a very difficult proposition. Reformers noted, sometimes with a heroic frustration, how resistant middle-class families are to integration. As one reformer says, "I wish I could say to some of these White families, 'Don't wait for something to change, for these schools to be good enough for your precious babies. You *are* the change that will make the school good enough.'" The power of White resistance, they admit, places barriers on their ability to actualize their vision of creating economically integrated schools. Many reformers admit feeling skeptical that mixed-income schools can really be created, since doing so depends so much on larger issues of neighborhood segregation. Some argue that in order for mixed-income schools to be created, mixed-income neighborhoods have to be created first. One reformer, for example, recognizes that in theory, White middle-class families in the district could be parceled out to low-income schools, as was done in the 1970s with busing and efforts to desegregate schools, but dismisses this idea as unacceptable since it would be "complete social engineering."

Instead of forcing the desired middle-class population into low-income schools, and instead of waiting for mixed-income neighborhoods to develop, almost all reformers argue that the next best thing is to replicate middle-class cultures in low-income schools. One reformer bluntly puts it this way: "Economic integration is not necessarily the answer. It's like any kind of diversity: the more diversity you have the better, ethnically and economically . . . but can it be done without it? Yes." As many interviewees explained to me, the way to do this is to intentionally create middle-class school cultures. Reformers characterize these as cultures that center academic standards with measured outcomes, and tight disciplinary mechanisms to which students must adhere.

For reformers, the standards movement, coupled with the creation of new cultures of discipline, is essential to creating middle-class environments for low-income kids of color. One reformer cites Geoffrey

Canada's widely touted approach to low-income students' success in
Harlem: "It's not that they have to sit next to a White kid, or a middle-
class kid, but they better be surrounded by that kind of value system
and that kind of support system or they're not gonna make it. I mean,
it's just kind of a no-brainer." As this reformer points out, the key is to
build a larger support system in the entire neighborhood, as Canada did
by bringing in community-wide wraparound social services for students
and their families. Even in referencing the concept of broader neighborhood resources, no reformers interviewed for this study elaborated on
the importance of those other community supports outside the school
environment itself. Rather, they focus heavily on individual interventions within the school. For example, another reformer describes the
importance of "giving" low-income students cultural capital:

> You probably don't need to test this empirically: kids come in the door
> without all the skills that a lot of us from middle-class backgrounds take
> for granted. And so we just need to teach those skills. We have to teach
> those skills *explicitly*. . . . There's cultural knowledge that has to be made
> explicit and taught because it's cultural *capital*. . . . You know, we say these
> kids lack [self-] discipline. But have we ever sat down and explained it to
> them? Or, how are you gonna introduce your parents to your advisor and
> to other people? You know what I mean? Teaching these social behaviors.
> And we're not assuming kids don't know them, we're just making sure
> that they do.

As this reformer describes his vision for establishing middle-class school
cultures in low-income schools, he imagines that this will provide students with much-needed cultural capital. Yet the vision of building
middle-class school cultures relies on a deficit model. Reformers like this
one assume that low-income communities lack the "behaviors, orientations, knowledge, and values that middle-class people take for granted,"
those that instill wealth, accomplishment, and individual mobility.
From this perspective, reformers imagine that the school must provide
what low-income parents and their larger communities cannot or will
not. In fact, this use of cultural capital ignores the fact that low-income
communities, immigrant communities, and communities of color also
have many forms of cultural capital (e.g., navigational capital, linguistic

capital, and familial capital), since these forms of capital are not valued by the dominant society.[25] The quest to build middle-class cultures in schools stands as a clear example of the paternalism characteristic of the reform movement.[26] Reformers elevate their own cultural values over the values of the communities they are trying to serve. Such paternalism undercuts their efforts to build community coalitions around possible shared values like urgency and accountability, and limits the potential for reformers to authentically align themselves with community struggles and promote racial equity. It also further marginalizes the families of those children they are urgently trying to "save" from substandard schooling. By focusing on socioeconomic class, reformers from middle- and upper-class backgrounds communicate their qualification to solve inequality in ways that erase the significance of race, thereby positioning market-based reform as the ultimate frontier of civil rights work.

The Disappearance of Race: Discipline and Standards as Social Justice

As the "real" reformers, these agents advocate neoliberal reforms in the name of racial equity, civil rights, and social justice. At times, reformers align themselves with racial justice activists whom they see as sharing their vision for how to end racial disparities in education. Yet at the same time, these reformers work diligently to deny the existence of systemic racism. One tool by which this happens is the focus on academic achievement as evidence of racial equity. Reformers posit that as low-income students and students of color embrace middle-class cultures, discipline, and values, they will succeed academically (as measured in improved test scores). Uniform educational standards, then, are the key tools that will solve racism in education. From this worldview, uniform expectations will result in higher academic achievement, which will in turn end systemic racial disparities. Reformers position high academic achievement—rather than a broader eradication of systemic racial bias in education—as the ultimate goal of the reform movement.

Rather than focusing on unequal resources at home or discrimination children and their parents may face in their neighborhoods, reformers see formal, race-blind expectations as the key to equity. As one reformer explains,

But to me, until you push to a set of instructional techniques, it really doesn't matter. I mean you can believe all you want that you're gonna achieve, this kid can achieve. Maybe they don't read the *Wall Street Journal* at home . . . but the beauty of the standards movement is if it were enforced strictly, we would expect every kid to achieve at this level and there are sticks and carrots. If the incentives are right, to really teach these kids well, then I believe the rest of the stuff would fall into place.

In this worldview, neoliberal accountability and standardized testing by default deliver color-blind educational equity and racial justice where traditional civil rights educational movements have failed. In the same breath, reformers dismiss culturally sensitive approaches to education by comparison, arguing that racist attitudes of teachers, school leaders, and school cultures are beyond the scope of what education reform can or *should* do. One reformer frames it like this:

Sometimes when I walk through the street late at night and there are a couple of African American, large boys walking down the street toward me, I cross the street. How do you fix that? And maybe you don't. Maybe all you can do is ensure that there are really high standards and ensure that those teachers are held accountable for making sure your kid reaches those standards, and that's the best you can do. You can't fix someone's soul, you just can't.

This reformer suggests that racial bias in education may be unresolvable. By relegating systemic racism to a defect of someone's inner life or "soul," reformers effectively deny racism as a social problem that could be dismantled through progressive social policy. Even as reformers see themselves and frame their movement in terms of civil rights and racial equity, they see standardization and accountability as the major mechanisms to eliminate racial bias in education. Systemic racism by comparison becomes an insurmountable and even *irrelevant* problem, falling outside the scope of what reform and community activism can tackle. Although reformers and institutionalized community movements converge in their calls for equalizing educational opportunity and closing the achievement gap, reformers' refusal to recognize racism as a systemic and central problem limits the extent to which they are able to engage in long-term coalitions with racial justice groups.

Universal high academic achievement is a social justice goal that *all* educational justice groups in this book share. But high academic achievement is but one facet of what "racial justice" in education means for grassroots groups. Other movement goals include the eradication of racist discipline policies that disproportionately push students of color into the prison pipeline; the use of culturally relevant pedagogies; and the inclusion of student voice in school decision making.[27] Much research demonstrates how the discontinuity between low-income students' home/community life and school life contributes to these students' decision to drop out of public schooling.[28] Yet, as reformers position high academic achievement driven by middle-class values as a *proxy* for racial justice, they erase the significant experience of racism that students and their families face. Their refusal to center racism as a central problem limits the extent to which reform advocates can effectively build coalitions with racial justice community groups that also view the achievement gap as one outcome of systemic racism that must be tackled.[29] Disregarding these concerns, most reformers argue that eventually parents and students will come to see the value in participating in these new school cultures. Even as they recognize the different cultures students may face between school and home, they reiterate their confidence that misguided parents will learn to stick with it and enjoy the results of higher academic achievement. For those parents who do not eventually buy in, one reformer suggests that schools will need to take a stand: "There's a line right here. When you cross into the school, these are the rules and values that you live by. And if you can't do that, you can't be here." In his estimation, parents usually rise to the school's expectations and accept what he characterizes as strong discipline and high expectations. Those who don't accept it exercise their consumer mobility and leave:

> And, you know, the parents buy into it because they send their kids, the kids either they buy into it or they don't. And they don't stay if they don't. But they have figured out that, even if there is a huge [dis]juncture between the two, the exchange that they make is that you will behave

here. We may be very strict with you, but you will also be safe here. It will be a safe environment where you can be as smart as you want to be, and it's safe.

Most reformers, like this one, often discuss the creation of middle-class cultures in the context of *discipline*. Sometimes explicitly, sometimes implicitly, reformers argue that strong and clear discipline is essential to building middle-class school communities. Through reformer narratives, it becomes clear that essential to the project of creating new school cultures is the creation of internal school communities, where students become bound to and accountable to each other, to the adults in the school building, and to the behavioral norms that dictate the boundaries of this community. Repeatedly when talking about instituting new school cultures in spaces where schools are deemed failing, reformers mention the necessity of building internal school communities of students and staff, and these communities become the bearers of these new school cultures. Without creating communities, they insist, there is no hope of creating new school cultures.

Inevitably, school reformers note that the key to creating these communities is to first enforce some kind of very clear structure of student discipline, essentially "disciplining" students into taking on the role of not only a student in a school, but also a member of a newly imagined community. Just as some school reformers speak about economic integration as "giving" students cultural capital, these reformers also speak about discipline as "giving" students social capital. They assume that schools can provide not just the values that middle-class people take for granted, but also the valuable social networks and connections to other people that help to determine a student's eventual success. Implicit in their statements is the belief that either students completely lack communities outside school—in their homes or neighborhoods—and need to be taught what it means *to be a member of a community*, or that their home communities do not provide valuable ties (and certainly not ties that will contribute to their academic and eventual job market success).

Another signifier of community and capital mentioned by all reformers in this study is the school uniform. These reformers admit that there is no compelling evidence showing a direct relationship between school uniforms and academic achievement. Nonetheless, reformers frame school uniforms as potent symbols, ways to discipline kids to see themselves as a part of an intentional school community. One reformer uses a football team metaphor to explain both the importance of a uniform and the self-sacrifice it requires: "For me, it's like a team. You know, nobody on a football team says, 'Well, I'm not gonna wear the uniform but I want to play in the game.'" In describing how the uniform communicates a sense of belonging in a learning community, he adds, "Yes, and a little bit of self-sacrifice. If I want it bad enough."

This reformer clarifies that this vision of a "team" or community is not easy for students and does not emerge organically. Instead, it demands some kind of self-sacrifice for the good of the entire team. Reformers promote a vision of community in which students subjugate both themselves as individuals and their membership in their home communities in order to "belong" to this internal and intentional school community. The school uniform then becomes the marker of membership and subjugation.

Another reformer explains the power dynamics involved in using school uniforms to discipline students into being community members. He admits that the clothes themselves do not predict educational outcomes:

All these schools that are way outperforming expectations, a large number of them have strict dress codes. But [it] isn't, like, the clothing, because, you know, I did my graduate work in my pajamas. Right? I mean, I locked myself in my room and I wrote. And how I was dressed did not influence the work that I did.

Instead, this reformer emphasizes that in these schools, power flows one way: from the administration down to the students. Uniforms are reminders of this power. They symbolically mark community membership, even as there is no empirical evidence that they actually affect performance. He continues,

In a community, it's like a uniform. It's one of the symbols. And it may be a factor that we ultimately determine in this complex social system we call school, as absolutely no influence in ten years from now, and all these schools that are really outperforming will drop their dress code. But right now all the high-performing schools that I visited, not only do they have dress codes, but they took it seriously. And I think it's the broken windows philosophy, that, you know, it's a symbol around which we can battle out who's in charge of what and who gets to set norms in this community, and if you want to be in this community you have to abide by the community rules.

In his narrative, this reformer draws a parallel between school reform and the broken windows thesis, developed by James Wilson and George Kelling.[30] The broken windows philosophy posits that the very aesthetics of minor forms of public disorder lead to serious crime. Therefore, by attending to these minor forms of public disorder, authorities can prevent more serious crime. In drawing this parallel, this reformer invokes school reform as a broader project of urban renewal, one that stands vigilant against minor infractions lest they lead to more serious crime and urban decay. Standardized, measurable education incorporates a broader standardization of children's self-presentation into the larger project of remaking urban schools, communities, and entire neighborhoods. Although the language of standards (whether applied to the formal curriculum or children's presentation of self) denies systemic racism, references to crime prevention as an educational strategy contain implicit racialized meanings.

The uniform, which reformers insist demonstrates the willing subjugation of children to White and adult-centered models of schooling, reveals an inconsistency in the trope of community: all students are expected to be "part" of this community, but clearly the rules of belonging are not decided by community members. Thus, the rhetoric of these schools as intentional learning "communities" becomes entangled in discussions of discipline, as school reformers argue that students must be disciplined into becoming community members, albeit particular *kinds* of community members. This power differential reflects the intentional creation of middle-class cultures in schools. Often these dress codes are designed to mimic middle-class dress norms, requiring all students to wear polo shirts, for example. Taken together, these disciplinary rules and symbolic gestures reflect the reformer construction of school communities that stand apart and above Black and Latinx students' home communities. Indeed, this creates a wedge between the reformer movement and the racial justice organizations with which they seek to align.

Reformers resist "socially engineering" schools in ways that forcibly mix gentrifying (White) families with low-income (Black and Latinx) families. This would be reminiscent of compulsory busing and its larger social and historical context in which racism was publicly named and tackled through progressive antiracist social policy. Instead, reformers advocate the use of uniforms and the creation of socially engineered school *cultures* as the next best thing to actual economic integration. The economic integration they imagine is more important than, and actually *supplants*, racial integration. While racial inequality may be intractable in the reformer imagination, new school cultures that teach values, community, and symbolic membership alongside high standards are imagined to stand in for the kinds of progressive antiracist policies (such as busing and racial integration) that were developed in the civil rights era.

"I Wouldn't Send My Own Kids There": Civil Rights and the Myth of Universal Standards

Reformers, in their narratives of school failures and needed intervention, criticize low-income parents for not being experts on educational quality, not asking for the right data, and not demanding ownership over the knowledge that "matters"—the test scores that they insist are the keys to accountability. As low-income community members aim to protect their neighborhood schools, reformers are dismissive of this form of "happy talk," which they believe reveals low-income parents' failures to understand the urgency of school reform.

Repeatedly, reformers emphasize in interviews that on an urgent school reform timeline, a student's happiness and comfort within a school are unnecessary luxuries. In fact, reformers explain that the strict discipline and structure of these reformed schools that may be confrontational or uncomfortable for students and their families enable new cultures of academic success to emerge. Reformers champion various structures of discipline, even those with more military-style structures that have been widely criticized for emphasizing conformity and zero tolerance.[31] Citing success in what they characterize as "beat the odds" schools, they argue that reformed schools with strict disciplinary cultures are compensating for the lack of structure and discipline in low-income kids' homes. All reformers in this study defend these discipline regimes and frame them as something the schools are "giving" to low-income kids to make up for something they lack in their own homes and neighborhoods. Most also preface this approval with the disclaimer, "I wouldn't send my own kids there." Reformers' willingness to champion schools that they themselves would never select for their own children underscores their belief in the fundamental differences between their children and the masses of low-income children of color who dominate the school system. As one influential journalist expressed,

> Just based on what I've seen in those schools and the results these schools are getting, I think they really are working. I went to visit one of these places and said, "I love this place, I think it's great, it's wonderful. I would never send my own kid there." I mean, I think different kinds of kids can be here, and it's not the school that my kid would have thrived in.

As they identify the ways children in reformed schools may dislike their schools, they describe them as a necessary compensation for what is broken in the children's families and neighborhoods. In contrast, reformers imagine their own children, who are seemingly intact, as needing inspiration and the freedom to problem-solve and critically think, more than they need discipline. A former city school board member who is now a board member of a reform advocacy organization describes this dynamic:

> Have you visited these schools? Well, they wear uniforms and look like . . . they aren't allowed to talk at all and it's very *mean*. But I think it works because you ask low-income kids what they feel about school, and they'll say they have little challenge and the teachers don't expect enough of them, and the kids that come from Mexico say school was better in Mexico. And I think when they go to some of the charter schools they feel they are really pushed. I mean, I wouldn't send my kids there because I would like my kids to have more of a free-flowing, problem-solving environment, challenging and not sitting still, "Don't do this, don't do that," you know. I want them to be creative.

For African American parents, the fact that these mostly White middle- and upper-class reformers will not send their own kids to these newly designed schools delegitimizes these reforms. As one African American parent noted, "I know that one of the buzz phrases is 'evidence-based.' For me, all the 'evidence' I need is that the people who tout 'evidence-based' do not send their kids to [the reformed public school]. So when you tell me that you're doing 'evidence-based' at [the reformed public school], and your kid, or you, went to a private school, then I know. I know you're looking me straight in the face and lying to me."

Indeed, most reformers admit that it is this very discipline structure they tout politically as the major reason why they wouldn't send their own kids to these schools. They recognize that the highly disciplined school environment is relatively joyless, rigid, and noncreative. Rather than conceptualizing joy and creativity as integral to creating successful learning communities, many reformers see these facets of schooling as luxuries available only to those who have already succeeded in meeting educational standards—their children. For example, one education reform consultant who helps to craft statewide reform policy explained how children in reformed schools need discipline in a way other children do not:

> It's different approaches for different needs, you know. And one of the things that I don't see in a place like [local charter school], I don't see a lot of joy, you know. I see a lot of serious faces, including on the teachers, and it's almost like an act that they put on. And the school will tell you, "We don't have time for this." I mean these kids are three grade levels behind. . . . Joy and happiness and all that is a nice thing, but we need to focus on other things right now.

To reformers, the emphasis on discipline—even at the risk of alienating students or creating "mean" or joyless educational environments—is rooted in the short timeline reformers feel they have to fix schools. In many reformers' eyes, low-income children's (but not their own children's) enjoyment of school and comfort are rendered irrelevant and unimportant on the urgency timeline.

These double standards—that some children need discipline while others need autonomy—reflect the extent to which reform activists defend segregated schools and differentiated learning environments. They openly advocate one model that is creative for their own families, and another model that relies on strict discipline for "others." In reformers' view, when low-income parents value happiness and want their children to find school and learning joyful, they are valuing the "wrong" things and are therefore seen as unworthy community allies. This reformer paternalism forecloses possibilities to effectively work in sustained coalition with community groups, and undermines their broader stated commitment to educational equity and social justice.

Conclusion

Reformers seek to move school reform forward, in part, by aligning themselves with select community organizations. As reformers work with private partnerships and reimagine education, they do so in ways that advance neoliberal projects in which public systems are individualized and privatized and individual choice and accountability substitute for access and equity. In thinking about neoliberal innovations, we must consider not just the ideology but also the specific figure of the "reformer" who exerts agency in neoliberal processes. As social and cultural scholar K. Wayne Yang argues, the reformer identity is "not reducible to the neoliberal apparatus" and has a "subjectivity in dialectical relationship to grassroots organizing from below."[32] It is through their racial consciousness, their identities as civil rights activists, their urgency and accountability framework, and paradoxically through the constellation of tenuous community alliances that this framework helps to forge, that reformers advance exclusionary and racialized gentrification projects.

Although neoliberal rhetoric relies on market-based language, privatization, and color-blind stances, these reformers are not simply translators of these goals. Their identities as activists and their articulation of education reform *as civil rights work* provide the potential for building the coalitions, political will, and public support necessary to move reform forward. Yet, as self-identified reformers talk about civil rights and racial inequality, they skillfully mesh racial and educational justice language with market-based reform rhetoric. In this sense, the reformer "identity" and the blending of racial justice and neoliberal rhetoric articulate with forces above the grassroots: the national foundations, think tanks, and hedge fund managers that Saltman describes as instrumental to national school reform.[33]

Recasting market values as civil rights values requires some rhetorical maneuvering. Local reformers de-center civil rights-era educational justice cornerstones such as racial integration and cultural competency, and instead center market values of *choice* (translated as "opportunity"), *economic integration* (rather than racial integration), and *standardization and accountability* (which are imagined by reformers to be immune to racial bias). These maneuvers enable reformers to perceive themselves and the national school reform movement that they represent as a continuation of civil rights work for educational equity. They also enable reformers to align with select community activist groups around specific campaigns for educational justice that also resonate with grassroots racial justice initiatives in schools. At the same time, these market-based perspectives—coupled with a neoliberal ethic of urgency that champions rapid change and experimentation—combine to systematically restrict their network of community allies and denigrate specific community activist groups that organize against school choice, dispossession, and gentrification.

In reformer narratives, the urgency of quick and drastic reform makes the prospect of broad community involvement difficult to reconcile. How does one make drastic changes to a school system and in the process authentically solicit input from multiple community stakeholders who often conflict with one another? Reformers frame the timeline for drastic reform and the timeline for comprehensive community input as ultimately at odds with one another, and cite the urgency of school reform as one reason why wider community input cannot and should not be solicited. However, this does not mean that reformers have no concept of the importance of community participation. Reformers use the central tenet of urgency as a guiding principle to distinguish "good" low-income community involvement from "bad" low-income community involvement, and worthy low-income partners from misguided and ignorant oppositional voices.

At first glance, this partial valuation of community participation seems to run counter to Lipman's broader claims that neoliberal education reform excludes low-income community participation.[34] However, I argue that reformers' *partial* valuation of community participation obscures two important and nuanced exclusionary dimensions of the neoliberal reform movement.

First, reformers' often public valuation of certain community groups obscures what is essentially a narrow vision of low-income community power, where "community" is imagined as both peripheral to and co-operative with the reformer movement, rather than a central force in the reform process. For reformers, "valuable" parent and community partners embrace the data and information that reformers value to reach the same conclusions, and then have enough faith in the good intentions of school reformers to know when to step aside and allow reformers to initiate swift reform experiments. They exercise their consumer mobility, "hold schools accountable," and even "raise hell" when reformers do not follow through on their promises. Instead of gauging their own children's everyday experiences of comfort or discomfort in education as a measure for what quality education is and should be, "good" low-income allies recognize that the "real" value of education lies in the test score data and other external, quantitative measurements of school success. Good community partners cooperatively facilitate the visions of school leaders and other reform "experts." They even embrace calls for urgency and voice their outrage when innovation is not proceeding fast enough. Above all, good partners understand the shared value of urgency, and know that for the sake of urgency they are not to be central reform leaders. Rather, they act as external forces to the reform process, and hold these experts accountable. The discourse of urgency masks a fundamental disregard for the many forms of cultural capital that urban communities of color could bring to the school reform discussion, as well as these communities' own assessments of educational injustices and prescriptions for educational improvement. A pervasive deficit narrative runs throughout reformers' perception of school failure and through the range of possible roles that low-income communities of color can play in reform. This deficit narrative undergirds assessments of low-income allies and foes alike.

Second, reformers' partial valuation of some low-income community collectives over others makes it difficult to see how the larger reform movement engages in racial exclusion, educational displacement, and

Black and Latinx community dispossession. Reformers' partnerships with select low-income groups of color allow reformers to identify and project themselves as racially progressive, rather than fully committed to neoliberalism, which makes their collective stake in neoliberal ideology and their role in racialized gentrification projects even more difficult to identify. Even as they easily draw on discourses of urgency and civil rights in their visions for school reform, reformers in this study could not think of one meaningful alliance they had with a local predominantly African American community group. Instead, reformers routinely dismissed or denigrated the perspectives put forward by African American educational justice activists in Denver, whose violation of reformers' criteria is the value they see in preserving their community fabric and accessing their neighborhood schools.

The heroism of reformer urgency also works to camouflage a persistent racial and class double standard throughout reformers' narratives. Urgency allows reformers to advance a racial and class double standard around issues of discipline and happiness in schooling, valuing happiness, comfort, and creativity for their own mostly White middle-class kids, but not for low-income Black and Latinx youth who are more urgently in need of "rescuing."

Finally, because the reformer movement distinguishes between "valuable" low-income community allies and "backwards" low-income community voices, it has the power to blunt what could otherwise be broader low-income Black-Brown community coalitions around educational and racial justice. As we will see, the potential for community groups like those African American neighborhood groups and those organizations who partner with reformers to coalesce together across their shared visions (such as ending "zero tolerance" policies and reducing police presence in schools) is continually hampered by their different orientations to such powerful and controversial school reformers and the gentrification projects they advocate.

Neoliberal education reform has been central to urban gentrification and globalization projects, and these projects are racialized. It is not only by aligning neoliberal *rhetoric* with calls for educational justice in low-income communities that reformers advance these agendas. They also accomplish these neoliberal projects by forging real alliances with select racial justice organizations that have their own agendas for educational change. Reformer-community alliances, forged largely by local reform agents who rely on an interpretive framework of urgency, may represent opportunities for some racial justice organizations to meaningfully impact the ways education reform is implemented in specific urban contexts. At the same time, these alliances also function as mechanisms for racial exclusion, as they help reformers to both legitimize and mask their marginalization of other critical voices that attempt to stand in the way of neoliberal education and urban transformation. These critical African American voices are detailed in the next chapter.

3

The Dispossessed

Neighborhood Activists Beating Back Gentrification

I am sitting with Mable, a woman in her early forties with a son in high school; Josephine, a grandmother in her sixties with grandkids in elementary school; Darla, a single mother of two in elementary school; and Lynn and Bennie, a couple with a blended family of four kids ranging from three to seventeen years old. We are crowded around a small table in a McDonald's restaurant, discussing school reform while keeping an eye on Darla's, Lynn's, and Bennie's kids, who are playing a blend of hide-and-seek and tag in the twisting plastic tunnels of the indoor McDonald's play place. This group, the African American Parent Project (AAPP), is small tonight. Informally organized and comprised mostly of women, the group meets every two weeks either in a public library room, a nearby rec center room, or a McDonald's to accommodate the needs of parents with children.

They are talking about their neighborhood high school, Central High, which had closed down after a momentous and disastrous school reform experiment that lasted just one year.[1] As described in the previous chapter, the closure of Central High School—a once beloved community anchor in the heart of what had been for decades a thriving Black community life in Denver—signaled the arrival of the school reform movement in the city. The closure of Central was ordered by the district despite massive community mobilization and protest, and on the heels of falling attendance and test scores after over twenty years of court-ordered busing to desegregate schools ended in the mid-1990s. What followed was a small schools experiment engineered by reform consultants and funded by a prominent national foundation, which did not look like anything that Black community members had wanted in their neighborhood. One Black community activist and longtime neighborhood resident described the Central High closure and reform as killing the very spirit of the school:

There was always one constant in the neighborhood, which was Central High School. If it was known for one thing, it was known that Central had a spirit. It was the anchor of the community and had that fire. You walked into Central and you knew you were in a high school. People had pride. When you walked into the three small schools, it was dead as Julius Caesar. There was nothing happening.

In killing the spirit of the school, the closure and reforms began to kill the spirit of a neighborhood already strained by White middle-class takeover. The links between urban renewal and education reform are rarely described or even acknowledged by self-identified reform advocates, whose language of reform as civil rights positions the reform movement as saving children from their presumably "wrecked" neighborhoods via the liberation of market choice. Yet the links between school reform processes, urban renewal, and gentrification are clear when we consider the involvement of development companies and capital in funding reform,[2] as well as the long-standing relationship between property values and school quality.[3]

This chapter examines the devastating impact of neoliberal education reform experimentation in African American communities. In this chapter, I outline the ways these communities experience reform experiments—especially those as destabilizing as the landmark reforms at Central High—in tandem with gentrification. I also detail the ways these communities mobilize to fight neoliberal school reform in their neighborhoods, as well as the steps reformers take to delegitimize their oppositional movements and marginalize their voices in school reform debates. I give special attention to faux community engagement processes, school choice, and new cultures of school discipline as the most significant dimensions of education reform that impact these activists. Their collectives resist neoliberal reform in their interactions with school personnel, in their fights against the erasure and the "renewal" of their community parks and neighborhood associations, and in their attempts to mobilize votes in school board races and other elections. They carry out their resistance on a terrain marked by the co-optation of geographical spaces like schools and parks, organizational spaces like neighborhood associations, and even the discursive spaces of civil rights rhetoric, a terrain on which few philanthropic foundations, formal nonprofits, or political leaders can be trusted. This distrust shapes their resistance, and even culminates in their resistance to movement institutionalization itself. I conclude this chapter by considering the implications of non-institutionalized grassroots African American and Latinx resistance in the larger landscape of school reform politics.

The AAPP, the networked group of Black parents and grandparents, aims to mobilize even more Black parents through face-to-face consciousness raising. AAPP members see their power in their ability to act as conduits of information to other parents they know in a quickly changing school choice climate where information is hard to come by and difficult to decipher. Elite White reformers in the previous chapter talk about parents who can negotiate the school choice system as "savvy consumers," and ultimately champion a "portfolio" of educational choices that will appeal to different consumer preferences. The repeatedly used descriptor "savvy" obscures systemic racial and class privilege, and infers that good educational outcomes will hinge on how nimble, informed, and plugged-in consumers are to the array of ever-changing local education choices for their children. In such an environment of "savvy" consumers, one must also imagine leagues of consumers who by comparison are not as savvy. In the neoliberal imagination, these might be parents who don't go the extra mile to do intensive research on different curriculums and school models, who don't take the time to tour schools on their lunch breaks or days off from work, or who don't read the latest education blog that critically analyzes the track records of various schools in reading, math, or science. In reform advocates' worldview, "savvy" is rewarded with better outcomes and better choices, while poor choices are assumed to be the result of less selective parents who behave as less savvy consumers.

At their core, AAPP members reject the implicit assumption that somehow they are not savvy-enough consumers and just need to learn how to be more so. Instead, they detail experiences of marginalization in their interactions with city planners, reformers, and school district representatives. They perceive themselves to be systematically and intentionally uninformed, misinformed, and explicitly excluded from key decision-making processes. Given these experiences, creating a new network for information sharing becomes a potentially powerful community intervention in the city's school choice processes.

Out of the wreckage of the Central High closure and small schools experiment came the AAPP and two other grassroots groups. One group, the Community Education Collective (CEC), is a group of Central-area neighbors and former teachers who meet to discuss how to resist reform rhetoric and the takeover of their other community spaces by newly arrived White neighborhood renters and home buyers. By doing so, they position themselves as protecting and supporting the Black and Latinx youth in the neighborhood. The other group is Democrats for Educational Justice (DEJ), whose roots are in the Central neighborhood but whose network represents a citywide effort to strengthen the Black vote and challenge White reformers in electoral races, placing the fight for community control of the neighborhood school as a central racial and economic justice goal in school board, city, and state politics. Along with the AAPP, the perspectives and movement strategies of CEC and DEJ activists will be featured in this chapter.

During the same wintry week we gather in McDonald's, Michelle Rhee, the former chancellor of Washington, DC public schools prominently featured in the documentary film *Waiting for Superman*, stands in front of a packed lecture hall in a posh athletic club about four miles from the McDonald's. Members of reform organizations, local foundations, media outlets, community organizations, and local philanthropic organizations fill all the chairs, and many have to stand along the edges of the room. She has been brought by a local pro-reform organization in Denver as a national icon of the reform movement. She pushed for an end to teacher tenure, a pay scheme tied to student achievement on standardized tests, the closure of several low-performing DC schools, and the termination of several school principals. A Teach for America alum, she had never been formally trained as a professional teacher, nor had she ever served as a principal before she was selected by Mayor Adrian Fenty to serve as chancellor for the DC schools in 2007. With the school board's decision-making power stripped that same year in DC, she occupied a powerful position in the city's school system. She instituted major changes to the city's education system without school board oversight or approval. She passionately argues that champions of school reform should not be afraid of controversy. "For too long," Rhee says to the predominantly White audience, "we have valued collaboration over conflict. If we only talk about the good stuff going on in our public schools and we don't talk about the bad stuff, we don't create a sense of urgency, a sense that our schools are in crisis." Her statement receives a round of applause.

Her call to action takes place only a week after hundreds of protestors crowded the last school board meeting, which lasted hours and ended in a contested vote to ultimately close down a series of low-performing public schools and replace them with charter schools. This decision was made despite the prior implementation of a school transition plan that included broader teacher, parent, and community participation. The plan had barely got off the ground before the district cancelled it. DPS favored the quicker pace of "turnaround" and school closure rather than the slower-paced "transition" reform. After Michelle Rhee's speech, an audience member asks her how best to involve parents, carefully adding, "especially those who are coming from neighborhoods experiencing pretty drastic school reform." Rhee's answer: "Change means you are always going to have opposition. Part of our challenge in DC was that the opposition was vocal, organized and mobilized. The problem is, opposition to change will always be vocal. We need to make sure that supporters [of these reforms] are just as vocal." Although the question to Rhee does not ask about parental opposition per se, the subtext of the question was understood by Rhee to refer to the problem of low-income parents' and community residents' *resistance* to reform. Rhee's answer focuses on mobilizing school reform advocates to be as vocal as the opponents (i.e., parents) who come from these neighborhoods. As I watch her speak and field questions from the audience, I notice that Rhee never explains how best to involve these "resistant" parents and community members in the school reform process.

I also notice that as Rhee exhorts the audience to mobilize in favor of quick-paced reforms and fight the opposition, nobody discusses *why* low-income parents of color are engaging in campaigns to resist these quick and drastic school reforms. In the popular media, the resistance to school reform has been largely portrayed as a battle between innovative reformers who want to do what is best for children, and the intransigent teachers unions that represent the status quo and the security of teachers' jobs.[4] On the ground, however, there have been multiple community mobilizations in opposition to school reform in the very cities where school reform successes have been touted the most: Washington, DC,

Oakland, Chicago, and New York City. Importantly, many of these mobilizations have been led by grassroots groups concerned with broader issues such as gentrification, and not necessarily by the teachers union. Echoing these mobilizations, the NAACP and National Urban League, in concert with other civil rights groups, issued a statement criticizing elements of the Obama administration's education reform agenda, specifically school reform experimentation in communities of color and the lack of sufficient community participation in school reform decisions.[5] These elements escalated in the Trump era with Betsy DeVos's championing of an ever broader expansion of charter schools.

For the low-income African American and Latinx activists detailed in this chapter, the rapid changes in public education (namely, the closure of schools, the opening of new charters, and the transformation of comprehensive neighborhood schools into autonomous schools) feel less like "innovation" and more like "experimentation," especially after the emblematic failed experiment at Central High detailed in the previous chapter. As one AAPP parent put it,

> I think that if they could model the schools after those that have been successful, from beginning to end, if those could be modeled, and not all these other things that they think are good ideas but haven't been put to the test yet . . . I mean trial and error, yes, but we have already errored too many people to keep trialing!

Although Rhee and other school reformers attribute community resistance to reform as a simple and backwards "resistance to change" and a misguided "blind loyalty" to one's neighborhood school, I argue that African American community resistance to neoliberal school reform signifies a larger resistance to gentrification, community fragmentation, and community exclusion from elite urban revitalization projects. When examined through the lens of African American and Latinx community critique, school reform can be understood as a practice of designing intentional school cultures and communities *within* schools while simultaneously dissociating schools from their surrounding low-income communities. The process of remaking former neighborhood schools into discrete communities that are disconnected from actual neighborhoods serves as a powerful tool for excluding low-income communities of color from school reform processes. It is also a central mechanism of gentrification.

Pauline Lipman has extensively examined the ways low-income African American communities in particular are equated with pathology and moral deficiency in the rhetoric of neoliberal education and housing policy. The language of poverty-as-pathology and moral deficiency hides the extent to which neoliberal attempts to revitalize the urban core are premised on a social engineering that systematically devastates African American community institutions and social fabric. As Thomas Pedroni also points out, pathology and crisis must be invoked by elites in order to "scrub clean" urban areas for displacement and then renewal. It is not enough to rehabilitate an area for residents of color; neighborhoods slated for development must first be declared disasters so that planners can remake urban territory as "fit" for affluent newcomers and capital investment.[6] This denigration of African American community life in the name of capital accumulation also marginalizes critical African American voices in school reform debates.[7] The question then, is not only how and why African American voices in particular are silenced and delegitimized in processes of neoliberal reform, but what insights we lose about the pitfalls and promises of reform when their critical voices are left out of these policy discussions. How are these communities differently imagining school reform, and how are they organizing to push back against it?

The experiences of African American exclusion culminate in a marked distrust of the district and the various reformers, reformer organizations, and foundations that drive school reform in Denver. These key categories of exclusion include the school choice process, new discipline policies instituted in individual schools, and school reform experimentation. This sense of profound exclusion and distrust drives their collective responses to school reform. These responses range from community consciousness raising and resistance at the local school level to larger community walkouts, protests, and community education forums. Gentrification and its resulting community fragmentation form an unstable yet powerful catalyst for activism, one that is not institutionalized in funded organizations or launched from stable community centers. Black community mobilization against neoliberal school reform is cultivated in noisy McDonald's dining rooms, quiet community libraries, and Black-owned coffee shops under threat of closure because of rising rents. Its power lies in its diversity of tactics (from the more micro interpersonal consciousness raising and information sharing to meso-level collective strategies to influence school board votes) and its refusal to be co-opted. The activism is undercut, however, by the forces of gentrification that are tearing apart community institutions. How does a community mobilize if the community itself is suffering displacement? As Nancy, a biracial Black and Latina activist, explains,

> You know, the myth of this all is that there *is* community. There's no community in the sense of how people talk about it as an entity or entities. The "community" is who shows up and who makes their voice heard. And so I think the challenge to the organizers is to make sure those who would otherwise not be heard somehow get their voice heard, because they don't have time to come to a meeting. So I'm conscious when I'm talking about "community," it's about those people who have an issue with school reform and it resonates. At that moment, *that* is community. When we talk about community we're talking about a larger vision that benefits everybody.

In Nancy's view, "community" manifests through the very act of resisting reform in ways that authentically resonate with a base of neighbors and kin who for various reasons cannot afford the time and energy to devote to the "triple shift" of activism.[8] The activism that resonates with community—indeed, that brings *community* into being—is unfiltered and uncompromising. It is a renewed community that arises specifically in the belly of a gentrified urban space, one that used to be forged by a shared relationship to a stable geographic location and stable community institutions, but now spans a network shaped by the push-out of urban renewal and is scattered across neighborhood lines. In this sense, African American resistance in a quickly changing urban landscape *is* the very act of stitching together a community that is at the same time being driven apart by urban development.

Critical race scholars point out that neoliberal school reform represents a racialized project of urban development, one that increases racial inequality between Whites and African Americans. However, political scientist and Africana studies scholar Lester Spence emphasizes that neoliberalism also generates a profound *intra*-racial inequality. Since the 1970s the class divide between downwardly mobile and upwardly mobile Blacks has grown wider than this same socioeconomic gap among Whites. He writes,

> The internal gap between black "haves" and black "have nots" is increasingly depicted in cultural terms rather than in structural terms by prominent African Americans, and black public opinion polls point to a growing value-driven disconnect between black populations. . . . And even when it is depicted in structural terms, black businessmen, political representatives, and thought leaders increasingly tout entrepreneurial solutions.[9]

This means that low-income Black activists resist neighborhood dispossession without the support or representation of prominent Black politicians and business leaders. Sociologist and labor organizer John Arena describes the elite's erasure of public housing in post-Katrina New Orleans, for example, and illustrates how this effort was led and negotiated by an alliance between a post–civil rights urban Black leadership and White elite developers. This alliance relied on the nonprofitization of grassroots movements to secure the consent, or at least to blunt the dissent, of poor and working-class Black public housing residents.[10]

In my research with these activists, many spoke at length about their perception that prominent Black leaders have "sold out" the community and have ended up touting education reform as a solution to long-standing educational inequality. Adolf Reed Jr. and Cedric Johnson attribute the "sellout" discourse to a faulty mythology stretching back to Black Power radicalism in the late 1960s.[11] Reed critiques Black Power radicalism— even as it manifests in contemporary movements like Black Lives Matter—for imagining Black communities as monolithic based on racial (and not) class interests. He writes,

> A politics grounded on antiracism simply cannot accommodate interest differentiation among black people as genuine and instead can conceptualize it only as the machinations of "sell outs" or "misleaders." . . . That discourse posits racial authenticity—who *really* speaks for the "black community"—as a standard for political judgment that is a vestige of

black power radicalism. That standard was inadequate then. It is worse than useless now as an analytic or programmatic tool in a contemporary period whose objective political fault lines . . . do not reduce empirically to a black/white axis.[12]

Johnson analyzes the fault lines within Black Lives Matter itself, a movement divided on education reform issues. Some organizers have taken pro-charter and Teach for America stances, while others have called for a moratorium on charter schools.[13] Both Johnson's and Reed's scholarship emphasizes the class variation within Black communities, and the rise of a Black political elite that has increasingly supported neoliberal attacks on public institutions based on its own class interests, even as elites justify these attacks using racial justice claims. For Reed and Johnson, dominant monolithic notions of what constitutes "Black community interests" leave the Black working-class and poor without a language to identify and discuss class interest variation among Blacks, while also positioning Black elites to speak on behalf of "the Black community" in ways that work against Black working-class self-interests. This is particularly true for educational justice issues. As Johnson writes, "Within the opinion poll context, if someone says she prefers government action to insure quality education for all, this expression tells us very little about how the same person would act in an unfolding battle over school reform where statist intervention could mean school closures or more 'Teach for America' scabbing, and charterization, or conversely better salaries, more job security and professional development for teachers."[14] Certainly in the Denver context, the Black political regime has aligned with the kinds of education reform measures consistent with the former set of social solutions. The notable absence of Black middle-class and upper-class solidarity and Black political representation also shapes and challenges these Black and working-class resistance movements.

Throughout this chapter I profile African American dispossession and resistance, especially as this resistance is launched from the historically Black epicenter of Denver. Even though the neighborhood is known for its Black history, there has been a sizable Latinx population in this neighborhood over the last several decades as well. These Latinx activists—pushed out by the same forces of gentrification that assail the low-income Black community in this city—also join forces with their Black neighbors to launch this resistance against exclusionary school reform and urban renewal in their neighborhood. In centering mechanisms of school reform exclusion and dispossession that align with African American experiences in particular, I do not want to render invisible the Latinx community members who also experience these dynamics with their African American neighbors and who periodically join their resistance movements. However, as Spence, Johnson, and Reed caution, there is nothing automatic about these kinds of Black-Brown alliances, since it is not inevitable that communities of color align on the basis of a shared racial positionality vis-à-vis White urban elites. There is variation both within and between racial groups according to different class interests within those groups. While many Latinx neighborhood schools activists in Denver find alliance with the Black working-class movements to save neighborhood schools, other Latinx activists in the city join forces with institutionalized nonprofits, and still others represent a Latinx professional-managerial class crystallized in organizations like Latinos for Education Reform. Like members of the Black professional-managerial class, these organizations and Latinx political elites align with elite White reformers on issues such as charter school accessibility and expansion.[15]

African American and Latinx Experiences of School Reform

Reform-Driven Community Forums: The Systematic Exclusion of Black and Latinx Voices

Central High is like the "Middle East" of Denver. You know the speech the new principal at Central gave? He referred to Central as "the historically Black school." He is asserting that there is ownership *beyond* African Americans, and you know, that's why I referred to it as the "Middle East," because the White alums who were bused in feel that it is *their* school. I know African Americans feel like it is *their* school, and I know there are other groups feeling like it is *their* school. Everybody feels like they have ownership. But I think the reformed Central High is *not* for the people that I am here talking about: the previous, the historical, the traditional, the Black students.

—Mable, African American neighborhood activist

Mable recounts her experience of participating in a community forum hosted by the school district regarding the fate of Central High. Mable had heard that the prestigious foundation grant had a provision that required community participation. The organization Family of Central, which was previously an entity that maintained records of Central alums, became activated as *the* representative community organization to help steer Central High reforms in tandem with the foundation and the central school district. Not coincidentally, Family of Central's membership was dominated by White alums from the long stretch of history when Central was a heavily tracked school, an era when its prestigious Advanced Placement track sent numerous White kids to Ivy League schools, while Black students occupied the vocational tracks. Some of its most active members had ties to local pro-reform think tanks and foundations.

At first, Mable, Josephine, and several other concerned Black parents, grandparents, and neighbors attended the community forum, which lasted for several hours. Participants were charged with creating a blueprint of what they wanted to see Central become. According to Mable, there was broad consensus among Black neighborhood residents that Central should be a comprehensive high school open to all neighborhood children. They agreed that most neighborhood residents would not understand or see meaningful differences between the various school designs that mark this era of "portfolio-style" school reform, including innovation schools and charter schools. Rather, their preference would be for a school that acted as a strong community anchor. Their vision also included culturally responsive education and a better mechanism for parent outreach. As they blueprinted their designs for the new incarnation of Central, they deliberately pushed against some of the new models for parental engagement in other schools they had heard about, as well as the old models of parental engagement that have failed low-income communities of color. As Valerie, a thirty-eight-year-old Black parent of a fifteen-year-old daughter, put it,

> For the schools in impacted communities, there's usually not a PTA. And nowadays, there's some fabricated artificial parent group that just makes no sense. They create these processes in schools that are artificial. They have no historical reference for it. I think it's a way for them

THE DISPOSSESSED | 105

to manipulate us, or somehow disenfranchise us. It's my experience that the parents in these communities don't have access to the information they need, so they're not going to set themselves up as targets to look stupid, to look uninvolved. So they just leave it alone and then before you know it other people are making decisions that we should be making.

Josephine, who also participated in the brainstorming session, remembered their collective insistence on establishing an innovative parental engagement model that grew out of the experiences of Black neighborhood residents:

> I have learned that in communities where there are significant numbers of poor Black and Latino kids, the problems are different for those families as opposed to White affluent families. And the problem is the relationship between time and money. So in poor Black and Latino families you may have two parents working two jobs, or three jobs, so the relationship is very different between time and money.
>
> White affluent parents will go to the schools and they can sit in the classes and they can volunteer. They can do this and that, so they have access to information and process, which is very different for Black and Latino families. There has to be a system in place that is specifically designed for those parents, and you have to *know* the population to be able to design that access for them.

In their vision for a reformed school, Black neighborhood participants in the district-run community forum specifically imagined that their ideal neighborhood school would include representatives from the community. They wanted people who knew their neighborhoods and their children to be institutional advocates within the school system. They imagined that these community representatives would be able to transform "reform" into an innovative mechanism that worked to their children's and families' advantage.

Despite the work they did that day to brainstorm their ideal school, they soon found that none of their visions for the newly reformed Central High were included in the actual reform. Instead of a comprehensive neighborhood school, the school reopened as three small schools. After that experiment failed a year later, the school was designated as an innovation school, and let in only one class at a time on a lottery system. For the first time in many decades, the neighborhood was effectively left without a comprehensive neighborhood high school. Community members like Josephine, Mable, and Valerie felt betrayed and became instantly suspicious of reform rhetoric and district processes around "community engagement." Valerie summed up the district-foundation partnership's approach to community engagement as an exercise in "placation" with a "scripted outcome." They suspected that the plans for school redesign were in place all along, and were scripted by local and distant elites with two major interrelated goals: to revitalize the city by drawing in affluent Whites to a handful of high-performing schools, and to establish shaky and poorly planned educational experiments like at Central aimed exclusively at low-income Black and Latinx students. Sheila, who decided to put her teenage son in a new innovation school centered on technology, bitterly put it this way:

> In my opinion what we are getting is "segregation with benefits." That's my description. That's what we are given in terms of poor Black and Latino students. We get to walk in the building and *they* are there in the building, so we are told, "Why should you be complaining about what is happening to your child if you get to drive up in front of a five-million-dollar building and he gets to walk out, to get out with a free laptop? You should feel lucky!"
>
> So if you are at Central, and you have a new principal who came from a White private school, the students supposedly get the benefit of the network that he is bringing into that building. That's the image they are creating and putting out there in the media. I'm not saying this is the truth or this is correct. I'm saying that this is the benefit I'm told I should be glad I'm experiencing.

After this initial forum cohosted by the school district and Family of Central alums, Black neighborhood residents felt even more distanced from the reform-oriented school district and an even deeper sense of distrust and betrayal. Many refused to go to subsequent district-sponsored community forums, sensing that they were shams with "scripted outcomes" and therefore a waste of precious time and energy.

Bennie, an African American man in his early thirties who spends his time as an electrician, musician, and a parent to his teenage sons and his partner Lynn's preschooler and third-grader, recounts his defeating experience trying to access another community forum on neighborhood development and school reform. He heard about the planned town hall meeting "from somebody who knows somebody who knows somebody," underscoring the complicated chain of information and communication upon which he had to rely just to get information about his teenage children's school, Central High:

> It bothers me so much! I can't get over this town hall meeting because Channel 9 was there, Channel 2 was there, Channel 4 was there, and the Food Channel! [*Laughter.*] And all this going on. And no parents are in there! There were no parents from any schools.
>
> There were construction companies at this meeting, but there were no parents. There were no concerned people who live in the area. And I'm sitting there, and they looked at me like I was crazy, like I shouldn't have been there. I walked in and they're like, "Can I help you?" And I'm like, "Did you ask that to anybody else? I'm just like everybody else!" But what I found out is that they had planned this for years. They had this planned to shut down schools.

Darla, an African American mother of a second-grader, agrees, criticizing the pace and the exclusionary nature of school reform: "So it seems like we gotta be at these meetings, because that is where the fight is. Because if you're not here in a meeting where they are saying, 'We're gonna close this school. Oh, we're passing us a bill. Oh look! It's passed.'" In Darla's and Bennie's view, reform opens only the shortest windows of possibility for "community" participation, in which "community" can just as easily mean urban developers and other private sector actors as it does Black parents of students in the neighborhood.[16] In her critique of public-private partnerships in Third World countries with decentralized states and wide socioeconomic gaps, urban planning and globalization scholar Faranak Miraftab writes,

> Private sector firms approach local governments and their impoverished communities with the message of power sharing, but once the process is in

motion the interests of the community are often overwhelmed by those of the most powerful member of the partnership—the private sector firms.[17]

In her analysis, Miraftab dispels the claim that public-private partnerships, whether leveraged in the service of Third World development or, in this case, domestic urban renewal, turn out to be an equal win-win for both dispossessed people and corporate interests. In the case of neoliberal education reform, the promised empowerment to parents able to engage in the educational marketplace also extends to private actors in ways that sabotage the broader civil rights goal of equitable educational access and outcomes.[18]

Nancy, one of the community architects of Democrats for Educational Justice (DEJ), remembers another pro-reform forum on Colorado's "Race to the Top" efforts. She recalls the distinct absence of grassroots community voices, and the strategic use of reformers' language of social change and their claim to authenticity as the "real" reformers. As Scott notes, reformers' claim of the term "real" reformers also positions "others" as simply propping up the status quo. This polarizing reformer worldview presumably takes aim at Black and Latinx neighborhood activists, teachers union activists, and others who criticize reform.[19] Nancy recalls,

> There were no other viewpoints. There were no organizers. There were no teachers. It was ridiculous. There were officials that claimed that they are part of the dialogue, but in actuality they're preaching to their choir. There is no other avenue for people who don't agree to get their voice heard.
>
> And there was actually one comment that I thought was very demeaning, and that was that "the current teachers are the problem and not the rest of us. We're good guys. We're trying to do the right thing." He said something to the effect of "the people who have low expectations of people of color are just as bad as the Klan members who try to deny Blacks their freedom." Then he went from there and leapt to "the people who are against school reform are just as bad as those people." Using that kind of inflammatory language was really problematic to me.

For these Black and Latinx neighborhood activists, the co-optation of civil rights and social justice language in spaces that are dominated by Whites is both problematic and endemic to the process of school reform. Spence notes that this co-optation is endemic to neoliberalism; it is the way neoliberalism as a mode of governmentality transforms the problems of racial injustice into phenomena that can ultimately be solved by market solutions:

> Attempts to fight racism are not privatized if by privatized we mean "made invisible." To the contrary, anti-racism becomes a public principle. However, the key distinction is that under neoliberalism the most effective means of combating racism are developing entrepreneurial capacities in populations, institutions, and spaces deemed as "non-white."[20]

In the most immediate sense, these activists view it as a process endemic to gentrification. As Georgette, a Black twenty-eight-year-old mother of three children, put it, "We got gentrification on the line, so now it's a strategic thing in place. And so when we talk about access, when we talk about being informed, if there is a strategic mechanism in place to keep you out of the loop, how do you fight a system like that?"

School Choice as Dispossession

In February 2018, DC public schools chancellor Antwan Wilson—hailed as a successor to Michelle Rhee's school reform agenda, which had become a national model for reform years before—was forced to resign after privately evading the same school choice process that he politically and publicly championed. Well-networked, Wilson arranged to have his own teenage daughter leapfrog over six hundred students wait-listed for a high-performing DC public high school. While this controversy made national news and exposed some of the inequities built into the choice system, African American and Latinx neighborhood activists voice criticisms of the choice system that stem from their own experiences with the process. While reformers champion school choice as a way to empower families by freeing them from their "broken" neighborhoods and unleashing their consumer power in a neoliberal model of consumer choice, neighborhood activists express a marked sense that rather than choosing schools, they and their children are ultimately the objects of neoliberal "choice." These neighborhood activists experience several exclusionary dimensions of school choice.

First, they point to early childhood education (ECE) programs attached to desirable schools nearby. If families can pay the steep tuition to send their children to ECE programs, then they have priority in gaining admission to the upper grades (typically K–5). In the same vein, neighborhood activists point to new innovation and charter schools opening that have selective enrollment, so applicants must either win a lottery to get in or qualify according to specific criteria (e.g., science and tech schools or schools for performing arts). These selective mechanisms stand in sharp contrast to African American activists' visions of an accessible, high-quality, comprehensive neighborhood school. While these choices appear to broaden the portfolio of choices that school reformers champion, these choices don't appear viable to low-income African American residents who are already experiencing push-out from their neighborhoods.

Second, African American parents recount stories of gatekeepers at the schools who dissuade them from trying to enroll, or district "choice" advisors who ultimately suggest a handful of low-performing schools from which to choose, rather than the ideal slate of *all* the city's schools. Betty, a twenty-two-year-old mother of a four-year-old and a two-year-old, recounts a disturbing story about walking into an innovation school across the street from where she lives to inquire about enrollment:

> I went into the school and the lady's like, "Can I help you?" and I said, "I'm going to the office to put my name on the waiting list for the ECE programs." And she said, "Don't bother." And I said, "I think that's my decision, not yours. I'm putting my child on the waiting list." And she's like, "No, I'm telling you, don't bother." And I'm like, "I'm gonna do it anyway." And she was like, "I'm asking you to leave the school grounds."
>
> And I was like, "Are you telling me the list is closed, or you're not accepting any more names?" She's like, "I'm telling you it's a waste of time. We have over sixty kids on that list, and we only have space for twenty-eight. Don't bother." And I was like, "What is your name?" You know, because this is not acceptable to have. And I was like, "It doesn't matter how big your list is, because it shows a need in that community, and you guys should be reporting that need to somebody."

As Betty underscores, there is no clear district process for ensuring that community need is reported and integrated into the creation of new school choices in the neighborhood. Olivia, a young African American mother of three children, one with special needs, called the district choice office to clarify which choices she should list on her choice form. In the end, the choice office suggested three subpar choices that would accommodate her daughter with special needs:

> So they said, "Okay, so your child tests at this level, these are the choices that you're given." Why am I limited to my choices when this is an open choice program? Why are you limiting me to three schools? What is that about? Why wasn't I given the fifty-eight schools in Denver public schools with their scoring to make my own choice? Why did you give me three?

Like the seemingly duplicitous community forums about education reform in their neighborhoods, the choice process itself, with its language of "choice" and ultimately parental empowerment, appears equally as duplicitous when parents begin navigating the process and find themselves preemptively locked out of their potential choices. Indeed, education policy scholars John Diamond and Kimberly Gomez found that middle-class Black parents tend to engage in school choice, see the process as a form of social inclusion, and subsequently develop a positive orientation to their schools of choice; in contrast, working-class Black parents are often relegated to poorer-performing neighborhood schools, develop a more critical perspective of these educational environments, and attempt to push teachers and administrators to reform substandard schooling practices from within.[21]

Beyond exclusionary, however, African American parents perceive the choice process itself to be one contributing force that further unravels and disconnects an entire community already undergoing disconnection and dispossession. With its emphasis on consumer savvy and knowledge, it is a system that demands much from parents who are already overstretched by work demands, underemployment, and the stressors that accompany living in precarity. Devon, a forty-nine-year-old father of two and grandparent of one, remarks on the burden that neoliberal reform brings. This burden is the shift from the school as a community institution that provides for the collective, to the single parent who is now tasked with responsibly "choosing" and providing for their own child:

Once you send that child to school at nine o'clock or eight o'clock—granted, yes, a parent is the first line of defense here. A parent is supposed to be the one advocating for their child. But if I have a condition, whether it be drug addiction or mental health or whatever, how can I truly advocate for my child? If a school system is supposed to give equal access to everybody, isn't the school system responsible for providing access to education for *all* students? What happened to schools being accountable to people no matter where they're at?

In reformers' worldview, "savvy" parents will ultimately be the winners in the choice process. Parents who aren't as "savvy" will be compelled by the new system to become more knowledgeable in order to find the best educational fit for their children. For African American and Latinx neighborhood activists, however, the choice process siphons the more active and involved parents from the traditional public schools. In this sense, choice represents one more form of community dispossession. As Darla observes,

> The parents that can do that and can be involved in that way. . . . That accountability on the regular public school just isn't there anymore. So you took that involved parent away from the traditional neighborhood school, and put them in the charter school.

These charter schools are the very institutions that often appear exclusionary to African American and Latinx parents. By siphoning active and involved parents from the traditional neighborhood public schools, choice effectively removes the biggest sources of community power from the very institutions to which parents still have unquestioned access: the neighborhood schools. Gone are the bodies and the voices of involved parents who can raise hell about their children's education. In a new choice landscape that is hard to decipher, especially for parents who do not have the time and resources to investigate schools outside their neighborhoods, choice also removes the potential for parents to share reliable information with each other and build community cohesion and power around educational justice. Valerie reflects on the neoliberal context of choice and how she perceives it to erode African American community power:

When you think about the oppression that our parents and their parents had to endure, but yet somehow got educated. Somehow were able to buy a home and buy land, and everyone was together. When you think about how these systematic things are in place now, and there's so much division. If I go to a meeting, and I know what's going on, what are the chances that I'm going to educate everyone on my block if half the time the kids on my block don't even go to the same school?

In this sense, the school choice process, like rising property values and rising rent, becomes both a reflection of and an engine for gentrification and displacement.

Equally as profound, the choice process also privatizes the promise of public schooling as a cornerstone of civil rights. When schooling becomes the province of individualist savvy consumption, it threatens the function of schooling to foster collective equity and community advancement. Criticizing the portfolio approach of reform, in which new school experiments are designed according to narrow interests and specializations that align with state and federal standards or individual advancement in specific industries,[22] Black neighborhood activist Mona says, "We are not putting our kids in an educational program that is going to benefit the entire community. We're saying, 'OK, what is it that you like to do? You like computers? Well, how is that going to benefit the whole? You want to make games?' That's not a good choice! We have to make strong hard decisions for *our* children." Reformers would claim that giving individual families more choice would accumulate into better outcomes for entire communities. However, Black neighborhood activists like Mona reject the model of savvy consumption that advances individual children at the cost of the collective well-being of the community.[23]

Neoliberalism as Neocolonialism: New Cultures of Discipline Inside Schools

Black and Latinx community activists advance a critique of reformed school cultures alongside their broader and systemic critique of district-wide school choice. The reform movement has pushed a shift from veteran, long-term teachers to temporary Teach for America (TFA) or other teachers from outside the community, sometimes bypassing training in credentialed university teacher preparation programs. These shifts are consistent with a neoliberal push to redefine quality teaching as how well a teacher can deliver testable content.[24] Au terms this a "new Taylorism" in which teachers' labor is controlled and prepackaged as corporate curricula geared toward the demands of standardized testing.[25] In schools serving low-income students and students of color, teachers are even less likely to have been trained in programs that explicitly foster equity-oriented and learner-centered teacher preparation.[26] Instead, these teachers are trained more as technicians delivering curriculum "with fidelity" rather than professionals with knowledge.[27] Reform advocates champion these shifts inside schools in order to shake up traditional models of schooling, and frame these changes as democratizing. As some reformers told me, these shifts represent a break from the past, when elite education professionals dictated curriculum and school design. Now, younger professionals from other sectors or start-ups, even without prestigious education degrees from Stanford or Harvard, can still innovate much-needed changes to a troubled school system. For critics of reform, these shifts in teaching personnel in newly reformed schools reflect larger patterns of deprofessionalizing and destabilizing the teaching profession in an era of neoliberal reform.

Community critiques of educational cultures *inside* reformed schools are consistent with community critiques of reform community forums outside schools; the perception is that a cadre of outsiders are deciding what is best for low-income Black and Brown communities without seeking community input or demonstrating an investment in building community trust. Invoking a perception of school reform as dispossession, a Black community member, Vivienne, likens reformers' discourse on educational justice to robbers offering to watch your house:

> So they say, "Well, we're gonna do this and it's gonna be wonderful," you know, "don't you worry about your kids 'cause your kids in good hands." Really? If you're telling me that, it really makes me wonder. Because if you tell somebody, "Oh hey, when you leave town don't you worry about your house. We'll take real good care of it." You didn't ask them to! I need to be more involved with what's going on because now, you know, usually when people do that there's something else going on.

Here, Vivienne likens the reformist message "Trust us, we have your best interests at heart" to a stranger planning to rob one's possessions. Black neighborhood school advocates witness high principal and teacher turnover at these new schools; lament the lack of authentic cultures of care cultivated in schools where teachers form caring relationships with students;[28] and sense that dispossession and the transfer of community wealth and property operate as hidden ulterior motives. Bennie characterizes reformed schools in his neighborhood this way: "I think a lot of these schools get these principals that aren't invested in their schools, and it's just a job to them. And that goes to the same thing with their teachers, you know, that they're not invested. And then you don't get good parent involvement." For Bennie, the perceived lack of investment from White personnel inside newly reformed schools further alienates parents.

Georgette, single mother of three children, underscores the price that *all* Black families pay when some choice out of neighborhood schools and leave the families at the least-resourced neighborhood schools. Instead of embracing the opportunity to benefit from the consumer power that school choice promises to offer, Georgette points out that White district representatives, White reformers, and White school administrators and teachers perceive all Black children as the same anyway:

> So then you pull your kid out and you end up with a school full of those kids that are just kind of left to the wayside with the teachers who don't care. My experience is that the teachers approach the children that are dropped off early and the children that go to the neighborhood school in the same way they approach *all* African American children. So in advocating for those folks, that is also advocating for your child because what happens is that even if you are in a charter school, they're gonna treat you the same way.

Georgette's perception is shared by many Black parents who argue that charter school children and neighborhood school children share the same fate under an educational system governed by White reformers and teachers. Instead of embracing school choice, Georgette and other neighborhood activists argue that a better strategy would be to advocate for the children left behind in the traditional neighborhood school after other parents choice out, since Black children and their families who choice out in the end do not always enjoy a better educational environment. They are not exempt from White bias in the schools, and in fact encounter newly reformed and instituted school cultures with militaristic disciplinary rules, cultures that foster a kind of citizenship that stresses personal versus communal responsibility.[29]

Reformers routinely dismiss low-income Black and Latinx community perspectives as "happy talk," a descriptive phrase widely used by reformers that characterizes low-income parents' lack of savvy around test scores and their simple reliance on their child's enjoyment of school to ultimately guide their choice of school. However, I witnessed very little happy talk when asking parents about their children's experiences of schooling.[30] In my research, I start focus group discussions by asking Black parents about some of the positive experiences with DPS schools. Many of them tell stories about specific teachers who challenged their children, pushed them to excel, recognized their strengths and talents, and proactively communicated with parents about their children's particular needs. But these discussions do not stay positive for long. These discussions turn to concerns over problematic disciplinary cultures in schools, many of which are characterized by "no excuses" or "zero tolerance" policies. While reform advocates argue that there is "no time to waste" and educational equity cannot wait for joy in schooling when students are significantly behind grade level, Black parents identify harsh discipline as a central mechanism for student disengagement and low achievement. Consider this focus group exchange among AAPP participants:

> BETHANY: It takes an enormous amount of courage, I have come to know, for many of our children to go to school.
> MULTIPLE PEOPLE: Yeah, it does.
> JACKIE: And it's sad that they have to jump through all this, just to be a kid. I mean, it's like they're putting adult situations onto these kids. They don't know how to understand some of these things!
> MABLE: It's like we're releasing them to a world of wolves. It's like, "Okay, when I release you to this school, Lord help you. I want to give you the values that mom has taught you at home, and hope that my love here can not so much shield you, but at least empower you to be able to withstand some of the things that you're going to endure

when you get into this school." But it's like, how do you help your baby? How will he be treated?

Rather than being "happy talk," these discussions position schools in stark contrast to parental and community values. They are places where Black and Brown children must gather their courage and even suffer in their pursuit of education.[31]

Black community activists like those in the AAPP described these emerging disciplinary school cultures in some of these reformed schools as nested in a larger context of scarcity and austerity.[32] In these settings, new experimental models of schooling are launched out of the ashes of shuttered schools, but with scarce resources. One parent of a sixth-grader in a nearby charter school remarks,

> I would like to see where the money has been allocated for all the schools that are being closed down. With all the administration problems, where is this money going back into the school? My daughter doesn't have music. They don't have half of the sports that we did. They don't have home economics, they don't have none of what we used to have. They don't have drama. They don't have art. I've asked this question more than once, and I haven't gotten an answer. I would like to see where this money has been put back into the schools!

These parents understand the narrowing of school curricula as one outcome of decreased school funding and divestment, rather than as an intentional outcome of carefully designed educational experiments, as reform advocates would argue. They harbor suspicions that monies saved from educational cuts and shuttered schools are being funneled away from students and toward bloated administrations. As one grandmother notes,

> You got all this administrative stuff going on and they're not being involved and walking through the class to see what's going on. They're having these other meetings. They're having power lunches. They're going over here doing this, and then these kids are sitting in these classrooms and learning nothing. And then when it comes down to it the administrators want to say it's the teachers' fault.

Black and Latinx parents tell stories about various versions of "no excuses"/"zero tolerance" disciplinary cultures that their children endure. In one instance, one child asked for more challenging homework after complaining to the teacher that the homework wasn't challenging enough. The child received detention for "questioning authority" and never received a more imaginative assignment. Another parent recounted a story about her son, who had gone on a fishing trip with his father and brought along in his backpack a memento of his trip, a miniature Swiss army knife on a keychain. One day the keychain fell out of his backpack and he was nearly expelled from school before the principal decided on a three-day suspension instead of expulsion. This was a student who loved learning and even tutored other children. After this experience, the child began to dread going back to school. Another parent described a color-coding system in her child's innovation school, where children are labeled according to a color each day according to their behavior. If they start the day on a "bad" color (yellow or orange instead of blue or green, for example), there is no redemption; that child is not moved from that color for the rest of the day. In this situation, this parent tries to counter the school's values with her own parenting at home as a way to shore up the child's pride and mitigate the child's negative experience of a "no excuses" type of disciplinary school culture: "But I had to teach my son, 'It doesn't matter what color you're on. You make the decision of what kind of day you're going to have. I don't care if she puts your color on the wall for everyone to see. You ignore that, because you're not going to determine your day by a color the teacher gets to put on you.'"

Many scholars have noted the links between punitive disciplinary structures in schooling and school push-out, especially in low-income communities.[33] Black parent narratives recount the experiences of their children's schooling as joyless and punishing, and their stories support the idea that some of these disciplinary school cultures actually push children out of their educations. Beyond this, parents also detail how many times they are called in to school because of these disciplinary structures. The more discipline their child is subjected to, the more time caretakers have to take off work and come in to the school to talk with the teacher or the principal about what they perceive are minor infractions that escalate into major punishments.[34] These parent narratives reveal that low-income Black and Latinx parents must do a great deal of work at home to counter these "no excuses" policies and keep their kids engaged in school. In this sense, these narratives also reveal how burdensome neoliberal school reforms are on low-income families. As they are routinely excluded from meaningful participation in their children's education, including school design and turnaround, they are also over-engaged in school disciplinary processes. Caught between these two extremes, parents note that this taxing over-engagement actually dissuades them from other potentially meaningful forms of parental engagement. One parent put it this way:

> It goes back to why parents don't want to be involved. If you're constantly at the school for these minute situations because of this no-tolerance, I mean they figure that *that's* their parent involvement. I definitely don't want to come back to school after I'm constantly out there for just stupid stuff.

Reform activists frame choice as empowering parent consumers, and discipline as giving low-income Black and Brown children something they are presumably lacking in homes characterized by "disarray" (see reformer narratives in the previous chapter). However, parents find themselves trying to explain, translate, and then counter seemingly senseless and capricious disciplinary cultural values in their work with their children at home in order to help them survive the experience of schooling and preserve their zest for education. They experience this increased burden at home in the context of a larger community exclusion from school reform decision making.

Some community activists explicitly frame the growth of charter schools and their concomitant cultures of discipline as an issue of racial injustice and settler colonialism. As one activist notes,

> It's almost like Indian boarding schools, to me. And it's sort of this philosophy [that] to educate the child you must kill the Indian. And that's what I see in these charter schools: to educate the child, you must kill the brownness in them. While that may work, they may have great test scores, what is the long-term implication for that child? I am so grateful for having been born and raised in a Latino neighborhood. I'm grate-

ful for who I am, and I wouldn't trade it. I wouldn't even trade it for a "good" education.

While reform advocates view low-income communities as deficient and lacking the cultural capital that middle-class Whites can bring to under-resourced schools, this neighborhood school activist's perspective emphasizes community cultural wealth as an important form of cultural capital. As critical race and education scholar Tara Yosso explains, these forms of cultural wealth include those that these very activists cultivate at home and in the community: *aspirational* capital, or the ability to maintain hopes and dreams for the future despite barriers; *familial* capital, or the community history held by family and extended kin; and *resistant* capital, or the sets of knowledge and skills that work to challenge inequality.[35] For these activists, school cultures governed by White middle-class logics actually work to subtract these various forms of community cultural capital from students in their quest to transmit dominant forms of cultural capital to low-income students of color.[36]

Community Dispossession: From the Self to the Neighborhood

For these neighborhood schools activists, neoliberal reform entails a multidimensional community dispossession. This dispossession takes place at the level of disciplinary cultures in reformed schools and even the cultural dispossession of the self. It takes place at the level of parental involvement, where more involved parents migrate out of the traditional neighborhood schools to more selective experimental schools and leave gaps in collective parent power at the less selective neighborhood schools. It takes place in the exodus of Black and Latinx teachers from upheaved, shuttered, and turned-around schools, especially when this exodus is replaced by a stream of White teachers who do not live in the neighborhood or know the community outside the school. For these neighborhood activists, this dispossession within and around schools cannot be understood outside other forms of community dispossession. When I asked Barbara, a former DPS teacher, Latina parent, and neighborhood activist, about school reform in her neighborhood, she told me a story about the nearby park with a handball court:

All these Mexican people were out there playin'. I always went down there, there was always a huge crowd of Mexicans. The neighborhood association—I don't participate in it because now it's almost all White and I think they're totally worried about their property values. They exist to protect their property values. Well, they complained about the Mexicans playing and they wanted to close it down. They said, "They're peeing out there. They're breaking bottles." So now they have it fenced.

Indeed, the handball court Barbara references has been transformed into a dog park. School reform represents one more urban transformation that cannot be abstracted from other forms of radical urban renewal that in the end push out Black and Brown community residents in the city's campaign to welcome more affluent residents to the neighborhood. Black and Latinx community activists recounted stories not just about schools, but also about parks, neighborhood associations, Black- and Latinx-owned businesses struggling to afford rising rents, and even churches. These institutions are valuable as vital spaces not only to cultivate community bonds, but also to cultivate community power through information sharing. The sharing of information is an especially salient community resource in an era when transparent, honest, and thorough information about school transformation and educational choice is hard to come by. As Valerie comments on African American community power back in the heyday of the struggle for civil rights, observing that "everyone was together" despite overt and explicit racism before the contemporary era of "post-racial" or "color-blind" racism,[37] Darla connects this power back to community anchors like the Black church:

Our power as a people was about our spirituality. Where do we get information about what's going on in our schools? Our communities? We communicate this information in our churches. That's where our community loves. And that's why we win. But now we have churches, *big* churches, that are run by, excuse me, White ministers, who are not conveying information that is relevant to African American communities.

For these activists, dispossession signifies a loss of community institutions, and with them, the loss of reliable networks for information

sharing. This is why the African American demand for known and reliable community liaisons *inside* reformed schools becomes especially
vital, though rarely does this demand sync with the vision of school reform advocates. As one reform-advocate journalist in this study remarks
about the promise of reform for low-income students of color,

> I think that the schools that are really succeeding with those populations,
> the message that those kids get is really clear and it is, "Whatever the
> rules and whatever the values and whatever else that you have at home,
> we have our own set of rules and values in the school."

As this reformer outlines, successful school cultures are predicated
on cultural separation between the home and school, rather than cultural continuity. Without reliable information networks, community
strategizing around central issues of civil rights such as public schooling becomes difficult for these neighborhood activists to launch and
sustain. This is why information sharing becomes a key community-
organizing strategy to counter the impacts of neoliberal school reform.
The sharp line reformers draw between low-income neighborhoods and
their schools precludes such a vital information sharing. This poses an
obstacle that neighborhood activists fight to overcome.

Information Sharing and Consciousness Raising: AAPP's Small-Scale Organizing

AAPP parents gather in libraries, McDonald's, and each other's houses
in order to first change the consciousness of other parents who are not
yet activated around education reform issues. In the context of the disappearance of Black community institutions, face-to-face consciousness
raising about reform becomes paramount, and stands as one example
of how parent activists advocate for themselves *against* the neoliberal
structures of new schools. These parents also organize face-to-face
in order to resist the reform rhetoric so often couched in civil rights
language. They encourage other parents to first trust their own observations of reform at schools to explicitly counter the marketing language
coming from these schools and the district. Josephine, a Black grandmother in the neighborhood, tells other parents to observe the football

field-turned-running track at the newly reformed Central High, for example. She challenges other parents to notice which children actually use the track (which now occupies the space formerly used by the school's football team for community games):

> So we got a track team over there at Central. Okay? Now how many Black kids do we have running around that track field? And so my question is when we say that something has done a good in our community, we need to go back to see if in fact it *has* done good. We're talking about how we get information, and it's also about how we process what is before our eyes. What are we seeing? Are we seeing little Black kids running around the track field? Are we seeing that? We can't just go off of the justification that the schools give us.

In their networking with other parents, many of these parents explicitly eschew formal organization. In fact, there are some AAPP parents who contrast their "nonpolitical" politics with the formal politics of other organizations. Making an impassioned argument for a network guided by "love" instead of "politics," Valerie explains her organizing approach to me:

> Like I said, we don't want formal. Because once it becomes formal, then it becomes a burden. We want familiarity, we want love, we want embrace. Just that, as simple as that. Grassroots, that's how it spreads. Love spreads. And it will happen. But if we're forcing it and trying to organize it, it becomes a political thing, and we don't want politics. We're looking for hearts. . . . The love that we have for our kids, it's a little tiny process.

This "tiny process," however, collectivizes the private support that parents give to their children when they return home so that they can withstand their experiences of schooling. It also encourages parents to trust their own observations and believe in their own power to advocate for their children. As parents talk at length in focus groups about how their children navigate punitive discipline policies in schools, they also discuss the extent to which they perceive themselves, *as parents*, to be the secondary objects of school discipline policies. Many parents recount their experiences of signing parental agreements with schools that spell out exactly their rights and responsibilities. These agreements often mandate that parents support the school's vision and methods of education as a condition of attendance. In these school-parent agreements, there is little room for parent and community critique or input; mainly the emphasis in these agreements is on the instrumental ways that parents can support student success in school. The promise of individual parental empowerment through school choice does not necessarily extend to parental empowerment within schools. These activists' experiences with exclusionary school cultures are consistent with findings that schools serving communities of color tend to not solicit parent engagement despite their inclusive rhetoric, and teachers prefer to solicit feedback from more advantaged White mothers in racially heterogeneous schools than lower-income parents of color.[38] In one Denver innovation school, for example, the parent handbook specifies that the school centers on a communication model facilitated by an advisory program. Advisors are assigned to groups of students, and become the primary contact for parents. They facilitate communication between parents and teachers. Parents are directed to the advisors first to resolve any concerns, rather than approaching the teachers or school administration directly.

The consumerist model of school choice, with its focus on individual consumer advantage in the educational market, renders individual parents as passive consumers. This also reflects the reform movement's larger ambivalence about the value of parental engagement, especially at the lower rungs of the economic ladder. When parents who sign these agreements take issue with their children's education, they find that they are often not believed or even reprimanded when they individually take their concerns to the teacher or principal.[39] Angie, a Black mother of a high-schooler and middle-schooler, comments on her own experiences of feeling delegitimized before she ended up pulling her younger child out of her middle school:

> I was there, and I was willing to be there whatever the circumstance was for my kid. But there were times when I knew that the system was not going to respond, because it was just me. And they would say, "Well, you're the only one complaining!" But you know, I talk to other parents and everybody's complaining! "What do you mean I'm the only one complaining? Everybody's complaining!"

AAPP parents, in their face-to-face organizing, join other Black parents when they go to meet with their children's school principal. AAPP organizers counsel parents to "never talk to the principal alone" and instead to always go in groups of at least three. This face-to-face organizing model aims to counter the subordinated position that Black parents find themselves in vis-à-vis reformed school cultures. AAPP organizers work to raise the consciousness of other Black parents in ways that encourage them to critically analyze school and district marketing, and instead elevate the experiences and perspectives of both parents and children as sources of legitimate knowledge. In this sense, they work to counter the subordination of Black children by countering the subordination of parents as they engage with their children's schools.

Finally, AAPP members act as a conduit for school reform information—especially school choice—by providing an alternative to relying on the school district for information. For example, Tanya, a twenty-six-year-old Black mother of two children (one with special needs), approached a newly opening charter school in her neighborhood about the possibility of her children attending. The principal of the school assured her that the school would be a good fit for her children, and even asked Tanya to spread the word about the new charter school to drum up enrollment. After Tanya talked to other parents and even distributed the school's marketing information to her parent networks, the principal then informed Tanya that unfortunately they did not have the services her special needs child required, and the school could not accommodate her daughter. She was told this as the deadline for school choice time was quickly approaching. Tanya was livid, and provided parents with this additional piece of information about the lack of special needs supports. This information is not given freely by the school district. The AAPP foregrounds parents' firsthand knowledge and experiences with schools in order to share information about attrition of Black children and school climate. Often, this firsthand knowledge runs counter to the official marketing and discourses of the district, specific schools, and reformers more broadly. For example, several high-performing innovation schools in Denver boast a high college acceptance rate for students who make it to graduation. However, information on student attrition at these schools is harder to come by. At one meeting, Mable brings her son's three yearbooks (freshman, sophomore, and junior year) from one of these schools. It is a school that she would eventually pull her son out of for his senior year. She shows AAPP members the yearbooks, pointing out through student pictures the disappearance of Black students at the school from one year to the next. The visual representation of push-out is a powerful illustration of her personal stories of the ways the school mistreated both her son and herself as a parent.

Part of this information sharing provides support to parents in their decision making to navigate the public school system or even pull their children out entirely. AAPP parents express frustration with not being able to trust the school system to meet their children's needs, and encourage parents to consider that there may come a point when they should give up fighting and pull their kids out of the public school system entirely. Consider this exchange between AAPP parents, after which several parents shared their stories about searching for the right educational fit for their children before deciding to pull them out of school and transferring them into a GED program and then into vocational training programs (e.g., culinary arts):

> MABLE: I'm being real. They system isn't doing it for our kids. And by the time you figure out how to *make* them do it, your child is in jail. And that's real. So what do we do as a group, for our children when the system has failed us? It's crazy for us to sit here and talk about the system not doing it. There comes a time when I need to be educating my child instead of just fighting the system.
>
> JOSEPHINE: Yeah, you oughta listen to the blues sometimes; Etta James sings about "sugar on the floor." And that's what we do to our kids: sugar wasted on the floor. Oh my god.
>
> DARLA: I think that there are ways, there are ways that you can get what your child needs. And we have to realize that that is *not* the public school system. They owe it to us, yes. But that is not the only way to access it.
>
> JEANETTE: You know, but it's frustrating to have to go to different grocery stores to get what we need.
>
> MAGGIE: I do it all the time.
>
> DARLA: But at a certain point that's what we have to do to educate our children.

This exchange underscores the tensions between collectively "fighting the system" and advocating for their own children's educational pathways that might take place outside the system. The AAPP functions as a collective support system to help other parents decide when it is time to cobble together different educational opportunities ("going to different grocery stores to get what we need") or pulling their children out of the public school system entirely. In one sense, this exercise of "choice" allows these parents to best select their children's educational fit. Like savvy and conscientious consumers who might shop at different stores to get what they need, these parents advocate shopping for different options that market choice might offer. However, their choice to support their children's entry into a GED program or vocational training also renders the prospect of a future college education and economic advancement much more distant. This is not the kind of "choice" that necessarily yields economic or educational advantage. This exchange also reveals the strain on parents who feel a tension between the need to fight an unresponsive and even hostile system for *all* children versus the responsibility they have to protect the success and dignity of their own children, even if it means exiting "the system."

Disrupting Hegemony: The Community Education Collective (CEC)

Darren Richards, a Black man in his fifties, has lived near Central High for three decades. With his wife, Ramona, he raised his three children in a small house just a few blocks away from the high school. Darren and his friend and neighbor, Joe, a Latino grandfather of four and in his early sixties, sit at the same table in the same community room of the local library every Wednesday at 5:30 p.m. They are the cofounders and main facilitators of the Community Education Collective (CEC). Darren and Joe formed the CEC in the wake of the Central High closure, after they and many others participated in protests and walkouts, and witnessed the school district make the decision to close their neighborhood school. Darren and Joe not only live close to Central, but they each did a stint there as workers: Darren had been an assistant coach there in the 1980s, and Joe more recently served as a counselor there for many of Central's academically struggling students. Darren and Joe, together with about fifteen other core members of the CEC, faithfully meet each week to discuss the status of Central High and the neighborhood. Through the grapevine they keep participants apprised of the quick changes at Central: the new community liaisons who come for a few months and then go again; the hiring of new teachers and assistant principals; the development of new school sports programs and educational models that shift, recede, and emerge year to year as school leadership changes annually. They don't have officers or formal positions in the CEC, nor do they have letterhead, newsletters, or a dedicated space to meet besides the community library. Yet they have been an enduring part of the neighborhood landscape since the district closed Central despite community protest. Ramona also attends these meetings, as do Vicki and Tony, a married couple who are neighborhood residents and former teachers at Central. Some members of the AAPP also attend each week. What is striking about the CEC is its concentration of former Central teachers, though its membership is much broader than this.

The group represents the city's pre-reform past, when teachers were local professionals and often lived in the neighborhoods in which they worked. Many of them knew the students both inside and outside the schools, and knew the students' families and lives in the neighborhood. They are teachers whose racial and ethnic backgrounds reflect those of the majority Black and Latinx kids they came into contact with every day as teachers and school staff. They also come from a community ethic in which *all* the kids in the neighborhood are *their* kids too; they are not simply property of the biological parents who are positioned as the sole savvy consumers in neoliberal reform's consumerist school choice model. In the popular debates over school reform, the teachers union, which supposedly represents the interests of teachers' jobs, is positioned as oppositional to the innovative reformers who instead have the children's best interests at heart. However, this polarized popular framing of the debate neglects to capture the broader variety of teacher activism that also happens outside the union. Given that reform has entailed an exodus of teachers from the public school system and an influx of Teach for America and other nonlicensed and contingent teachers,[40] many of reform's casualties are teachers who also have strong ties to local neighborhood communities that have been impacted by reform. Because of this concentration of former teachers in this sector of neighborhood activism, the CEC offers some unique critiques of reformer discourse from the vantage point of former educators. They position education reform as an important manifestation of gentrification, but it is not the only manifestation. As neighborhood residents, they also organize to halt the takeover of their community parks, neighborhood associations, and businesses.

Together, the CEC stands as a collective that marched, along with student-led walkouts, when the district announced that it would close Central High. As Joe remembered,

> To some extent the CEC started with acts of civil disobedience. We marched to the school board and basically took over the meeting without being on the agenda, without any permission to do it. It was very passionate. It was very strong. And so we were asking the relevant questions like "Why are you closing it? Why are you lying? Why did you not invest in our community?" But they never invest in our communities. They never invest in our schools. And then they turn around and they make it as if it is *us* who have failed.

According to CEC members, the district had pledged to track the students who were lost in the closure and in transition, but as the months after the closure wore on and the media's spotlight began to wane, the district failed to demonstrate investment in the fate of the former students of Central. As Joe put it, the CEC arose as a "watchdog for the students of color" to protect them from the vagaries of a majority-White and elite reform movement. In the wake of these walkouts and marches, the CEC continues to resist reformer narratives that position reformers as the "real" change agents and neighborhood opponents as simply the champions of the mediocre status quo. As Vicki, a CEC member and thirty-four-year-old former Central High teacher, explained to me,

> So for those reformers who say we're not offering alternatives, we don't have to. They're already there. There are existing models. What we're fighting back against is a form of imperialism in our neighborhoods. That's what we're reacting to, and the whole Great White Savior complex.
>
> There's no mystery to kids doing well in school. Rigor, accountability, good teachers, helping students focus on being college-bound-minded,

high expectations, small class sizes, right. . . . I think that neighborhood schools that are well-performing are doing much of what Catholic schools are doing, and what well-resourced schools have always done. But those neighborhood schools are not very well resourced, especially since the school reform started.

In Vicki's view, reform has accelerated the divestment in neighborhood schools, setting them up for failure.[41] She and other members of the CEC believe that with more resources and political will, neighborhood schools could be successful models for educational equity and success. Reform experimentation is unnecessary, unwarranted, and capricious, in her view, since there have always been successful models of public and private schooling. CEC members emphasize resource divestment as a key precipitator of educational failure, rather than the inherently flawed bureaucracy of a centralized school district that reformers commonly identify as the cause of educational inequity.

As I began attending weekly meetings, I noticed that the CEC's rhetoric as a community collective is much more politicized than that of the AAPP network. CEC members explicitly frame education reform—as a major mechanism of gentrification—as imperialist and racist. In their meetings, they tackle the ideal of "urgency" so pervasive in reformer rhetoric and process, and work to delegitimize it. At one meeting, Darren shifted the group discussion from DPS's marketing to the larger issue of reform rhetoric around urgency and civil rights:

> We need to talk about how the term "civil rights" is now being used as a weapon against us. I am third-generation DPS and the fact that it's suddenly an urgent issue *now*, when it wasn't such an urgent issue not only for my mom, but for my grandmother, right? We have learned how to raise kids in a racist school system. So don't tell me it's urgent now. Don't tell me it's all right. When we have the debate on school reform, I just want to say stop co-opting!

Members of the CEC take their confrontational politics not only to the school board, but also to the local neighborhood association meetings that are now majority-White. CEC activists challenge White residents on their perspectives on the Brown and Black residents of the neighborhood. Barbara, who had cherished the neighborhood's hand-ball court as a welcoming space for Latinx and Black youth in the neigh-borhood, tried to intervene in neighborhood association discussions about closing the handball court and reopening the space as a dog park. She remembers,

> When I found out about the dog park, several of us from the CEC went to the community center for the meetings and fought against it. I said, "You're puttin' dogs above kids. This is a small park. The kids play there." And the argument they came up with was, "We're helping to fight crime. There's a lot of gang members that stay there, and if we put the dog park there, it's going to help reduce crime."
>
> I'm like, "I go there every day. I've never had a problem. I take my nephews and nieces there. I've never had a problem. My neighbor took her kid there. She never had a problem." So they come up with these things. "It's good for you, and we can also help kids come to learn about our dogs." It was really pathetic, very elitist.

Barbara complained to her city council representative, who in the end defended the dog park and suggested to Barbara that in fact it was *she* who was racist since she was "making this about racism." This inter-action is reminiscent of legal scholar Ian Haney López's conception of "dog whistle politics" in which racist policies are suggested and supported by politicians without directly mentioning race, and then further veiled by the charge that critics are *making* it about race and are therefore the "real racists."[42] Barbara signed up to be a neighbor-hood watchdog (no pun intended) when the dog park was opened as a pilot project, since she learned that the dog park could be shut down if residents did not clean up after their dogs or follow the rules. She documented and reported the many piles of dog excrement littering the park in its first few months of operation, yet the park was allowed to remain open.

The fight over the dog park signifies a deeper fight over the future of Black and Latinx families and especially Black and Latinx youth in the neighborhood. During the discussions of the dog park, CEC activists challenged White residents on their framing of neighborhood youth of color as "criminal." Ramona remembers,

You have all these White people talking about how afraid they are. Me and these other organizers were sitting in the back of the room going, "Ugh. Oh my God." Then finally we were like, "You're talking about our families. You're talking about our friends. You're talking about our children. Most of these kids are not hard-core gangbangers. We're not L.A. We're not Chicago. If you're so worried about gangs, how about you write a check to [local organization] to help support the anti-gang work that they're doing?"

From their weekly meetings in the library to their presence in White-dominated community spaces such as the school board and the neighborhood association, CEC activists collectively question and boldly delegitimize reformer rhetoric. They engage in a kind of culture jamming by refusing to allow this rhetoric to completely permeate public processes around education and neighborhood development. But they do so without organizational stability or structure. A sense of hopelessness and bitterness pervades their meetings, even though they faithfully meet each week. Tony articulates this hopelessness in the context of an absence of community-anchored Black leadership in the city:

Bottom line is, we know we're gettin' screwed, but nothing's gonna change. It's just that feeling of powerlessness. You can't fight them. They're not gonna change their minds. That's the way I feel. The powerful people I know are not gonna get in there and do anything. They're just not. The CEC will, but the others have been bought.

The pervasive hopelessness in the CEC is also fueled by members' lack of faith in Denver's major media outlets and traditional community institutions like the neighborhood association to spread important information and tell their stories. I attended one meeting where the CEC discussed the possibility of distributing its own newsletter, since members recognized that the city's major reform-oriented papers would not print their op-eds or articles. They quickly concluded that collectively, they did not have the resources to generate *and* distribute their own newsletter.

The CEC is not about building something new. It is not necessarily about expanding or recruiting more members. It is about vigilance and presence. It is about interrupting hegemony—reminding reformers, urban developers, and the gentry that racism is replete throughout their visions of saving and reviving a "troubled" neighborhood and its disadvantaged youth. As Vicki puts it,

> People ask me, "Why should I go to a meeting? You guys aren't doing much either." But we voice our concerns. We go to the school board, the neighborhood association. At least that way they have a little bit of a fear that we're still here.

The CEC represents agitation without infrastructure or formal representation. It organizes on a political landscape where few entities (the press, local foundations, city councilors) can be trusted not to collude with the moneyed interests of White elites coming into the city. Although the confrontational politics of the CEC makes it known to various reformers and reform groups, Darla, a core AAPP member, critiques the CEC as a functional community organization:

> I just have to be as blunt about them as I am about anybody else. They have no structure. I don't know what their mission statement is. There is no strategy. They have been good people who have gone into these meetings with consistency, and they hang in there as long as they can. But you've got to create some formal structure. So the end result is that our kids are *still* not getting what they need because they [the CEC] are not in a position to be able to help them.

But as Vicki notes, even without structure or strategy, the CEC's power lies in persistently reminding moneyed interests that consent is not total. This public withdrawal of consent may not in itself transform power relations, but a counter-reform movement cannot exist without it.[43]

Capturing the Vote: Democrats for Educational Justice (DEJ)

Democrats for Educational Justice (DEJ) was founded by a group of Black and Latina women who argued that DFER (Democrats for Education Reform), a national education reform organization with state chapters across the United States, represents a troubling fusion of the

Wall Street hedge fund–backed reform movement and party politics. The DEJ is a loosely organized network of Black and Latinx Democrats struggling to take back the party from the pro-reform Democratic wing, and center the fight for neighborhood schools as the cornerstone of their Democratic vision. Their reclamation of the word "Democrat" signals the break in apparent consensus that Democrat has always meant pro-reform, a consensus that has dominated state politics since reform's inception in the early 2000s. Journalist Erica Meltzer reported in 2018 that a new wave of leftist Democrats is now rising up within the party to push against the Democratic brand of education reform that has dominated the Democratic Party in Colorado.[44] Even before this massive pushback within the party, however, DEJ activists were organizing and networking to begin this pushback from the ground up.

Already activists for drug and criminal justice reform, voter engagement, health justice, and broader economic justice, members of DEJ leveraged their organizing networks to try to integrate Denver's education reform's crises into these broader movements. They also conducted voter education drives across multiple neighborhoods during school board races and state elections. They showed up to protests and neighborhood meetings around school closures in Denver to support localized fights for neighborhood schools. They leafleted parents about the influence of DFER in Denver; the background on specific school board members and candidates for school board races; and information on local reform-aligned think tanks and foundations, as well as these actors' instrumental role in Denver's school reform politics and urban renewal. Their struggle represents a larger struggle to maintain and strengthen the progressive wing of the Democratic Party and the Black and Latinx vote. Like the AAPP and the CEC, DEJ does not have stable funding or a formal organizational base. Like the AAPP and the CEC, it works to delegitimize the power of the reform movement in Denver by educating predominantly low-income communities of color about the national reach of the reform movement, and primarily by disrupting the hegemony of reform rhetoric. Unlike the locally rooted AAPP and CEC, however, membership of DEJ spans neighborhoods across the city, and between election cycles the group exists mostly online. By running an online newsletter and providing a web-based clearinghouse for smaller and localized struggles around particular neighborhood schools slated for closure or turnaround, DEJ has attempted to connect these localized fights together. Given the influx of outside money into Denver's school board races over the last decade,[45] DEJ's efforts to organize Black and Latinx voting power has helped to produce limited wins on the Denver school board in certain instances, even though the pro-reform majority has maintained its edge on the school board throughout most of the last decade. Between election cycles, DEJ recedes as its main members focus on their activism in other spheres.

Significantly, as a progressive voter education wing of the neighborhood schools movement, this group is almost completely organized by and comprised of women of color. Black women almost exclusively lead the AAPP as well. In a larger city context where the Black churches have been dismantled or pushed out and Black leadership has grown estranged from the communities it claims to represent, Black and Latina women's political power addresses this void. One main DEJ organizer, Nancy, questions the legitimacy of Black leadership in Denver:

Every time someone says that, it bothers me. I mean, for instance, Black people who say they're speaking for the Black community, I'm like, who are those folks? They'll say, "The Black community stands for this." Well, I don't stand for that, so what does that mean? For so long, the "Black community" has meant Black men, and Black men would speak for the community.

And in some ways I'm an anomaly of Black leadership because I don't fit the mold. I'm a woman. I don't come from the civil rights era. I don't go to church. But I want to make sure that we're expanding our goals so we're not just going to this person with the ministerial alliance or that person—that we have several leaders in our community that aren't recognized and we need to raise up those voices.

With this, DEJ activists, who are the most likely of the three groups featured in this chapter to become involved in electoral politics in the city, advocate a multivocal movement that foregrounds Black and Latina women's leadership. These women are integrated in broad movements for social change around the city and state, including movements for affordable housing and prisoner reentry programs; movements for economic justice and an increase in the minimum wage; and movements to halt the expansion of new highways and other projects that displace low-income communities.

Not only is this a contrast to the hegemonic models of Black leadership in community organizing for civil rights and the neoliberal Black professional-managerial class, their organizing represents a major contrast to the White, male paternalism of the elite reformer movement.[46] It is largely because of this race, gender, and class contrast—and not only the contrasting ideology of the neighborhood schools versus the charter schools debate—that elite reformers and dominant media outlets can consistently delegitimize these fights for strong and accessible neighborhood schools. At one point, the DEJ organized a community education event at a local church about the history of education reform in Denver. The *Denver Post* commented on this event in its coverage of school reform in Denver, and referred to the DEJ as "a shadowy group." In other dominant narratives, elite reformers have dismissed the efforts of DEJ and other neighborhood schools activists as misguided and uninformed. When I ask self-identified reformers to illustrate their version of a "power map," that is, who holds the most power in deciding the direction of school reform, and who holds the least power in Denver school reform politics, often the non-institutionalized groups like DEJ, the CEC, or the AAPP are not even on reformers' maps. In contrast, local community nonprofits often are.

Organizing without the leverage of the city's traditional Black, male, ministerial leadership, political representatives of the Black professional-managerial class, or the formal structure of the nonprofit, these women neighborhood schools organizers are the most delegitimized players in the landscape of school reform politics. It is a landscape dominated by neoliberal reform rhetoric that champions school choice, experimentation, turnaround, and innovation as part of a larger project of urban renewal. It is difficult to imagine this kind of elite dismissal of local opposition to neighborhood schools if the major organizers were White middle-class men advocating for strong and accessible neighborhood schools, though chapter 4 does explore the stories of such activists. Indeed, reformers cite White middle-class backlash against more radical forms of equalizing education (such as a return to busing, rezoning, or changing property tax structures for school funding) as an unmovable barrier to educational justice. For example, one prominent pro-reform foundation representative uses the civil rights frame in his explanation of why reform policy must ultimately work around the formidable threat of White middle-class resistance to equity:

> It's a huge civil rights issue. A *huge* civil rights issue. And the fact of the matter is, that the people who have what they want, aren't going to willingly give it away. So the problem is, if you really wanted to make a difference, you would first of all completely change the way that schools are funded. If the system were to really say, "Okay, we're removing the following ten teachers from this wealthy school and bringing them to this poor school, and we're moving some of those teachers (from the poor school) over to the rich school," they would, trust me, the school board would get so much pressure, the superintendent . . . that I'm not sure they'd survive.
>
> So the only way for them [neighborhood schools activists] to really get quality schools is by fighting the political battles that are stacked against them. I don't know how else to say it. I mean, 'cause the real answers are very radical. If you really want to solve this, . . . well, nobody *really* wants to solve it enough. People—I mean *middle-class* people—don't care enough about your kids to be willing to sacrifice their own kids' education.

In this unusually candid moment, this reformer recognizes the root causes of educational inequality, but frames the solutions to these root causes as politically impossible since they are "too radical." In this unusual admission, this reformer notes that the deeper vision for equity would be to change the formula for school funding, or to swap resources from better-funded to poorly funded schools. And yet the anticipated pushback from more affluent families means that such a redistribution of resources would be an untenable solution.

While White backlash is framed in reformer narratives as politically undesirable and simply too risky for the viability of a given education policy, Black resistance is clearly worth the risk. The subtext of reformer narratives is that the reform movement and the school system can withstand Black and Latinx resistance. That this resistance is launched mostly by neighborhood Black and Latina women is significant, and demonstrates how the reform and counter-reform movements are profoundly shaped by race, gender, and class dynamics. As in the case of

Roy Moore and the 2017 Senate upset in Alabama, Black women have been central to organizing Democratic voters around racially just and racially responsive candidates and policies. Their organizing often takes place outside formal party networks, and yet holds the potential to tip the balance of power in local and state elections.[47] For most of the last decade, the reform movement has been successful in winning most seats on the school board and infiltrating the central school district. But the few neighborhood schools advocates on the board over the first several years in the new millennium—and certainly the November 2019 school board election that for the first time "flipped the board"—have served as a reminder that reform hegemony is not total, nor is it uncontested. As Vicki of the CEC put it, "At least that way they have a little bit of a fear that we're still here."

Conclusion

There are many mechanisms that enable reformers to minimize the scope of Black resistance. As explored in the previous chapter, the reform movement delegitimizes Black resistance with its polarized rhetorical framing of its own activists as the "real reformers" and opponents as the deplorable "defenders of the status quo." The reform movement also racializes this "real reformer" rhetoric, framing reforms like school choice, discipline, and the standards movement as the vanguard of a new era of civil rights struggle.[48] The co-optation of civil rights language and mission enables reformers to claim that they are working for racial justice even though their movement is largely White, and the very neighborhood schools advocates they regularly discredit are largely Black and Latinx.[49] Reformers are buttressed by outside connections to national reform organizations and financial resources and enjoy widespread media and foundation support.[50] This serves to further discredit, overpower, and render invisible the widespread community resistance to neoliberal reform.

There are larger forces at play, in addition to the reformer movement's rhetorical, organizational, and financial advantages, that further work to challenge Black and Latinx resistance to neoliberal reform. One is the impact of community fragmentation as a result of gentrification's displacement in the urban core. Each of these groups—the AAPP, the

CEC, and DEJ—all struggle with being able to share reliable information about reform, and to root out common experiences of living with reformed schooling experiments in their communities. Information sharing becomes a political goal and a political act in and of itself, as decades-old community anchors disappear. These anchors include the neighborhood school, the Black church, neighborhood parks and community centers, and even neighborhood associations. They also include the loss of trusted and representative Black leadership. Any evaluation of the relative success or failure of these grassroots efforts to counter neoliberal reform must take into account the conditions under which people labor to organize in environments with disappearing resources and organizational stability.[51] Dispossession undermines the very indigenous networks, organizational homes, and resources that are essential for launching counter-hegemonic resistance. As Arena underscores in his study of how New Orleans's public housing was dismantled in the wake of Hurricane Katrina, dispossession erodes the basis of Black working-class and poor people's political power.[52]

It is also important to recognize that for many of these neighborhood activists, school reform is experienced as another form of community dispossession. It is a dispossession that cannot be abstracted from other forms of dispossession like rising rents and public spaces that were once governed by Black and Latinx residents and are now occupied by White newcomers. For many, school reform is not experienced or enjoyed as consumer freedom. It is experienced through the faux community forums that in the end discard Black and Latinx input and facilitate urban development projects with school reform at their cores. It is experienced through the choice processes predicated on models of individualist consumer savvy, and in the disciplinary cultures in schooling that end up alienating many students of color and their families through the institutionalization of dominant cultural values and White teachers. In the end, the AAPP, the CEC, and DEJ represent anti-gentrification movements that are not simply trying to preserve the "status quo"; rather, they are trying to advance the vision of strong, well-resourced comprehensive neighborhood schools that are accessible to all neighborhood children and families, that are rooted in and not separate from community processes, and that are culturally competent and culturally responsive. This is a vision of educational empowerment tied to community advancement, and in the case of the DEJ, the integrity and strength of the Black and Latinx vote. As educational critics and community movements alike have pointed out, and despite what the reformer movement would claim, this vision never represented the status quo of what was already widely recognized as unequal and substandard public education even before reform landed in Denver.

Even with these challenges, these neighborhood schools movement groups create new networks for information sharing. They validate and collectivize their experiences of reform. They push against the power of reform agents and supporters both inside the schools (e.g., in meetings with principals) and outside the schools (neighborhood association meetings and electoral politics). More significantly, all of these groups remind reform agents and supporters of reform, as well as the public, that Black resistance will not go away quietly and that the reform movement's hegemony is not total. It is always subject to challenge from below, and cannot take over neighborhood institutions or even the Democratic Party without a fight. These very fights also bring "community" into being. They stitch together individual experiences of and frustrations with school reform, and transform these into social injustices that must be collectively tackled. This cognitive liberation is an essential component of movement mobilization, and turns private problems into collective political issues.[53]

These movements also remain largely outside the boundaries of formal and stable organizations. There are surely advantages to this lack of institutionalization. In the case of the AAPP and the CEC, their activism is deeply connected to the families experiencing the brunt of quick reform experiments. Instead of serving as paid organizers charged with mobilizing members of a community, they *are* this very community mobilizing itself. They answer to proximate community needs instead of funders and specific campaign or grant requirements.[54] Because of this, their organizing is uncompromising and their message is unfiltered. In the case of the DEJ, these activists can emerge and recede quickly between election cycles, and they can flexibly move between other stable movement organizations that represent various social justice initiatives. They work to connect these other struggles to the fight for strong neighborhood schools and race- *and* class-based justice. As Arena points out, movement institutionalization, or *nonprofitization*, encourages a narrow fragmentation of identity groups along single-issue lines that are ultimately unable to effectively mount a collective challenge to neoliberal capitalism.[55] Non-institutionalized movement networks like those represented by the AAPP, the CEC, and DEJ have the capacity to link multiple issues (e.g., urban development, housing justice, educational justice, and racial justice) and multiple identity groups that share a similar working-class location.

However, there is a high cost to this non-institutionalization. Their organizing takes place in a context where few funders can be trusted, and where few funded organizations will take on the fight for strong neighborhood schools as a central social justice issue. Bruce, a young director of a statewide progressive racial and economic justice nonprofit, shares with me that some of the DEJ and CEC neighborhood activists had approached his organization to take on market-based reform as one of its major campaigns. Although he is passionate about the movement for neighborhood schools and views the issue as in line with other organizational campaigns related to dispossession such as payday lending, wage theft, and private prisons, he is hesitant:

> This group of community members are coming to us and telling us that there are no organizations representing our side. And I know this. We have no infrastructure for us in this fight, for our place . . . and personally, education is still on the top of my mind. But I don't want to set us up for failure, because the opposition is strong.
>
> I feel sad that I'm not going to be able to fight this fight, but the funding isn't there right now, especially locally. And it's a danger for us to engage in this locally because we will offend a few of our local funders. We just can't afford to do that.

As explored in chapter 5, formal community nonprofit organizations can empower even the most marginalized community members, such as youth of color, to speak on behalf of their own educational experiences and even push reformers to adopt explicitly antiracist policies in their quest for neoliberal reforms. As sociologist Suzanne Staggenborg has persuasively argued, movements that are made up exclusively of informal movement networks rather than formal social movement organizations (SMOs) are unlikely to survive, so the structure of the SMO gives movements a chance to endure into the future.[56] But there is a price to pay for this funded organizing. These community nonprofits must walk the line of holding reformers accountable to reform's missteps, while periodically coalescing with them on shared visions and values for educational justice. In these long-term relationships, they also run the risk of being co-opted by the reform movement, which in the wake of failed educational experiments increasingly seeks community buy-in. As Bruce's quote above also reveals, funded movement organizations must tread carefully in terms of their messaging and alliances in order to survive in a political climate in which most funders, even those who identify as progressive, support the movement for education reform. Arena notes this reality in his critique of nonprofitization's role in post-Katrina New Orleans:

> The hard reality faced by nonprofits, radical or otherwise, is that to obtain funding they have to fit their agenda into the issues and guidelines laid out by the funders. The liberal foundations, who are the major provider of funds for the 501(c)(3) sector, . . . encourage applicants to develop and forge campaigns with reasonable goals that do not represent a radical challenge to the status-quo. The nonprofits are generally encouraged to approach social problems as technical in nature, requiring the application of expert knowledge, rather than to frame issues as deeply rooted, class-based conflicts. Any deviation can result in a cutoff of funds.[57]

The non-institutionalized Black resistance, in contrast, remains profoundly local, under-resourced, and difficult to sustain and grow. Because it is not tied to a recognizable organization and recognizable funders, it is a multivocal resistance mostly shouldered by low-income Black and Latina women that is attacked and easily dismissed by the mostly well-resourced White male reformers who are tied to national organizations, resources, and support from the dominant media. It is also a resistance that is not represented by the city's traditional Black male leadership. Because reformer discourse publicly and broadly claims the moral high ground and the "reform versus status quo" framing and co-optation of civil rights rhetoric, it is an uphill battle for community organizations like those featured in this chapter to reclaim civil rights discourse and successfully redefine what this means in a neoliberal era. At its most powerful, this Black and Latinx resistance is cultivated by the women organizers who work to center school reform in other struggles for economic and racial justice. But they too encounter major roadblocks in the reluctance of institutionalized movements to take on these fights.

As a passionate social justice warrior and always a bridge builder, Bruce sees hope for the neighborhood schools movement to take off (and more importantly, for the funding to follow), as soon as it hits White neighborhoods. He believes that the funding for the progressive fight for strong neighborhood schools will come when the movement can shift into a multiracial antiracist struggle, supported by White affluent urban newcomers who are also motivated to fight for access to neighborhood schools. In the next chapter, I explore such a White resistance to school choice in a historically Latinx neighborhood quickly gentrifying right across the river.

4

Fragile Alliances

Cross-Racial Solidarity and Conflict in Community Claims to the Neighborhood School

Adam, one of the most prominent reformers in this city, meets with me in his top-floor office of a downtown skyscraper, where he talks about the advantages conferred by race and class:

> I mean, even in a crappy urban district, unless it's a place like Detroit, we find we are advantaged. So we will find the magnet program, we will find the AP track, we can always count on little islands of excellence here and there. Most of us are going to care more about opportunity for our own kids. It's really about protecting access. It's actually okay for many kids. For the White middle- and upper-middle-income kids.

Adam's prediction, that White middle- to upper-middle-income families will always find "little islands of excellence" even in a "crappy urban district," is certainly supported by a literature that suggests that school choice advantages those who already have racial and class advantage. School choice, as a major tenet of neoliberal reform, has been widely criticized for the racial segregation and disparities it creates. The school choices made by White wealthier families in the context of neoliberal school reform often lead to increased racial and economic segregation in the neighborhood schools attended by students of color.[1] School choice has accelerated the resegregation of schools in recent decades; schools in the United States are now even more racially segregated than are their surrounding neighborhoods.[2] Less advantaged parents who are not plugged into these special networks tend to rely on other parents in their communities for information regarding school choice, but lack the information furnished to more privileged families.[3] Furthermore, some researchers argue that "choice" is not completely free but is circumscribed by class and race inequalities. Poor families and families of color often do not have the same array of choices as wealthier White families.[4] Indeed, rather than perceiving themselves as empowered agents of choice, the low-income Black and Latinx parents featured in the last chapter perceive themselves to be the disadvantaged objects of the choice process. Their stories suggest that from their vantage point, the schools "choose" them, or even screen them out completely.

With neoliberalism's emphasis on consumer choice now guiding school reform policies, advantaged families are theoretically free to live anywhere they want in the city. Although a good school undoubtedly boosts home values, the children of White-flight suburbia who are refusing to go back to their suburban roots are instead opting to settle in more diverse urban neighborhoods, even if the schools have a reputation for low performance. Close to transportation, jobs, and "culture," these families have access to local urban gardens, eclectic mom-and-pop stores, grand parks, old theaters, and a walkability of a kind they did not have growing up in the crush of suburban America. Widely recognized by proponents of urban revitalization as the "creative class," these relatively affluent newcomers are demanding and generating urban renewal.[5] Yet school choice allows these families to settle in and reshape neighborhoods that were formerly Latinx or Black, while still protecting their access to quality schools and their children's educational and future economic success. According to this reformer, school choice enables these advantaged families in particular to work a school system to their benefit in order to escape a failing neighborhood school, while still enjoying the diversity of older urban neighborhoods. White newcomers' willingness to settle in a racially and economically diverse neighborhood while electing to send their children to schools outside their neighborhood echoes sociologist and human geographer Tim Butler's argument that gentrification by the creative class "values the presence of others . . . but chooses not to interact with them. They are, as it were, much valued as a kind of social wallpaper, but no more."[6]

What neither the critical literature nor Adam's prediction can explain, then, is why some of the largest community opposition to neoliberal school choice and corporate reform is being led by the very members of Florida's so-called creative class. If these are the beneficiaries of neoliberal school choice, why are some of these people mobilizing to actively resist it? Even more importantly, what does their resistance lend to the broader community resistance against neoliberal reform, especially when this resistance is largely sustained by leagues of low-income Black and Latinx residents who are so often left behind by processes of urban renewal? This chapter examines such a White resistance to school choice. By analyzing the rise and fall of these gentry-led micro-mobilizations around specific beloved neighborhood schools, I demonstrate in this chapter the possibilities for these advantaged activists to coalesce with other community neighborhood schools groups into powerful multiracial alliances against neoliberal reform. I then trace the underlying reasons for the unraveling and decline of such nascent coalitions.

Just across the river from the historic center of Black community life, where Black and Latinx residents are organizing to oppose school closures, turnarounds, and the establishment of charters in their rapidly gentrifying neighborhood (see previous chapter), I am sitting in an old community theater on a Saturday morning in the belly of such a resistance. A White woman in her thirties with a tattoo of a serpent climbing up her arm, who I will later get to know as Janeyl, warmly welcomes me to this community meeting. I introduce myself as a researcher, a member of the community, and a parent of two small children who lives in this neighborhood. Urns of coffee and paper cups are neatly stacked on a foldout table in the corner. The room is buzzing with multiple conversations between thirty, then fifty, then roughly seventy people who have trickled in, until Janeyl says above the din, "Okay, everyone, let's start the meeting! There are too many people crammed in this room. Let's go back into the theater." We head back into the old theater, where there is a well-worn stage along with several rows of comfortable, tattered theater seats. Typically, this theater hosts eclectic events like punk shows, hipster string quartets and bluegrass jams, and local film festivals. Just a stone's throw from a Venezuelan sandwich shop, a Thai restaurant, an Italian pizzeria, three wine bars, four beer taverns, seven art galleries, two independently owned bookstores, a bicycle repair shop, a natural baby shop specializing in cloth diapers and environmentally sound baby toys, a high-end pet store, and two yoga studios, this theater is one of the cultural centers of a neighborhood that is quickly rising in reputation as one of the city's most "charming" areas of town. On the first Friday of each month, this neighborhood is packed with visitors who join the neighborhood locals to frequent the galleries serving wine and cheese, enjoy ice cream in the neighborhood park, listen to homegrown bands play on street corners, and dine at any number of eateries within a mile radius. Thirty years ago this neighborhood was mostly Latinx. Homes were affordable, and the neighborhood hosted a few small coffee shops, some family-owned Italian and Mexican restaurants, and the city's oldest amusement park.

Within the last two decades, this neighborhood has rapidly developed. Now large duplexes selling for up to half a million dollars each are replacing small, dilapidated houses, and they tower awkwardly above the homes next door that have not yet succumbed to this fate. Few residents have lawns anymore. Instead, many have opted for less water-intensive colorful xeriscaping with native plants. Anglo children regularly play in the newly renovated playground, though there are very few White teenagers to be seen. Instead, small groups of Latinx teenagers also try to carve out space in these parks, especially at night, at the picnic tables away from the playground. The new, mostly White settlers in this neighborhood are overwhelmingly two-parent families with small children. With a few high-profile elementary schools in the area with highly gifted and talented (HGT) tracks, these new families have found local choices for their children. But when their children age out of elementary school, these families have typically either left the neighborhood for higher-income neighborhoods with higher-performing middle and high schools, or have elected to stay in the neighborhood but commit to driving their kids across the city to higher-status schools. In doing so, they effectively exercise the advantages that their creative work brings (their time, job flexibility, and transportation) to choice out of their neighborhood schools. That is, until the recession of 2008.

The Rejection of School Choice and Renewed Commitment to Neighborhood Schools

After the recession, a number of knowledge-production jobs disappeared or were consolidated, leaving these families with slightly more precarious employment or without a second wage earner in the household. At the same time, home prices skyrocketed in the neighborhood, and these residents knew that they would be priced out of the neighborhood forever if they left. They were no longer as easily able to relocate to a higher-income neighborhood, and were resentful of the time and energy it took to drive a child to another neighborhood for a quality education. The contraction of the economy was the final straw that solidified an already growing ethic of localism among these new settlers, and a belief that all families deserve a good neighborhood school. Shortly after 2008, several Anglo parents organized to push for change at a low-performing elementary school, and on the coattails of that victory, a notoriously low-performing middle school. At the middle school in particular, these Anglo parents activated their resources to push for a strong school leader who could unify a diverse student body through rigorous academics paired with Spanish-language programs and a culturally sensitive arts and music education that reflects the culture and history of Latinx students. As one Anglo organizer marvels,

> We kind of had connections with one another, but we didn't know we had these same ideas. And we ended up together, and we ended up with this group of people that had some complementary skills, it was incredible. An urban planner, a couple of district employees who have an inside understanding of how things work, a PhD in math, a PR person, and myself. All of us getting together and bringing our skill sets to the table. We didn't have a formal name, but we had a vision and were willing to talk about that constructively, make some demands, but not make them in a way that would close the door to an opportunity.

Fueled by the successes of community mobilization at the elementary and middle school levels, an ever-growing network of gentrifying Anglo parents, along with some key Latinx allies, decided to take aim at the grand high school located in the neighborhood. Built over a century ago, Ridgeview High School is a hulking and ornate building with beautiful old windows, marble-floored hallways, and the aesthetic of an old capitol building or a city central library. And yet, like many large comprehensive neighborhood high schools in urban areas, the grandness of Ridgeview did not match its declining reputation, attendance, and test scores. By the new millennium and after several decades of White flight, Ridgeview was identified as the lowest-performing high school in the entire city district. Within a decade after that, the high school had gone through a landmark failed reform that received widespread media attention and was premised on the controversial firing of most of the teachers and staff.

Years after the reform, test scores and enrollment were even lower than they were before. Facing declining enrollment, the reform-oriented school district proposed to co-locate a charter high school within the walls of this traditional neighborhood school. This college-preparatory charter organization, which already operated middle and elementary schools geared toward Spanish-speaking immigrant families, applied to open its first high school. Many of the Anglo families who had worked so hard to push for improvements at the elementary and middle school level began organizing against this co-location. They argued that co-locating a charter school in a traditional neighborhood school would result in two bad outcomes. First, it would breed animosity between the two student bodies and their families, fomenting divisions in the neighborhood. Second, the co-location would also rob the traditional high school of its capacity to accept the coming wave of affluent families that were already committing to the public neighborhood middle and elementary schools, and would doom those families to choice out of the neighborhood for high school. In their view, co-location kills the promise of public education, and a traditional neighborhood school is a public asset and should be a public (not private) right for everyone. As one Anglo organizer remembered,

> It was a panic, because when we finally came to realize that this co-location was gonna be announced in May and voted on in June, we thought of it as a panic. The house is on fire. And fortunately, it was a different fire drill, but we had already been through fire drills with [middle school]. And we all have different strengths. So we mobilized.
>
> And then there was a bigger circle, all these alumni who had been shouting in the wind for twenty years to try to get the high school back to what it was. We finally show up and they're like, "Where the hell have you guys been?" [*Laughs.*] "We've been trying to get this school back on track for years." So we came together, alumni and parents.

As this Anglo organizer described, their voices were joined by some long-time Chicano activists in the neighborhood who had been organizing around educational justice at this high school long before the gentry began mobilizing. In the view of these Anglo organizers in particular, the rapidly gentrifying neighborhood was just on the precipice of making a new commitment to send their kids, their cultural, social, and financial capital, and all of their resources to what had been touted in the media and by the district as failing neighborhood schools. Co-location, in their minds, would prematurely kill this move toward equity in the neighborhood. Another White organizer detailed how the gentry's resources would be the key to achieving neighborhood equity for *all* children:

> We're gonna increase enrollment, we're gonna get proficient and above kids in the building and restore balance. We're not looking to just run a school that caters to "proficient" or above kids. We have a passion for helping kids that are below proficient. But just the reality of the world is, if that's all you have in your school, you can't move the numbers. Then you look like a failed school and you're no longer the principal and they put a charter in there. So we made it very clear, we want our fair share of every type of kid in the neighborhood, the kids in our own backyard.

These activists perceived co-location as an intentional siphoning of public resources into a private charter organization, as well as the district's refusal to recognize a growing neighborhood commitment to public education *for all*. On the one hand, this neighborhood movement, mostly led by gentrifying parents but also supported, to an extent, by a contingent of Latinx activists, argued that public schools *should* be community anchors. They should reflect the cherished diversity of the neighborhood, the very reason these families *chose* the urban core over the White, "community-less" suburbs. On the other hand, these members of the gentry argued that the district and the larger corporate reform movement were making an unwise move, since they were wasting the unprecedented opportunity—made possible by community mobilization—to attract "better students" and more "proficient students" to failing schools, a move that would surely benefit *all* students (new immigrant, second- and third-generation Latinx, and Anglo) in the neighborhood. It is this dual message of the gentry's movement for educational justice—the call for strong, diverse, quality neighborhood schools open to everyone in the neighborhood, and the subtext that there are more valuable community voices than others, more valuable enrollments than others, more valuable students than others—that contains the seeds for powerful multiracial community mobilization around public education, as well as the undoing of these same fragile cross-racial alliances and the demobilization of these educational justice movements.

If the School Is Diverse, Why Aren't We?

Back in the community theater, Janeyl sits on the stage with one child squirming on her lap and another older child leaning against her, looking out at the packed theater. Flanked by five other co-organizers of the meeting, she starts by explaining why she and the other men and women have called this community meeting around the reform at nearby McDonwell Elementary School, and why they have decided to address this issue through community organizing rather than through the school's PTA structure. Together they explain the timeline of events: the district removed a beloved principal who had been heading the majority-Latinx school for many years. She had lived in the neighborhood, and by all accounts had good relationships with the many families attending McDonwell. The district replaced her with a principal who had no experience as an educator and very little experience in educational administration. A rumor circulated that this new principal was a close neighbor of the superintendent, and was handpicked to radically turn around the school although she had little prior experience doing this. For several months, neither the parents nor the children knew who the principal was, as she did not go out of her way to introduce herself. Paul, an engineer standing next to Janeyl, said he knew something was wrong when his seven-year-old daughter pointed at the principal one day after school and asked, "Daddy, who is that lady?" By then, the principal had been at the school an entire semester, and Paul was alarmed that his child did not yet know who her principal was. Janeyl, a graduate student earning her PhD in the sciences, approached the new principal to volunteer part of her days in several classrooms and enrich the science curriculum with her own resources and expertise. Janeyl was rebuffed by the principal, who barely looked at her and dismissively muttered, "Maybe another time." Janeyl was shocked. The previous principal had enthusiastically welcomed her help in the classrooms.

Shortly thereafter, the school's test scores were publicly released (as they are annually, to assist parents with school choice decisions) and it was revealed that test scores were actually dropping. McDonwell was now one of the lowest-performing elementary schools in the city. The principal held a meeting with concerned parents and teachers to announce that the school would be adopting a new learning model for the following year. Instead of a dual-language Montessori model, which was the model promoted to prospective families who had already choiced in to the school, the principal abruptly announced that she would be switching to an expeditionary learning model. Instead of facilitating an open discussion at the forum, the principal only allowed parents to write questions on a piece of paper and hand them over to the assistant principal, who then handed them to the principal. Because she professed not to know much about the expeditionary learning model, she committed to hiring an outside consulting firm to guide the school through this transition. Even more controversial was her next decision to lay off almost three-quarters of the teachers. Many of these teachers had been at the school for years, and some were at this meeting today. The families came to know and respect these teachers, and were upset that their children's favorite teachers would not be returning to the school. For Rob, a financial analyst and parent, the firing of these teachers whom he understood to be beloved and effective underscored what he called the district's corporate and financial "agenda," and woke him up to the duplicity of neoliberal school reform:

> Well, every school is trimming the budget. This teacher of seventeen years, this is her career, $80,000. This teacher, seven days out of school, $32,000, and she'll only stick around for two years. I'm a math man. I know what the bottom line is. And I know how pensions work. Following the money at the expense of our children. Fixing the bottom line at the expense of our children. And it's like, wait a minute. You're cutting out the teachers and the people who—and you're telling the parents, "Sorry, go along with it"? It really boils my blood.

Although this meeting in the community theater is led and organized by parents themselves, some of the teachers in the audience speak up about their shock at being laid off, and express their suspicion that they were fired because they were vocally opposed to the rapid reforms at McDonwell. One parent says, "This isn't just McDonwell. This is going on everywhere. This is corporate reform and all they care about is privatizing the schools. That is what this is all about." There are audible murmurs of agreement and side conversations.

Another parent, James, interrupts the explosion of conversations:

> We have to push back. First, we have to demand that the district get rid of this principal. She's terrible! She's tearing this community apart. I mean, how do you have a challenged school with 80 percent poverty . . . how do you bring in a principal who's never even been an assistant principal or a classroom teacher and expect her to manage this entire school? This isn't a place where the kids who go here get extra help and they have parents with resources and things like that. This is a struggling, high-poverty school. I don't understand how you dump this corporate person over here who doesn't want anything to do with kids.

He then asks the folks attending to come to the next city school board meeting to voice their disappointment and outrage with the forced reform at McDonwell. Rob scans the mostly White audience and says, "We know that if the school board sees that most of the parents are *not* behind these reforms, they will listen to us. But right now, look at this room. I mean, the school is majority-Hispanic and this room is mostly White. Where are the Hispanics? We need to figure out how to get more Hispanics to these meetings." In the back of the room sit five older Latina women who have been listening to the meeting but have been silent. Rob cranes his neck and for the first time addresses them directly: "Can you all do some outreach to other parents you know? Can you get other parents to come to these meetings and to the school board meeting?" The room grows palpably tense as everyone turns to look at these women in the back of the room. Up until this point nobody has spoken directly about race in their critiques of corporate school reform. Rob identified the few brown faces in the room—women he did not seem to know—and had placed the burden on these women to diversify their efforts to save their neighborhood school.

Rudy, a lawyer who lives in the neighborhood with a long history of Chicano activism and a sharp critique of neoliberal education reform, reflects upon these White activists in our interview. One of the handful of outspoken Latinx allies to this Anglo-led neighborhood movement, Rudy defends these activists by drawing a sharp line between their presence in the neighborhood and more pernicious forms of gentrification:

> A lot of them are coming in not because they want to gentrify. That's the result of them and other peers who are coming in at the same time. They're not trying intentionally to gentrify. They're coming to the common denominator—they want to live in a diverse community with other ethnicities, with other cultures. They made a conscious choice to come that way, not to make the community reflect them. They came to *join* it. You could group them with the newer Anglo parents who come in. There are a few who have come in and want to make the neighborhood look like them, like where they grew up in another place that wasn't very diverse. Push people out they don't like. But they're not organized.
>
> That's what's beautiful about this part of the city. There might be some subtle and a little bit of overt bigotry, but they're always put in check. They just can't keep doing it. Their peers will call them on their privilege, on their bigotry, so it rears its head and everybody jumps on top of the monster and it goes away.

Rudy's perception points to the delicate balance in this neighborhood between the more organized, forward-thinking, and racially conscious Anglo residents and the overt bigotry of their less forward-thinking gentrifying peers. This echoes education scholars Maia Cucchiara and Erin Horvat's insights into the distinction between middle-class residents who are motivated by individualist orientations toward neighborhood school reform and middle-class residents motivated by an ethic of diversity and collectivism. In their view, the value of White middle-class involvement in improving neighborhood schooling outcomes for everyone is mediated by these two different orientations, which can either further escalate school inequality or work to ameliorate it.[7]

This balance, however, is precarious. As Cucchiara and Horvat note, motivations for middle-class involvement in neighborhood school revitalization can be mixed, and can therefore produce mixed outcomes. In their study on Boston White residents' motivations for choosing their neighborhood schools, for example, sociologists Shelley Kimelberg and

Chase Billingham argue that White parents who desire a diverse educational environment tend to cluster in a select few urban schools, which ultimately *increases* racial educational segregation.[8] In fact, Billingham's study of the ways Boston school assignment policies work to collude with gentrifiers' preference for neighborhood schools demonstrates how curtailing school choice can actually promote an "exclusionary social closure" that exacerbates racial and class educational inequalities.[9]

Even the more collectivist-oriented White parents, such as the ones featured in this chapter who are able to find solidarity with some Latinx activists in the neighborhood, still exhibit a persistent racial and class privilege that often goes unrecognized and unchallenged, and guides their struggles to protect comprehensive neighborhood schools. I argue that these two factions of newer White settlers, and these two orientations (individualist and collectivist), are not as distinct as they might seem. Even collectivist orientations to school reform may not be enough for White newcomers to produce the kinds of multiracial alliances in a neighborhood that would sustain high-quality, diverse schools over time. As education policy scholar Linn Posey-Maddox reveals in her examination of middle-class commitments to diverse urban public schools, the consequences of a school reform policy that relies on middle-class involvement in the public school system are far-reaching: they can produce new patterns of educational exclusion and inequality, *despite* these parents' commitment to diversity and their good intentions to work for the collective.[10] Middle-class mechanisms for school fundraising, for example, enable middle-class parents to have greater control over school decision making and budgetary decisions, and can further exclude working-class and poor student interests. When cities rely on middle-class engagement as a mechanism for filling gaps in eviscerated educational budgets, the onus shifts from governments to middle-class families—who have their own class interests—to ensure equitable education for all children.

Two of the Latina women sitting in back of the room nod their heads at Rob's request. Before they can say anything, Janeyl says, "We need to offer food at these meetings. That's one way to bring in more people. We also need more people who can speak Spanish so that whatever outreach we do, we can translate it to Spanish." Although everyone agrees that these could widen the net and bring in a broader coalition of people affected by these reforms, the parent organizing meetings against the McDonwell reforms that take place over the next four months are plagued by a notable absence of Latinx voices, and a constant vexation among Anglo organizers over the lack of racial diversity in their push against reform. These parents know that if they rally against corporate reform without the support of the overwhelming Latinx majority in the school, their push against reform will fail. Because of its co-optation of multiracial and civil rights language, the reform-oriented district will claim that its own corporate reforms are on the side of racial justice, and done for the good of the very children that have been the most maligned by public school failure: low-income kids of color (see chapters 1 and 2). Meanwhile, these parents will be portrayed by reform advocates as White neighborhood obstructionists who are standing in the way of educational opportunity for less advantaged students. They will be portrayed as elitists trying to take over public schooling for their own affluent children. With a commitment to racial diversity and traditional, comprehensive neighborhood schools, and with a strong critique of corporate educational privatization, it would seem that these Anglo voices could coalesce with the Black and Latinx community activists described in chapter 3 in a larger fight against neoliberal reform, and could join more effectively with dissenting Latinx voices in their own neighborhood. Yet these parents hardly know about the battles being waged by African American and Latinx low-income residents in the heart of the gentrifying community across the river, nor do they succeed in bridging the gulf between themselves and the Latinx parents they see every day dropping their kids off at their shared neighborhood school. Why? What explains both the potential for these cross-racial coalitions and the limited success of such coalitions? And what does this portend for neighborhood movements such as these to counter neoliberal reforms in gentrifying areas?

White Activists' Rejection of School Choice

Like the Black and Latinx parents in chapter 3, the White parents active in these movements to counter neoliberal reforms at their neighborhood schools express a strong preference for quality schools they can walk to over the prospect of more choices. They also express nostalgia for their own experiences of schooling before this reform movement hit their city. In these recollections, the neighborhood school of their youth was more than just a place of quality education. It was also the community anchor. Kevin, a strong neighborhood schools advocate and software developer, grew up in a relatively diverse California town, and remembered his own experience with public schooling growing up:

> Our little city had three schools. There was no choice. You had to make the high school you had work. *Everyone* had to make it work. There were a couple of private schools in town, but by and large at our one big high school, people made it work.

Kevin expresses nostalgia for a community that shared a commitment to make public schools work for everyone. In Kevin's view, the absence of school choice exerted a healthy pressure on the community to come together and bridge their differences. Whatever the particular educational needs of each family, every family made an effort to "make it work." For Kevin, school choice enables families to take the easy way out, and to no longer make this effort. It dissolves what could have been a shared commitment to making public institutions work, and dissolves the nascent bridges between diverse communities.

Another neighborhood schools advocate, Lacey, draws on her own suburban, segregated public school experience as a guidepost for what she wanted to *avoid* for her own family:

> I moved here because I wanted diversity. I feel like the suburbs, not all of them—I'm totally generalizing here—but we don't live there because we want variation in our life. I also feel like—I went to one of those schools that had the token Black person and the token—I don't think we had any Hispanics. We had a lot of Asians. I went to the school where your parents were either doctors, university professors, accountants, or lawyers. It was boring.

Lacey wants to live in a more diverse area and have her children attend a more diverse school so that they won't be "bored" with exposure to only upper-middle-class White people. Although Lacey wants the same quality schooling for her kids that she received, she rejects the vanilla segregation that came with it.[11] Importantly, Lacey does not view her decision to send her kids to her failing neighborhood school as a consumer choice she distinctly made for her kids; she views this choice as stemming from her own desire to settle her family in a diverse neighborhood. When I framed the question as "Why did you decide to send your kids to McDonwell?," she answered with her rationale about why she *herself* moved to the neighborhood, instead of framing schooling as a consumption choice for her own kids.

In these White activists' narratives, protecting neighborhood schools is part and parcel of the larger project of protecting neighborhood diversity. It is fundamentally about fighting for diverse community cohesion, a kind of utopia that feels so precarious in a rapidly gentrifying neighborhood. Notably, many of these activists' zest for neighborhood schools is also premised on nostalgia for a comprehensive neighborhood public school model that was largely racially segregated and dominated by White neighborhood residents. Thus, there is a tension that runs throughout their narratives. This tension between longing for a simple past when nobody had a choice and "everyone made it work" on one hand, and their rejection of that same past, which deprived many of these activists from early exposure to more diverse communities and perspectives on the other, drives their activism for strong neighborhood schools in the new gentrified urban neighborhood context. As Cucchiara and Horvat note, school choice is a cultural and social process; it is not simply a direct cost-benefit analysis based on raw test scores and ratings.[12] Like the parents in their study, the White middle-class parents that choose to commit to McDonwell make their choices in part based on their identities as liberal urbanites. Leila, a White architect and former Peace Corps volunteer, emphasizes her reasons for joining the community struggle to improve the failing middle school in the neighborhood and to fight against district-led reforms:

> My concern is not just about my own children, it's about the larger population and what opportunities are we creating or taking away by giving a select few access to a program that is really stellar. That is segregation, choice segregation. We're all living together, why aren't we all going to school together?

Here, Leila explains why she rejected the individualized model of school choice that promised White families like her own "little islands of excellence," and instead put her energies into mobilizing her parent networks to fight for a de-tracked, comprehensive middle school that catered to both Anglo parents' desire for diversity and worldliness, and Latinx parents' desire to see themselves reflected in a diverse curriculum.

Fundamentally, the narratives of these Anglo activists, though sometimes premised on a nostalgia for their mostly racially segregated public school past, reveal a marked desire and respect for diversity, as well as a turn toward a collectivist orientation to schooling. In their rejection of school choice, these parents privilege community cohesion over an individualized search for the best educational product available on the market. As Pamela, another White neighborhood schools advocate, puts it, "It was not so much what the school could do for my child, but what we can get involved in to make it a better place for not only my child but the entire community. I feel like maybe it's like my community volunteerism, to make the community better." Kevin boils down his philosophy about public schooling to this:

> What's important to me personally is, the way I think about it, when I go into [middle school] or [high school], I shouldn't see any different mix of people than when I go into Safeway or Auto Zone. I should see the same mix of however you want to measure people.

Rather than perceiving the reform movement as giving an advantage to their families, these neighborhood activists perceive the corporate reform movement as posing a huge threat to the community cohesion they have worked so hard to build. Carl, a financial advisor and a major organizer of the movement to save McDonwell Elementary from reform, cannot hide his anger at the school district. He now views the district as a tool of the reform movement. Carl remarks on the rift, or what he terms the "scorched earth," created by the district between the parents at McDonwell who were alarmed by the school's failing scores and wanted to give district reform a chance, and the parents who felt alienated by the reforms:

Oh, my gosh, people used to smile at me, and I know this one couple used to have dinner with this other couple, and now I see they're like, really cold with each other. And that's what the district system, marching through neighborhoods, leaving that scorched earth, is doing. And I don't think they care. If the schoolhouse is the heart of the community and your process to improve the schoolhouse is dividing the community, what good are you doing? If we end up with the best school in the city in a community divided, will that best school stand? I don't think so.

These narratives of White neighborhood activists suggest a radical move toward surrendering some White middle-class educational privilege in the name of authentic community cohesion. Their ethic of diversity and their rejection of school choice create the potential for cross-racial alliances in neighborhood movements against neoliberal reform. This potential is sometimes realized, especially at the high school and middle school levels. Even though their movement networks are majority White, these activists do succeed in forging alliances with some key Latinx critics of neoliberal school reform in the neighborhood.

Ironically, however, it is the cultural capital and unexamined privilege drawn from their racial and class status that undergird these White activists' refusal of school choice and their rejection of the neoliberal search for the best educational product for their own children. In choosing a collectivist orientation to neighborhood schooling, these activists must first rationalize the risk they know they are taking in choosing to pursue community cohesion over the "little islands of excellence" for their children. In their rationale, these activists often rely on their privilege and class mobility to fill in the gaps.

It is this same unexamined privilege that convinces these activists that their vision of a strong neighborhood school will benefit *everyone*, even if they don't achieve greater racial diversity in their movement. In the case of the McDonwell school mobilization, the lack of diverse voices in their movement continually baffled and concerned them, yet their conviction that they were doing right by the communities of color that shared their neighborhood schools prevented them from pursuing authentic and deep community alliances with these very same families. Interviews with Latinx critics of neoliberal reform in the neighborhood who choose *not* to align with these Anglo-led movements, or who decide to align with these movements but then find themselves marginalized and tokenized by Anglo organizers, reveal that at times the White middle-class bias of this activist movement is too much to overcome. Just as this bias is evidenced in rationales of White middle-class parents who exercise school choice to maximize their own children's advantage, it is also evidenced in these White activists' rationales for choosing community cohesion over educational excellence.

Community Cohesion over Educational Excellence: Banking on Cultural Capital

In a surprisingly humble admission, Josie, an Anglo mother of an eighth-grader and a sixth-grader and one of the major organizers of the community-led effort to revitalize both the middle and high schools in the neighborhood against the tide of corporate reform, rationalizes her surrender of school choice: "Let's face it," she says, "not all of our kids are geniuses. Not all of them are the next Bill Gates or Jimi Hendrix. Not all of them belong in an exceptional school. But they *will* be okay." At first glance, her view exemplifies a humility that opens a door for educational equity, a realization that one's child is no more special than other children, and doesn't necessarily deserve a distinguished education. It is the remarkable relinquishing of the very class and race privilege that has long characterized educational inequities in the United States. However, it is the last piece of her statement that undermines this humility and the sharing of power that comes with it: "they *will* be okay." These members of the creative class, buttressed by their own experiences of creative success, innovation, and economic payoff, see schools as community anchors rather than institutions that can directly ensure social and economic mobility. They believe that whatever the school lacks in rigor, they can make up for with their own dominant cultural capital, social capital, and family values.[13] It is precisely because these families have more resources at their disposal that they feel they can take the risk to refuse educational advantage.

Janeyl tells me about how the reforms at McDonwell Elementary, much like the reforms in the historically Black community across the river, have been implemented with little community input and are geared toward pulling up test scores by disciplining low-income students of color and their families (see chapter 3). She recounts a moment when she found herself, a White mother, on the receiving end of this discipline after the reform:

> [After the reform] my kid could not handle his class and his new teacher. So he started having problems. The first two weeks of school, my boys had to miss a couple of days. They were stressed. We had a Friday off, and the school attendance lady comes to my house, unannounced, no phone call from the school, nothing. We had school off that Friday. I was in the backyard taking care of my garden and saw this lady pounding on the door, so I walked up there, and she introduces herself as the social worker and tells me that my kids have missed too many days. The lady says, "At this school, we are striving towards educating our kids towards being college-bound. You need to send your kids to school."
>
> And I told her one of those days he was struggling, my five-year-old, it was a new situation, we were having a hard time getting him down there, and she said, "Next time you need to force him." I said, "Whoa there, cowgirl! You're on my doorstep, and I appreciate you coming to my house and caring about whether my kids come to school. That's wonderful. I hope that's your intention. But I feel like you're telling me how to parent, and believe me, I know how to get my kids to school. We're *good* learners."

In Janeyl's recounting of the school's efforts to discipline both her children and herself as a parent, Janeyl expresses her outrage that she has been singled out, erroneously, as a parent who doesn't foster good learning. In Janeyl's mind, the reformed school bureaucracy had misidentified her. Just because she allows her children to miss school here and there does not mean that they are not educated, nor does it mean that they are not learning and are therefore not college-bound. For Janeyl and many of these other parents, "learning" happens in multiple places, and educational advantage is ensured in the home as much as it is ensured through formal schooling.

Even as these parents fight for their comprehensive neighborhood school, they do so while recognizing that sometimes their children's integrated classrooms do not move at the pace that they believe fits their own more advanced children. Nance, a mother of a preschooler, recounts the reports from her child's teacher:

She would always say—and this is totally me, the bragging parent here—but she would be like, "Your daughter's so far ahead of the other kids." She'd been at a daycare that had done a preschool the year before, so she knew her alphabet and her numbers. She was pretty much ready to start learning how to read when she got to preschool. But the teachers were like, "Okay. This is an A." The teacher kept saying, "I'm afraid she's gonna get bored. We're gonna try and maybe put her in a kindergarten because she might get bored." But then she never did any of that. And then it turned into this "your daughter doesn't sit still for twenty minutes during carpet time." And I'm like, "Well, maybe she's bored!"

Instead of interpreting this as a reason to choice out of McDonwell, though, Nance rationalized her mild frustration with the pace of her child's class in this way: "I'm one of those, like, 'This is how school is. You have to learn how to adapt to whatever situation. In life, you don't always get to pick who your boss is, your coworkers are.' Does all the learning take place in the classroom? I think it is more *social* learning that takes place in the classroom, more than anything else." In Nance's mind, even though she perceived the academic rigor to be lacking, the school still offers valuable socialization for her child and even "life lessons" in adaptability that can benefit her child in her adult life. Nance also knows that she can fill in the gaps academically at home.

Of course, it is much easier for parents to downplay academic rigor in a preschool or kindergarten setting, where the emphasis is indeed more on learning social skills and emotional self-control. However, the White parents leading movements for quality, comprehensive neighborhood middle and high schools also bank on their own dominant cultural capital and familial resources to buffer against any risks they would incur by sending their children to low-performing schools. Rather than chasing an advanced academic track for his kids, Kevin admits that his kids are not particularly advanced, and has made peace with this: "By any test measure, they're not [gifted]. And that's fine. Honestly, in a way I'm happy they're not. I see the other end of gifted and talented people in the workplace, and workplaces are not meritocracies. They're not run by the smartest people. There's a lot of skills that go into being successful. Smart is just some of it." For parents of the creative class who enjoy a measure of economic success, especially the kind born from more autonomous and creative knowledge-work, there is not a one-to-one relationship between academic success and economic success.

Rose joined the successful community movement to commit the gentry's bodies and resources to the failing neighborhood middle school, and is candid in sharing her memory of how she calculated the risk involved with sending her kids to a low-performing school. In Rose's rationalization, she mitigated risk by challenging the district's designation of this middle school as "failing." It was important for Rose to realize that not *all* students in the school were failing. When I ask her how she made the decision to commit to her neighborhood middle school even though her children's peers were choicing out of the neighborhood and going elsewhere, she admits,

> I knew that the test scores were low, but I also felt that my kids were smart enough, or that we weren't gonna get left behind. We saw data about the breakdown of performance. It broke it down by demographics by each category, including children with disabilities. It broke it down by income, by race. I was going across the sheet of paper and looking at our income bracket and our race, and saw that those kids were *not* failing at this school. So I also knew, whatever happened, that my kid would survive it.

Even though Rose was committed to the shared vision of establishing a diverse school for everyone, her more private admission evinces a reliance on privilege that runs counter to her expressed commitment to living in a diverse community and engaging in a de-tracked, diverse neighborhood school. Rose cannot articulate why exactly she believed that her kids would *not* get left behind. Simultaneously recognizing and obscuring her racial and class privilege, Rose muses that it was perhaps because her kids were "smart enough" that they could weather a low-performing school, yet vaguely understood that this smartness had something to do with race and class (and ability). Rather than challenging these clear racial, class, and ability inequities in student success and failure at this school, Rose admitted to using this information instead as reassurance that her children's educational advantage would be protected, serving to mitigate her risk of committing to this neighborhood school. Although she recognized and banked on her privilege, she also believed that her privilege was a resource that could serve the needs of all community residents. If more resourced people like herself would commit to the neighborhood school, *everyone's* success would be assured through the influx of "more proficient" students, higher test scores, and "smarts."

Although many of these neighborhood activists are fighting to re-make their schools into quality public institutions that embody the di-versity that drew them to the neighborhood in the first place, they know they can still count on their mobility if they fail in their efforts to take back their schools from neoliberal reform. Lacey explains to me how she mitigated the risk of choicing in to her neighborhood school by relying on her resources, as a last resort, to choice *out*: "And I was definitely like, 'Let's try preschool here, and if that is horrible after a year, then we choice into kindergarten. If that sucks, we may possibly be guaranteed a spot for first grade somewhere else.'" Lacey, in fact, was wrong. She would not have been guaranteed a spot for first grade somewhere else. According to this city's choice system, she was only guaranteed a spot at her neighborhood school, McDonwell. This guarantee system effectively maintains residential privilege and protects educational advantage even in a choice system, insofar as wealthier people still have first access to more resource-intensive schools, and the relationship between property values and educational quality is still assured. Although Lacey herself did not fully understand how the choice system worked, she still fell back on her ability to choice in to a better school, as well as her belief that she would be guaranteed a better education elsewhere if her neigh-borhood school failed her. This perspective reflects an unspoken confi-dence in the choice system that low-income Black parents in chapter 3 do *not* express. For many of these Black residents, the district and the schools were choosing *them* (or more to the point, *rejecting* them as they tried to exercise their consumer mobility in search of better schools). In Lacey's case, this perspective also betrays an underlying ethic of supe-riority, since she assumed that the district would rescue her from edu-cational failure (but presumably would not rescue "others" who live in her neighborhood from that same fate). Indeed, the same resource used to mitigate the gentry's risk of committing to neighborhood schools—the threat of flight and the exercise of mobility—was the very resource that escalated movement demobilization around the neoliberal reforms at McDonwell Elementary. Just one year after the community initiated its organizing, most of the parents who led the fight against corporate reform at this school opted to end their fight and leave the school when they realized that they weren't gaining traction. Despite their organizing efforts, the district still refused to replace the contentious new principal or rehire the beloved teachers who were laid off. More importantly, their demobilization, predicated on their ability to abandon McDonwell and fall back on their individual range of choices, killed their collective motivation for more aggressively pursuing the cross-racial coalitions that would have lent strength to their movement. This more formidable challenge to neoliberal reform, buttressed by more and different community voices, would have also helped to forge the diverse community connections and trust that they so desired in their everyday lives in this neighborhood, but that continually eluded them.

Fragile Coalitions and Movement Demobilization

As their movement dwindled, the parents who had been so committed a year earlier to reclaiming their neighborhood school from corporate reform began, one by one, to reluctantly make their exit plans. Rather than being excited about their new schooling prospects, these parents overwhelmingly saw their exercise of school choice as a defeat. I ask these neighborhood advocates about their plans, and whether they are worried that they will not be able to choice out of McDonwell. With the same hazy understanding of school choice that characterized Lacey's decision making to choice *in to* McDonwell, Janeyl responds,

> I think the other parents are more worried for me than I am, 'cause I tend not to worry. Or maybe, I worry on the inside. I have a friend at another school, he helped to cofound it, so we're on the [wait] list there. And I'm not sure how much he can help me, I don't think much, but we have a chance. I don't even know where we are on the wait list for our other choices. My plan is at the end of the day . . . if we're not in a school, I'm just gonna go on hands and knees and beg outside until I find a school! Worst-case scenario, I'll bring them home. I'll do something. I can help them cover some of it. It's not my preference, and I have a strong feeling that the social situation at school is really important. But my kid doesn't want to be there anymore.

Like Janeyl, James also withdraws his child from McDonwell and decides to home school until he can figure out what his next steps will be. As he discusses his plan, it becomes clear that his ability to home school, even as a temporary plan, can only be possible with the financial and temporal resources available to his family:

> We're in a unique situation. I don't come into my office from 9:00 to 5:00. I sometimes go out into my backyard and sit in my sanctuary and watch the sunrise and get some things done and then go hang out with the kids. So we have that flexibility and we could do a lot of home schooling where things are falling short, but we're blessed in that. Not everyone is.

The experience with reform at McDonwell, for many, drives parents away from the city's school district entirely. Even though they sought this neighborhood for its promise of more diverse city living, Paul's family decides shortly after the failed McDonwell battle that if they move to the suburbs, they might not be subjected to the whims of experimental corporate reform. As Paul puts it,

> I don't trust this city. I don't like all this up and down. You never know when your school will get blown up and redesigned. What if next year your school moves to red [failing] and then the district wants to come in [and] basically trash all your teachers? 'Cause that could certainly happen. This city wants to redesign, they want to keep going through this for some reason.

Carl, another parent who finally opts to move out of the neighborhood in the wake of his failed activism and relocate to a nearby suburb, said that the biggest lesson he learned from this battle is that the city's school system is completely corrupted at its core by a corporate power that profits from crisis:

> We privatized prisons, and what's happening? We've got a lot of damn prisoners. We privatize mental facilities. Oh, my goodness! It's ridiculous! There's lawyers and insurance companies and then when there's bankruptcy, that's exactly what they do. So when we privatize school, there will

be problems for the consumer. I don't want Wal-Mart educating my kids, but guess who's one of the largest business donors to this school system?

Even as these White neighborhood activists express concern about their inability to draw more Latinx families to their movement, they are unable to build the kind of broad-based multiracial coalition that they know would hold greater potential to convince the district that the very families that the reformers are trying to save (the low-income children of color) are instead siding with the newer neighborhood residents around a unified call for diverse, comprehensive neighborhood schools. Instead of working to actively build these bridges, these White activists default to their individual mobility to choice out of the neighborhood, city, or school system entirely when they recognize that their outrage is not gaining any traction with the reform-oriented district. And because they believe so strongly that their racial, class, social, and cultural capital are undeniable assets that can better *everyone's* lot, the absence of Latinx activists (and in the case of the high school battle, the exodus of Latinx activists from their movement networks) puzzles them.

When I ask Annie about why there are not more Latinx parents drawn into the battle at McDonwell Elementary, she responds with some guesses:

> The things that I've heard are—but I hear them from other White people, so I don't know if it's the truth—is that Hispanics don't feel welcome, Hispanics have a different perception of school. They see it as a building that they drop their kids off at, it's an institution that they don't get involved in, what happens there happens there and they don't feel like they have a say. And there's always, "They work two jobs, so they can't come to meetings." Which I also think is just generally things that are just assumed and not necessarily real. Or they don't understand what's going on because they don't speak English. So I don't know. I would love to know more.

Just a few others recognize that perhaps the low representation of Latinx neighbors has something to do with experiences of racism and mistreatment, and therefore a reluctance to engage in oppositional activism. As Rob muses,

I don't understand all of the moving parts, but I do get the feeling that there is the fear of an authority. Latinos traditionally as a population tend to have more fear of banks and financial institutions and government entities and law enforcement and things like that because they haven't been treated right by those things.

Although these activists are perceptive enough to recognize that systemic racism might engender some reluctance for Latinx people to step out and organize around social justice issues, this explanation does not square with the long history of Latinx activism that characterizes this neighborhood and city. Even more problematically, this explanation does not include a recognition that they, as White affluent settlers, might be contributing to this systemic oppression. When these Anglo activists reflect upon gentrification in their neighborhood, they often portray it as an inevitable phenomenon, something they simply witness going on around them but that they themselves do not participate in.

Carl shakes his head, thinking about the Latinx families at McDonwell under the new disastrous reform: "I think they're probably gonna roll with it and see how it goes. For some of 'em, it's just that their kids can walk to school. That's what makes it so sad. Some people don't have choices." Although Carl recognized the sadness that some people don't have choices, he is unable or unwilling to recognize the socioeconomic and racial dimensions of what marks this inequality, nor does this insight prompt him to think about his own advantages in relation to these disadvantages.

James offers a mixed view of gentrification in this neighborhood, removing himself as an agent of gentrification and instead framing it as an inevitable wave of change:

I don't know, it's—this is a Hispanic neighborhood. The roots of this neighborhood are Hispanic. Every neighborhood has its own demographics. I'm sure the neighborhood's getting gentrified and they're building these frat houses around here, condos, whatever you want to call them, the blocky things. It's an evolving neighborhood. Change happens. But unplanned change sometimes ends up good.

When James offers his incisive and powerful critique of corporate school reform, I ask him what role, if any, racism plays in the reforms taking place at McDonwell. He answers,

> I don't want to throw the "racist" thing out there. It feels like, to me, I think the Hispanic population is going to pay more dearly than the more affluent yuppies here. You know, the thirty-somethings who are moving in, buying the $600,000 properties aren't gonna know what happened at McDonwell.
>
> But this is just one more way to wipe off the culture of a cool neighborhood. If you get rid of a whole bunch of teachers, you're not just wiping off culture, you're hurting the pulse of the neighborhood. We might have gotten rid of them down the road, but let us be involved. It's *our* school, not yours.

James's quote captures a curious valuation of "diversity" and a simultaneous refusal to recognize systemic racism in gentrification processes. James knows on some level that the Latinx families will be more adversely impacted by the poor leadership and district reforms at McDonwell. Even though he previously defended gentrification to an extent, he also laments the ways the school district's reforms are "wiping off the culture of a cool neighborhood." In his mind, the fact that this is a Latinx neighborhood is what makes the neighborhood "cool" and "cultural." It is the Latinx presence that constitutes the very pulse of the neighborhood. And yet James claims this neighborhood as "ours" even though he is an Anglo newcomer. He sees himself as protecting diversity, much as he sees his own organizing around McDonwell as protecting the interests of the Latinx community members curiously absent from the movement.

Neighborhood schools activist Kevin reiterates the perception that these White-led neighborhood schools movements *protect* diversity, half joking that he wants to be the "Anglo who's trying to sell people on Latino":

> We love the history of it. We're very comfortable with the Latino majority. We feel it's safe. We weren't feeling like we were moving into—our friends, who had moved in in the '90s, a little different. [*Laughs.*] . . . We skated in

behind them, and we paid for it as well. Which I always find funny about the gentrification argument, that somehow we're less deserving. I paid four times as much for my house as someone that might complain about me! I want to be the Anglo who's trying to sell people on Latino.

Here, Kevin distances himself from charges that he is just trying to reclaim neighborhood schools for the more affluent White gentry. He feels that this charge is unfair because he truly values the Latinx majority in the neighborhood, and even though he is not of this majority, he deserves some right to and ownership over these neighborhood institutions because he paid his way into the neighborhood.

This simultaneous show of respect for the Latinx roots of the neighborhood and the insistence that White middle-class resources should entitle one to equal ownership over neighborhood institutions (and furthermore that these resources will unquestionably ameliorate inequality) obscures their key role in settler colonialism,[14] and prevents these White activists from recognizing that perhaps their resources and their presence in the neighborhood are connected to larger systems of class and racial inequality. These systems play out in Latinx activists' experiences of this city and within these neighborhood educational justice movements.

The Fight for Neighborhood Schools: Critical Latinx Voices

The question of why more Latinx residents steer clear of these neighborhood movements is a crucial one. This neighborhood has a notable history of Chicana/o and immigrant rights activism, and many of these Chicana/os remain active around a variety of social justice issues. Certainly, many of these activists share their Anglo neighbors' critique of school choice and corporatized education reform. Situating his critique of neoliberal school reform in a larger critique of capitalism, Roberto, a longtime Chicano activist, expresses his disappointment with the proposed co-location at the high school:

I think what's happened is, high-level people have balanced the budget. And in capitalism, economic efficiency is a value that's a sacred cow, so they come out as heroes because they balanced the budget. But how did they do it? They invite charters schools to come into a space that's not occupied, they give them the money to take them back, and they go, "Look, we balanced the budget. We're spending these monies prudently and wisely, and the public says thank you." [*Applauds.*] But there's never any real reform, or certainly education revolution. It's back to the same old model.

Another Chicana educational justice activist in the neighborhood, Juanita, characterized neoliberal school reform this way:

Look at where we've come to. The more liberal education model, it's not there. Humanities, reading, writing. Reading and writing, but humanities is gone, literature is gone. It's math and science. That is such bullshit. That doesn't make the whole person. And then the way we teach it is in silos. That's not how you learn math and science. That's why people don't do well. Math and science are learned being integrated in the humanities. Only the elite get that kind of education. The masses, we get the factory model of education, one size fits all.

If these activists share a critical view of corporate school reform, why are they not mobilizing in greater numbers with their Anglo counterparts? Roberto chose to attend some initial meetings about the high school, as he was also concerned about the district's proposal to co-locate another school in the building. He explains why many immigrant parents refused to participate, and links their absence to their undocumented status and increasing fear of criminalization and deportation:

I do not believe that immigrant parents wanted to participate. They live in constant fear. During the time that we worked the coalition, a family was deported, and people came to me and said, "What are we gonna do? *Qué vamos a hacer?* Our people don't want to go to these meetings. How can we go to these meetings and feel safe when they just deported a family?" There was a fear that I don't think people could relate to, even myself, at that level. So how do you integrate this voice if you can't get the information and there's a level of fear?

In the conversations among White settlers about how to draw more Latinx people to movements for neighborhood elementary, middle, and high schools, I never overhear anyone mention the importance of building bridges between educational justice and immigrant rights issues in order to form successful coalitions with Latinx neighbors. If these activists had shown a concern about deportation and immigrants' access to educational equity, as well as police harassment and a host of other immigrant rights issues, there might have been a broader basis for trust across racial, class, and ethnic lines and a lasting bedrock upon which to build an alliance.

Beyond bringing immigrant rights issues to White neighborhood activists' attention, Latinx educational justice activists in the neighborhood challenge White assumptions that what is good for the gentry is good for everyone. For example, in the fight for the neighborhood high school, activists decided to survey community members about their vision for the neighborhood school in order to better craft their demands to the district. One activist, Javier, remembers,

> There wasn't a lot of attention given to the linguistically different in this neighborhood coalition. If I hadn't brought it up that the data they were doing was not a representative sample, they would never have taken the time to get the information they got. It would have been a skewed sample and ineffective data. There's no question methodologically in my mind that that would have happened. That's when I went to one of the organizers and I said, "You have a skewed sample, you know that, don't you?" She said, "What do you mean?" "You have no Spanish-speaking people. You can't generalize that to everybody. We're culturally and linguistically different."

By the time Javier brought this to some of the White organizers' attention, many other Latinx activists who initially shared a concern about corporate school reform had stopped coming to the meetings. The issue of language proved to be a divisive issue in the community process to envision their neighborhood school, and this precipitated an exodus of Latinx activists from the nascent coalition. Although both Latinx and Anglo activists supported the vision of a school offering multiple languages, they did so for very different reasons. Anglos wanted their kids to be "worldly," but Chicanos envisioned bilingual education in particular as a strong stance against the kind of "subtractive schooling" that public schooling often represents.[15] Alicia, a Chicana activist, under-scores this distinction:

> For liberatory education, that to me means I take you, you're enrolled here. I honor who you are, what your history is, what your culture is. I honor it so much that my teachers are going to learn about it, they're gonna ask your parents and relatives to come in and teach others about it, and we're gonna honor things that are important and special to you. Certainly the Anglo power structure wants their children to speak other languages. They're not stupid. They know that that's an asset, and they want their children to learn Chinese and French and all that. So do we. But why take away our language now? Why don't you just add the English?

Below the surface of a shared vision for a linguistically diverse school, some Latinx activists realized that the motivations for this shared goal were too vastly different to overcome. One Latino organizer who decided to exit the coalition reflected upon his experience:

> I enjoyed being part of the coalition. I've met some awesome people, some dedicated people. They're fighters. But for me, there's assumptions that what's good for one is gonna be applicable to everybody, and that's not the case.

Many of the activists who left disillusioned asked Javier, who decided to stick with the coalition, "What keeps you here?" Javier responded, "I'll tell you about me. You call me to a fight, I'm gonna stay till it's over. I will not leave. That's just the kind of leader I am. And I want people to know this is a multicultural fight. We've got to give the impression that we've got all these people of all colors."

Juanita, one of the Chicana activists who returned to some of the high school organizing meetings, defends her continued participation in these networks as a chance for her to maintain active relationships with others in the neighborhood, while also holding other activists accountable and making sure that nobody speaks on her behalf:

> I think it's important for people to be very engaged in the whole educational environment in their neighborhoods. I want to have an under-

standing of what's going on and create a relationship. I don't have to, but I want to. So it's about maintaining active relationships and interaction. That's very critical. Or the reform will take the direction and path of those most involved. That's where it'll go. And they'll say they speak for everybody, even if it isn't for you. That's where you get the conflict. That's when you get people saying, "Wait, we haven't been paying attention. Now this is happening. Oh, hell, no! You don't speak for me!"

Like Juanita, Roberto grew to respect some of the White organizers in the effort to save the high school from co-location. But he also experienced tokenization in the movement:

I think we've held hands in solidarity, and in the end, we may think differently, but I think we all put our hearts into it. But I even admitted to them: "I'm tired of feeling like window dressing here." Because the truth is that when they needed representation, I was there, and I felt selected for that. Will I look back and say that was my role in all of this?

In reflecting upon his experience in this community coalition, Javier drew an important distinction between "diversity" and "competency," a distinction that helps to explain the divergent values of the Anglo and Latinx activists who tried—but could not successfully bridge—their parallel educational justice movements for access to neighborhood schools:

We shouldn't confuse diversity with competency. Diversity implies numbers. Competency implies behavioral change and attitudinal change and skill development, where you're able to put culture into context and work with people from a different group. That to me is cultural competency. Diversity is, we look diverse, but is there equal education? And there isn't.

In the end, the Anglos' collectivist ethic of diversity that initially drew some Chicana/o activists to the fight against corporate school reform and into the struggle to save neighborhood schools did not translate into the cultural competency that would have forged a more sustainable multiracial coalition. Some Latinx activists came to distrust the Anglo neighborhood activists almost as much as they distrusted the school district, which had failed them much longer than it had failed the Anglo families. This school district had long assured the success of White, affluent city dwellers over and above their own children, and these activists had actively challenged the district in previous eras of educational injustice. As Cucchiara notes, neoliberal reform policy in the urban core is increasingly geared toward drawing in more affluent families back to the city's school system, on the presumption that their social, cultural, and economic capital will ensure school reform success.[16] In many ways, these collectivist, diversity-seeking White neighborhood activists who rally for comprehensive neighborhood schools also hold this core belief. Although these activists position themselves as oppositional to the district's brand of neoliberal corporate reform, both movements value middle-class White resources as a *solution* to educational problems, instead of identifying these as a *contributor* to educational problems and neighborhood inequity. Perhaps this is also why the gentry's movements around access to local neighborhood schools hold the potential to exacerbate racial segregation in diverse urban neighborhoods.[17] Indeed, these disproportionate resources are an outcome of previous iterations of this same inequity perpetuated through media, schooling, housing, employment, health, and policing.

Conclusion

In the end, the initial movements to revitalize an elementary and middle school in the neighborhood were successful in creating a "buzz" and gaining a reputation for being untracked, diverse, and rigorous neighborhood schools worthy of rising White enrollment (though Latinx activists question whether or not those community-led reforms are really benefitting the low-income Latinx kids in the neighborhood). White parents were able to mobilize resources and attract the ear of the district, which had not yet laid out plans for these low-performing schools and was eager to collaborate with neighborhood activists promising resources to struggling schools. Their activism is in line with a school reform philosophy that seeks to keep these resources within the city school system, while also enabling market-based choice within the district. In the case of the Ridgeview High School co-location and the McDonwell school turnaround, however, the community was reactive to a prescribed neoliberal school reform initiated unilaterally by the district, and its mobilizing did not prevent either reform from happening, even though the Ridgeview High movement did succeed in *stalling* the co-location in order to force the district to consider other options for the charter school's location. In these examples, the reformist district ultimately rebuffed the affluent parents, and reformers in power did not honor their wishes.

When compared to the parallel mobilization around neighborhood schools in the less affluent Black and Latinx communities across the river, however, these informal neighborhood-based networks do enjoy some success in remaking neighborhood schools into viable local choices. Unlike Black community members who lead community meetings, protests, and walkouts yet *still* cannot compel a reformist school board member to show up to their meetings for a dialogue, these White parents are able to compel several members of the school board, as well as other key reformers in the city, to come to their community forums and discuss school reform plans. Although these White residents draw upon nostalgia for a simpler time when their families did not have a choice about where they would send their kids to school, this nostalgia for the neighborhood school—though premised on a fundamentally segregated past—is not delegitimized by reformers as it is in the case of Black nostalgia for community-centered schools. This periodic alignment between elite reformers and White neighborhood community activists is enabled by a shared belief in the inherent value of White middle-class resources as engines for school, neighborhood, and city improvement.

Although there are important differences between individualist and collectivist orientations to reform in the movements of affluent parents to revitalize their neighborhood schools, these differences might not be large enough to explain why some affluent movements to reform neighborhood schools either facilitate or sabotage educational equity.[18] Perhaps a better measure of this would be to examine how well these neighborhood activists succeed in maintaining broad, deep, and sustainable cross-racial alliances with other concerned parents in the neighborhood, especially in the midst of pervasive racial and class tensions in their everyday relationships with each other. Undoubtedly, this kind of sustainable coalition would necessitate a reevaluation of the taken-for-granted notion that White middle-class resources will lift *all* boats, and that what is good for these settler families is good for all families. This notion refuses to recognize the sources of unearned privilege, and how this unearned privilege stands in relationship to historical and contemporary manifestations of class and racial inequality. This sustainable coalition would also extend beyond school revitalization and reform, and would consider police harassment, immigration reform, affordable housing, food politics, healthcare access, and many other pressing issues to be worthy of community organizing as well, since these issues would affect a sizable portion of those in this coalition and therefore would impact the health of the neighborhood. It is this kind of "cause affirmation" on the part of the gentry that would place the experiences, grievances, and commitments of those who are the *most* marginalized at the center of such a coalition.[19]

This sustainable coalition, then, would require its members to become long-term activists on many fronts, something that most of these White parents are unwilling to do. Neoliberal school choice, as a policy, and middle-class White privilege, as a pervasive paradigm, enable them to retreat from activism. James reflects on his activism with a tone of regret:

> I'm glad I got involved, but it took time away from my children, and that really sucked. My thought was, "Really? This?" It's one thing after another of all this sort of like, "Ugh, really?" You peek behind the curtains, and it's like, "Really? This is what's going on? This is the future?" It got me irritable and angry. And all of a sudden my son's like, "Dad, you said you weren't gonna miss any Cub Scout meetings or basketball games or basketball practices. Why are you lying to me?" I spent my energy fighting the system, and it made me angry, and it made me not a good neighbor. So I think that if somebody wants to fight it, that's what they're in for.

In contrast, the retreat of the Latinx activists from the neighborhood schools movement does not necessarily signal a retreat from activism. As Roberto explains, "The difference is that for lifetime activists, fighting for true social change and social justice for the people, when this fight's over, we lick our wounds and go to the next battle. Some people say, 'It's over, we've done, let's go vacation.' That's the big difference." Indeed, several of these lifetime activists detailed in the next chapter find more hope in the formal community nonprofit organization, which provides more structure, more political education, and more strategizing on both the policy and the grassroots levels. This context also provides support for the kind of holistic, multi-issue activism that would have strengthened the gentry's fights for neighborhood schools. For many activists, this context holds more promise than do the loosely organized neighborhood movements to effect meaningful social change in an era of rapid educational and urban transformation.

5

No Permanent Enemies, No Permanent Allies

The Politics of Reformer-Community Nonprofit Partnerships

I don't call myself a "reformer." But we do believe in this idea of "no permanent enemies, no permanent allies." We have a job to do, and that's to better our education system altogether, and that's what our mission is here. We want all kids to succeed. We want them all to be prepared to go to college, but within that there is some conversation about how we get that done. Not everybody will agree with me. But I'm working with parents to make change, and that is reform in itself for me. I look at it more from that standpoint, and whatever folks label that as, that's the work that we're doing. I'm committed to the mission of making change and changing the status quo.

—Rafael, community organizer

Rafael is a seasoned community organizer in his forties. He came to work in educational justice after many years working in labor and immigrant rights movements. He doesn't call himself a "reformer," but he does work with reformers to shape education policy. Rafael's organization, along with a handful of other community-based nonprofits, worked diligently on Senate Bill 191, the Teacher Effectiveness Bill, which passed in the early 2000s and tied teacher pay and promotion to test scores and student performance. It produced the ProComp pay system, which was eventually the target of the Denver teachers' strike in 2019. Rafael's job is to organize a groundswell of support among low-income Latinx people for expanded school choice and high-performing charter schools. In other nonprofits, organizers who came from the immigrant rights movement, youth organizing, and labor organizing now organize various low-income communities of color to rally for innovative transportation policies in order to realize the promise of school choice. They organize for weighted student funding, so that funding follows low-income students instead of schools and neighborhoods. They organize for revised discipline policies in reformed schools so that fewer students of color are targeted by police in schools and are pushed out of their education through the kinds of "zero tolerance" policies put into place in the 1990s.[1] They organize for longer school days, and alignment between state college standards and high school standards in order to reduce remediation rates once high school graduates get to college. They organize for in-state tuition for undocumented immigrants in order to ensure that out-of-state tuition does not defer an undocumented student's dream of going to college. They organize for student voice in teacher evaluation processes and school reform policy decision making.

Many of these goals align with reformer visions for educational change: expanding school choice, establishing more charter schools, and aligning secondary education with college requirements through mechanisms like the Common Core standard. Some of these goals do not necessarily echo reformer goals: changes in discipline policies and practices, for example, or new tuition rates for undocumented students. Certainly integrating student voice in school reform discussions is not a cherished value of the reformer movement. Yet whether or not they align with reformer visions for educational change, these campaigns, in many instances, arise from years of racial justice organizing within the school system. Many of them are part of broader social and racial justice platforms that have been developed in community organizations, independent of the rise of the neoliberal reform movement. These are not visions for privatization and marketization. For many groups, these represent visions for racial justice in education.

This chapter investigates how the nonprofit-reformer relationship facilitates low-income community activists'—especially low-income *youth* activists'—participation in school reform. This chapter also examines the costs to nonprofit activists of maintaining such a delicate relationship with reformers, since these activists aim to do several things at once: hold reformers accountable to their promises of radical educational success; push elites to incorporate racial justice into their metrics and ideologies; and strategically aim to become active partners with reformers in the course of executing various grassroots nonprofit campaigns. While pushing activist campaigns forward, these organizational ties to reformers, paired with the organizational constraints of the neoliberal nonprofit, can also end up hindering activists' broader visions for educational and racial justice. By examining the frustrations of nonprofit activists themselves to tamp down their own language and political critique as they become networked into the reform movement, we gain some insight into the ways that the neoliberal context provides the possibilities for, but also undermines, nonprofit activists' efforts to bring racial justice to the forefront of neoliberal education policy change.

Like the self-described reformers who have jumped into the fray of the reform movement, these established nonprofit organizations also see this historical moment as unusually open to community involvement. One nonprofit organizer in this study reflects on this new urgency to address failing schools:

> I think it is encouraging. It's encouraging that within the last few years there's been greater attention. There's greater resources being tied to addressing this, and with the urgency that it deserves. I would argue that maybe for too long beforehand it wasn't being treated with the same degree of urgency. Where it was an acceptable thing, that in certain cities that just was the graduation rate, in certain cities that was the dropout rate. But then to have political officials stand up . . . and folks say that this is not good. They make the economic argument. You can make the moral argument. But no matter what, I think it's welcome.

Many of these groups, some steeped in the Chicano student movement and the immigrant labor movements of the 1960s and 1970s, see this as a critical moment in which they can change long-standing institutional racism in the public school system. Now institutionalized in the nonprofit structure, these organizations are funded by grants, and their calls for racial and educational justice culminate in focused campaigns that aim to affect broader policy and not just individual school communities. Unlike the Black parents in chapter 3 who appropriate free (or almost free) meeting spaces in McDonald's restaurants and community libraries, these organizations have their own meetings spaces and offices. These are stable home bases from which to launch formidable community campaigns for educational change.

In one such office, news cameras are poised, ready to capture what could be a contentious community meeting. Roughly eighty community members, mostly Latinx, are waiting to hear from the four White men sitting in a line of chairs at the front of the room. The men are leaders in the school district and are key players in the city's larger reform movement—an amalgamation of foundations, think tanks, business leaders, political rising stars, Teach for America alums, education journalists, and even district representatives—which has spearheaded the rapid redesign of many schools throughout the district over the last decade. Also at the front of the room, to the side of the four men in chairs, are seven Latinx and three Black high school students, both boys and girls, wearing jeans and black and red T-shirts with graffiti print that reads, "Educate, don't discriminate!" They will be leading this meeting. Importantly, the meeting is not being held in one of the drab, stuffy meeting rooms at the district's central headquarters. The meeting is held on these kids' turf, in a community room housed inside the nonprofit youth organization where these activist kids from area high schools gather during their busy weeks to work on various racial justice issues in the education system.

The youth have gathered their families, friends, and community members—as well as the media—to bear witness and confront these education leaders with their own assessment of how well (or not) these leaders have done to reduce various racial disparities in academic achievement across the district. Although these reform leaders have previously given lip service to reducing racial disparities in school suspension rates, education funding, college AP course offerings, and remediation rates, they have not followed through with their promises to the community that swift reform would deliver equity on all these measures. Despite the tension in the room, and despite the tough stance of these youth who are standing over the seated adults at the front of the room, the fact that the reform leaders are also wearing identical "Educate, don't discriminate!" shirts suggests that reformers and youth activists of color ultimately converge in their calls for racial justice in education reform. These matching T-shirts powerfully demonstrate elites' symbolic alignment with youth of color and the formal nonprofit organizations they represent.

Outside this nonprofit context, however, other youth of color across the city have participated in walkouts and rallies to protest neighborhood school closures, often in conjunction with the parents and community members detailed in chapter 3, who have been left behind in these seismic school and neighborhood transformations. In contrast to the tenuous relationships that reformers have forged with the nonprofit activist youth described above, school reformers rarely ever align with these neighborhood youth in the same ways, and in fact often characterize their community movements as knee-jerk neighborhood reactions that "defend the status quo" instead of working collaboratively with reformers to solve educational failure in low-income communities. Why is it that these education reform leaders, without fail, show up to these highly publicized youth activist accountability meetings, as well as other community meetings hosted by nonprofit community-based organizations, but routinely dismiss broader community campaigns for racial justice and community claims to neighborhood schools? When powerful education reformers wear the same T-shirts that youth activists wear, it is unclear whose victory this really is. Does this empowering display mean that nonprofit activists have successfully forced elites to examine entrenched racial disparities and foreground these in their education reform agendas? Or does it mean that reformers have successfully cloaked neoliberal moves to reshape schools and cities in the activists' calls for racial and educational justice?

The nonprofit organizations I highlight in this chapter are not anti-reform. They, like reformers, are eager to make radical and rapid change to the school system. Even though their campaigns vary, these organizations all hold a consistent guiding coalition philosophy: "no permanent enemies, no permanent allies." This phrase was popularized by legendary organizer Saul Alinsky, who through his community-organizing model has left an indelible imprint on the contemporary political left in the United States. Alinsky, who had a distain for orthodox political ideology as a guide for popular resistance, took the lessons he learned about political wins from his experience in the Congress of Industrial Organizations (CIO) and imported them into other community organizing campaigns in the wake of the Great Depression. The full phrase "no permanent enemies, no permanent allies, only permanent interests" guided his philosophy bringing together the Industrial Areas Foundation in 1939, a motley coalition of various religious, racial, ethnic, and labor groups knitted together into an unlikely but powerful coalition organization for poor people's campaigns. Neither identifying as reformers or loyal allies to the reform movement, nor identifying themselves as fundamentally counter to the reform movement (as in the case of the non-institutionalized community activists detailed in chapters 3 and 4), the nonprofit organizations featured in this chapter view reformers as potential allies as long as reformers support the basic goals of a given nonprofit campaign. In theory, this means that key reformers could be allies for one campaign but could be targets for another campaign. Like reformers, these community activists view the public school system as a crisis that must be fixed on an urgent timeline (see chapter 2). Alliances must be forged to carry out the educational justice campaign like a surgical strike, which can impact school change on a broader policy and systemic level. Importantly, nearly all of these nonprofit organizations have a significant youth activist component to them. As the ultimate objects of school reform "saving," Latinx and Black youth in particular have an important role to play in school reform discussions. These youth are on the receiving end of substandard public education, and are the ones who stand to lose the most from educational injustice. Their voices, or at least their symbolic presence, carries weight. Part of the aim of these organizations is to transform high school youth from objects of school reform conversations into active subjects within them.

In practice, however, reformers need nonprofits as longer-term allies, especially in the wake of so much community upheaval and outrage after elite reformers initiate quick school turnarounds and closures. Reformers take advantage of photo opportunities they have with community activists, and especially youth of color, who organize from within the bounds of the funded nonprofit. In practice, nonprofit organizations find themselves moving from outside agitators, to valued allies, to longer-term reform partners. In the end, this shift undoubtedly helps community nonprofits to secure campaign victories and gain a foothold in education reform policy making. This foothold is significant, especially for the Latinx and Black youth who are positioned centrally in education reform discourse and imagery but whose voices are rarely heard. Neoliberal strategies that are often promoted through color-blind, market-based language reproduce racial inequality by leaving larger racial inequalities undisturbed and un-interrogated.[2] Given this context, the interventions of community activists, especially youth of color, hold the promise of forcing reformers to attend more closely to racial disparities in education. For youth especially, there are few other organizational structures besides community nonprofits that can effectively provide campaign scaffolding, funding, and mentorship to youth dissent. For many champions of the youth activist nonprofit, this structure promotes a model of positive youth development that relies upon young people's political activism and civic engagement.[3] Indeed, social movement theorists such as Doug McAdam argue that movements are at their most powerful when they are organized out of indigenous networks into social movement organizations.[4] Alinsky himself championed the figure of the organizer, who holds the power to frame social issues, mobilize disparate groups of people, and appeal to divergent interests in the name of launching winnable, single-issue campaigns that improve the lives of the have-nots.

Yet a host of critical scholars have long argued that movements lose their power when they are institutionalized. For example, sociologists Frances Fox Piven and Richard A. Cloward argued that movements, especially those waged by poor people, are not meant to last. Instead, they are meant to be disruptive in specific periods when they can win the most concessions from the state. However, once they are institutionalized into static organizations, they are more easily co-opted and mollified by elites.[5] In her analysis of the women's reproductive rights movement, for example, Suzanne Staggenborg surmised that formalized social movement organizations (SMOs) help to keep movements alive in historical moments when constituents become complacent, and are better prepared than informal movements to take advantage of opportunities to mobilize when the political environment changes. However, these formalized SMOs also tend to engage in strategic action that aims to stabilize and expand their organization as much as it aims to make political change by targeting external threats.[6] More recently, sociologist Dana Fisher argues that the progressive left has organized and outsourced grassroots activism in ways that burn out young, passionate activists.[7] The authors of *The Revolution Will Not Be Funded* claim that under neoliberalism, progressive movements have been institutionalized into the "nonprofit industrial complex." This institutionalization has tamed the power of social movements by compelling them to adopt less threatening reformist approaches rather than radical forms of dissent.[8] Asian American studies scholar Soo Ah Kwon also persuasively argues that the "nonprofitization" of youth activism in particular functions as a form of "affirmative governmentality" that burdens youth activists with solving social problems triggered by neoliberal state divestment over the last few decades.[9] She writes, "Youth of color organizing is not a panacea for social injustice and inequality: rather, it is the latest technique in a long line of youth management strategies."[10] This critique suggests that nonprofit youth activist organizations actually blunt the power of youth organizing, while protecting and masking the state's responsibility in disadvantaging youth of color.

These critiques suggest that there are limitations to the ways community nonprofit organizations can take back reform from elites and steer it toward community ends.

Finding Common Ground: Accountability and Urgency

As discussed in chapter 2, the self-identified reformers in this study do not express a universal distaste for community participation, although they certainly denigrate non-institutionalized Black and Latinx neighborhood schools activists in particular. Many reformers, in their interviews and public statements, stressed that community and parent involvement are important, and are the most powerful when this involvement (1) collaborates with school and reformer leadership and (2) functions as a mechanism to hold elites accountable. The reformer emphasis on two key elements of neoliberal education reform, *accountability* and *urgency* (see chapter 2), are also shared by some of these community movements. Although Pauline Lipman and Nathan Haines studied the ways neoliberal reform excludes critical African American perspectives in Chicago school reform, they also point to the presence of community supporters of neoliberal policies, supporters who have identified the need for an urgent remedy to persistent educational inequities and see the neoliberal reform movement as holding the potential to deliver these. They write, "It is important to understand their perspectives because this gets to the heart of the 'good sense' [of neoliberal reform], . . . In a Gramscian sense . . . those aspects of dominant policy that resonate with the lived experiences of the people affected."[11]

Counter to Lipman and Haines, however, I argue that the neoliberal context also provides an opening for community movements to authentically demand, from the ground up, that their institutions and their leaders be held accountable to their promises for radical change. These community groups are not simply supporting the reform movement's agenda out of desperation. They are finding common ground with reformers in the context of their own autonomous social justice campaigns, some of which have developed over decades. Furthermore, because local reformers actively seek community alliances and legitimacy in a landscape of growing distrust of school reform, the neoliberal context presents new possibilities for community demands to be *heard* and publicly respected. Accountability and urgency are two cherished values of the reformer movement that dovetail with community calls for real policy change that delivers educational equity. However, just because community movements and reformers find common ground does not mean that community movements ascribe the same social or political meaning to urgency and accountability. Even as these are mutually guiding principles of both reformers and some low-income grassroots activists, these principles are assimilated into a larger racial and social justice framework for the community activists who work on broader social justice issues. This is not true of reformers, who champion *accountability* and *urgency* in the absence of a larger social justice framework and discernible movement legacies.

One example of the ways accountability and urgency provide common ground for reformer-community partnerships is in the case of the Urban Parent Network (UPN). As I described in chapter 2, when reformers spoke of community organizations they respected and considered to be allies, one organization they repeatedly named was the UPN. The UPN largely represents low-income urban White and Latinx parents and youth. Its goals have included organizing parents at newly reformed schools, increasing student funding at low-income schools, helping to design new transportation systems, and championing innovation, reform, and school choice for low-income families. Although some of these initiatives resonate with reformer priorities, the UPN sees these changes as steps toward ensuring college readiness for *all* children. The UPN champions these changes by linking them to other calls for immigrants' rights in education, including in-state tuition for undocumented students. It pushes for new transportation policies to ensure that low-income families can truly exercise school choice without worrying about the logistics of how they will get their child to a better school further away from their own neighborhoods. Framing school choice as fundamentally a class and race issue, one UPN organizer explains the difference between how she views school choice and how reformers view school choice:

> What about the parents that don't have the means [to take advantage of school choice]? Can't look up online what the highest-rated school is? Can't drive every morning across town to get their kids there? They deserve access. This is an example of a community taking initiative and saying, "Let's make sure school choice really works for us." So that's a very different situation.

All reformers consider the UPN an example of a cooperative and not "angry" community group, and view it as an important school reform ally. In contrast, UPN activists view these reformers as potential allies in a given moment and within the context of a given campaign. As one UPN activist explains, "We're not gonna discredit a good idea that might offer something to our community because some person who is not familiar with our larger worldview *also* likes it. That would be kind of crazy, right?" These institutionalized activists try to walk the line of pushing elites, holding them accountable, and finding common ground to advance their own agendas on an urgent timeline. With their guiding philosophy of "no permanent enemies, no permanent allies," they enter into alliances in order to advance specific campaign agendas. Although commonly misread by the neighborhood reform opponents like those described in chapters 3 and 4, they do not enter into these alliances unconditionally in order to blindly support the aims of the reform movement.

Lifting the Veil on Color-Blind Neoliberalism: How Youth Activists Demand Racial Justice in School Reform

As described in chapter 2, elite reformers regularly refer to the achievement gap and the deplorable failure of low-income schools in their calls

for swift reforms (especially in low-income neighborhoods). However, there is a marked absence of a racial justice narrative in reformer
visions of educational excellence. As a result, even middle-class White
reformers who see themselves as civil rights advocates and as advocates
of low-income Black and Latinx youth note that the reformed schools
they championed for these youth are not necessarily the same schools
where they themselves would send their own kids. In their rationales,
reformers espouse a separate-but-equal vision of school reform in which
their own children should have more opportunities for free and critical
thinking, and less structure/discipline, than should low-income youth of
color who presumably come from family "structures that are in disarray."

Racial justice, as a key component of education reform policy, looks
much different to youth activists of color engaged in reforming discipline policies; fighting for college access, school transportation, and a
voice in teacher assessments and evaluations; and changing the ways
schools are funded. These youth do not believe in the standards movement to address entrenched racism, and they push reformers to "keep
it real" and explicitly discuss racism and racial disparities. As one
seventeen-year-old Latina activist explains,

> You have to keep it real with them. You have to let them know because
> obviously you can't turn a blind eye to racism. 'Cause it still exists. And
> you can't act like you don't know what's going on. And so, for us, in our
> testimonies and everything, it was easy for us to tell them, "Look, there's
> a huge disparity between Whites and minorities."

These youth, in their accountability tactics, test the boundaries of reformers' rhetoric of "equality" and "equal opportunity" by pushing reformers to more explicitly recognize racism and racial injustice. As one
sixteen-year-old African American woman explains,

> They do acknowledge disparities. They do acknowledge a lot of different
> factors that go into that. But I think that the end of the day they have to
> respond to all audiences: to White parents, to Latino parents, to Indian
> parents, to African American parents. They talk about "equality for all,"
> but when we need to call it out, then that's when we say, "You do want
> equality for all, but let's be real and let's be honest and look at the achieve-

ment gap. Let's look at, you know, the quality of education at different schools, and the specifics of everything." And so instead of avoiding it, instead of pretending that's not what it is, let's face it straight on.

Here, youth activists recognize reformers' proclivity to discuss the achievement gap and "equality" in color-blind terms, and see their own mission as "keeping it real" and bringing back racial (in) justice to the forefront of proposals for educational improvement. In this sense, youth activists' bold insistence on speaking truth to power holds enormous potential to interrupt the enforcement of neoliberal color-blind education policy, and frame discussions of educational excellence in racial justice terms. As these youth host elite reformers on their turf, hold them accountable to their commitment to "equity," and speak with support from their communities, their words are powerfully mirrored by the images of civil rights leaders and protest art lining the walls. The physical space, mentorship, and resources that this nonprofit structure brings to youth mobilization provide leverage to these young people's challenges to elites.

In doing this, and forcing elite reformers to address racism head-on, youth activists who find themselves in proximity to reformers and listened to by reformers (especially reformer policy makers) experience a marked sense of empowerment. One eighteen-year-old Latino man remembered his victory in the state legislature around a school equity bill:

> I was excited. Excited to know that I was finally getting a chance to make a difference in somebody's life. And it was kind of cool to see—to know that potentially, if this bill gets passed, everything that I've worked on and everything that [our organization] has worked on could change the lives of every single student in the state.

Because of the leverage that the youth nonprofit provides, these youth find themselves in an unusual position of authority vis-à-vis White reformers. As the specter of Black and Latinx youth figures centrally in reformer narratives about saving schools and saving youth from educational failure, these very youth find their voices and experience respected by elites in power. Moving from their usual institutional roles as depoliticized, silent, and powerless students to more skilled, powerful political representatives of the funded community nonprofit and its campaigns, many of these youth communicate a sense that they have broken through both their own political powerlessness and the adultist (and racist) perceptions that so often delegitimize their political potential. As seventeen-year-old Tanisha boldly puts it,

> We're not ignorant children. We know what's going on in our world. Just because you have a perception we don't know what we're talking about doesn't mean we don't know what we're talking about. Don't underestimate the power of a teenager.

Another youth organizer underscores the necessity of elites hearing from the very students who have been the most marginalized by substandard schooling practices:

> So when we talk about emerging leaders, it's not the honor roll, and it's not student government. Emerging leaders are not the traditional leaders. You can't have a student tell you how to engage them unless those students have experienced being disengaged.

Darius, an eighteen-year-old African American youth activist, explains his sense of empowerment and authority as someone who has actually experienced the injustice of being targeted for administrative punishment and expulsion at his school for a relatively minor infraction:

> It's better to hear from the students as opposed to talking *about* them. Because then you get a clear perspective from them. Like, "This is what's happening to me. And I'm going to tell you about it. I'm going to explain to you why it's a problem for me as a student." So it's cool to be able to speak.

As youth voice becomes more respected and listened to, youth in nonprofits find themselves in the position of entering into a mutual relationship with reform elites, and even partnering with them. Seventeen-year-old Bobby, whose youth organization collaborated with other nonprofits to draft a state student funding bill, remarks on the fruits of his speaking out in these adult-dominated political forums:

Well, for me, since I was able to speak to the committee about it, since I framed my messages in a different way, I was able to personally know some state representatives and state senators. . . . Now we know each other's perspectives and they understand where we're coming from and they were able to get the chance to take a step back and say, "Yeah, you guys are right." Like, hear from our perspective from the way we framed our message. And now we have so many people, so many politicians in support of our bill. It's incredible.

Genie, a nineteen-year-old from a different organization, explains,

Just, like, the first meeting we went to, to where the adults weren't so much interested in what we had to say. Now, to, like, the last meeting, they asked us, "What do you think?" or "How do you feel on this topic?" Like, it was a huge change. It felt good to know that, like, we changed their opinions on student voice. Like [at first] they easily didn't really know much about student voice, they didn't care. . . . To now, where they are asking us what we think. So that was a huge change. And I think that's what it is. We just don't go away!

As discussed in chapter 2, reformers describe why they respect these community nonprofits—many of them with youth activist contingents—who "don't go away." They contrast these groups to what they perceive as the ineffective "angry community groups" that continually seem to stand in the way of positive change. From reformers' perspective, these "angry" groups criticize reform from a faulty logic (blind loyalty to failing neighborhood schools) and their own deficient lived experience of schooling. In contrast, these youth activist groups are seen as valuable collaborators and partners in school reform; they are community players who are willing to speak the same urgency and accountability language that reformers speak, and value the same goals that reformers value. At the same time, they translate these goals and language into explicit calls for racial justice.

As nonprofit youth activists refuse to "go away" and continually show up to reformer meetings, strategy sessions, and policy discussions, they demonstrate that they can "become knowledgeable" and push for their vision of educational and racial justice while being able to "have a conversation on the same level." With the support of the funded nonprofit, teen activists of color begin to take their political education, skill sets, and training out into adult-dominated education policy discussions, town hall meetings on school turnarounds, or immigrant rights rallies. These students take pride in not just participating in ready-made political processes, but actually confronting the ageist and even racist mechanics of political decision making that are typically embedded in those processes.

At the same time youth challenge these dynamics, however, they are also cultivating key alliances with elite reformers. Cassie, a seventeen-year-old Latina student involved in a youth organization focused on integrating youth concerns into education reform policy, explains her strategy to keep showing up at key meetings and forge alliances with specific policy makers. Her organization's demand for students to have a real voice in teacher evaluation processes began to gain traction in state-level policy discussions about school reform. Locating the political power of her voice in the alliances she strategically made with adults in power, she notes,

> So, like, if I wouldn't have had those few allies, easily my comments would have been thrown out the window. And the allies would not have been there had we not showed up in force over and over. So it's really a bunch of legwork, a bunch of little things that make it so that our voices matter.

The longer these youth are "at the table" with reformers and the policy makers whom reformers try to influence, the more entangled they become in reformer networks. These networks value—and *need*—their continued partnership, and as a result these youth experience pressure to soften their messages for racial justice. It becomes much more tricky to navigate the seemingly simple philosophy of "no permanent enemies, no permanent allies," especially when they see the value of making key alliances with reformers.

Getting to the Table and Not Going Away: The Creeping Permanence of Partnerships

Gaining a seat at the table is no easy task. It is a fight in itself, as twenty-four-year-old Sylvia, a staff organizer, emphasizes:

> As an organizer, you have to create the space to get you to the table, first place. But I want to be clear that having a space at the table isn't anything that's just given. People don't really invite you and say, "Hey, I hear you guys work on education reform. We're thinking about this policy, what do you think about it?" Our experience historically has been that we have had to demand a space at the table. And if the question is how do you get to the table, the answer is that you demand it, because rarely do you just get invited to it.

However, the pressures to keep nonprofit activists at the table with elites through the course of long-term campaigns can steer community movements away from radical possibilities and toward the kinds of modest reforms that are carefully crafted to not alienate elites. In one sense, bringing youth voice "to the table" is what organizing is all about, as Rayanne, a youth organizer, observes:

> We should be working alongside teachers, alongside principals, alongside educators to find solutions together. Because I think that's what organizing is about. To bring in all the decision makers, all the players, all the people that have a say and that play a role in shaping our education. And together coming up with solutions.

But this organizing approach does not always leave room for youth activists or paid staff organizers to express political outrage and dissent. One twenty-five-year-old organizer remembers, "When I first came on board I was saying, 'Why isn't this city on fire? Why aren't people burning up garbage cans and throwing them in the streets, saying, we are not moving until the graduation at [local high school] goes from 30 percent to 80 percent to 90 percent?' That's a frustrating thing to think about." Over time, this organizer learned that a tactic like this would probably sever fragile relationships with elites in power who could be important campaign allies. Another organizer, James, expresses his ongoing frustration with targets-turned-allies who do not follow through on their promises: "So you get frustrated with different outcomes with whatever they're doing. But at the same time they're so nice to you and they want to work with you to address it. So that is difficult."

In one organization, youth activists help to cowrite a report on racial disparities in academic achievement rates, and they are preparing to target specific education officials with this report. In a meeting, youth organizers and youth activists grapple with how aggressively to word the report, since this document is one public mechanism to hold adults in power accountable. Yet the report cannot be so aggressive that it would alienate these very same adults. Several youth activists in the room favor the use of the word "demands" to push elites to more aggressively tackle racial disparities in education practices. A youth organizer asks students how they would feel about framing these as "recommendations," since "demands" might damage the relationship they are trying to build with high-profile education movers and shakers. After a protracted debate, students and the youth organizers agree that "a call-to" was a good way to phrase their messaging in order to assertively (but not aggressively) hold education elites to their word. As Hannah reflects afterwards, "We could have made this report scathing, but now it's, like, very nice. It all depends on where we are in that relationship [with elites]. Ah, it's hard."

Softening the Message

Select nonprofit activists are asked to enter into longer-term partnerships with reform entities, even as their own coalition philosophy is "no permanent enemies, no permanent allies." As one youth organizer explains,

> We also sometimes struggle a lot with how aggressive to be. What tactics to use. So it's kind of like, what tone to take. Should we straight up call them out and just say, "You haven't done anything! How dare you! You should be ashamed of yourself!" Or should we say, "You're doing some good things, but you know, this little progress is not enough. Let's work together to close that gap."

And I think it all depends on the time, place, and conditions. When you have [a target] that is moving in the right direction that is pro-change, sometimes in organizing you shouldn't be so "anti" with those people in power. Because in the end, to move things into power, sometimes you have to work with them. And in organizing, sometimes that's really hard to see. When you don't know how aggressive or how mean you should be towards your target.

In these partnerships, nonprofit activists' challenges to White elites can become risky as they try to sustain their status within elite education reformer coalitions. Several youth organizers express this ongoing dilemma of how to address "targets" who value ongoing change and reform, and are willing to listen to youth and communities of color in the process. For the sake of working together, youth learn to carefully tame their outrage and charges of racism, and also frame racial injustice as an *educational opportunity* issue rather than a larger social justice issue that extends beyond schooling. As eighteen-year-old Daniel puts it,

You definitely have to let them know, "This is going on in my life right now. And it's keeping me from school." Like, "I want to graduate, I want to go to college. I don't want to have a criminal record when I'm in high school 'cause I care about my future and I want to go and get my diploma and be ready to get my college degree without anybody questioning me about something stupid that happened in high school." So you do have to link it to that because it also gives more of an emotional feeling. Like not just saying, "Oh, kids are being criminalized in school." You know? Instead you say, "These kids aren't being able to get to go to school."

Although framing the problem of zero tolerance, for example, as an issue of educational access and opportunity is one way of maintaining a narrative about racial justice, this young man explains that he has to frame it as an educational access issue rather than a larger racial justice issue. He frames punitive discipline policies as something that keeps *him*, as an individual, from accessing education and future success, rather than something that impacts an entire community and connects to broader social justice issues such as the expansion of the prison-industrial complex, deportations, and immigration reform, among other issues. In this way, youth find themselves having to shift their message slightly to resonate with reformers' emphasis on education as mobility and individual consumption, rather than as a social, communal, and even human right. As a result, the careful and intense political education, mentorship, and youth leadership development work that youth nonprofits do—the "backstage" radical speak—begins to dissipate as it drifts toward the "frontstage," where youth directly confront adults in power over educational injustices in policy forums.[12] This means that youth tamp down their own political outrage and political analysis in a roomful of education reformers. Depending on the players in the room, it can also mean framing issues less collectively and systemically, and couching them in more individualistic and aspirational terms. This messaging also blunts the radical edge of their campaigns, and keeps them from coalescing with other racial justice groups on initiatives beyond education reform. As one seventeen-year-old Latina from another organization notes,

> So of course we all want to be like the Malcolm X type or Martin Luther King or Caesar Chavez type people. Like in our discussions with each other. But we can't be, like, extremely radical with them because then they would take that as, "Oh, you're totally against our government."

While youth activists push reformers to recognize racial inequity in existing educational practices, and press these mostly White reformers to value racial equity as a worthy goal in local education reform decisions, their public presentation for these increasingly valuable and powerful partners must walk the fine line of pushing adults in power toward racial justice goals without alienating them. These nonprofit youth activists find ways to assimilate racial justice goals into neoliberal rhetoric in ways that also require them to narrow the scope of their racial justice activism in public conversations, to undermine the leverage of their own coalition philosophy of "no permanent enemies, no permanent allies," and to frame issues according to their increasingly complicated ties to reform elites.[13]

Lost Coalitions

About thirty parents and community members sit on folding chairs arranged in a semicircle in the main office of a community organization, a converted house nestled between an old church and a gas station on a tree-lined street about three miles from the downtown skyscrapers and city center. Teen activists and older youth organizers in their twenties lead a workshop on racial disparities in education, citing racial disparities in curricular resources, discipline policies, mentorship and tutoring resources, graduation rates, and college attendance rates. Although the organizers are discussing disparities between White youth and Latinx and Black youth, there are mostly Latinx and White community members in the room. Out of thirty, there are just two Black women sitting in the circle. They are Darla and Mable, two of the women featured in chapter 3 who are at the helm of organizing against school closures, new charter schools, and the expansion of school choice, as these are experienced as part of a wave of gentrification projects across the river. The youth organizers take out a huge swath of butcher paper and post it in front of the semicircle, asking everyone to brainstorm which organizations or key individuals would be good allies to their campaign to reform schools to more adequately prepare low-income youth for college. "Who should be in our coalition?" As they post the butcher paper, we see that it is not empty: they've already started the brainstorming. One youth organizer says, "We started to think of community groups who are also concerned with school change and education reform, and we put these up here. These seem like groups we can get on board with our campaign. But we would like help from you in thinking through other potential allies." The room is quiet, as everyone is deep in thought. On the list are prominent school reform groups like Students First and Reform Now!, the very groups that regularly blame low-income Black community members for their "backwards" championing of the status quo and for holding back reform (chapter 2). Darla and Mable have spent many hours talking with neighbors, friends, and coworkers about these groups, holding them at least partly responsible for the dissolution of their neighborhood schools.

Mable respectfully raises her hand. A youth organizer smiles and calls on her. "I don't really think Students First and Reform Now! are gonna be on board with this. I'm sorry, but I just don't think they really care about Black and Brown children." Not wanting to alienate Mable, the youth organizer leading the workshop thanks her for speaking up, and pauses before speaking. "I think our strategy is to just brainstorm as many groups as we can to put on the list of possible campaign partners, since you never know what an organization will support until you engage them on the issue. Can others think of other individuals or groups that we need to reach out to? And could any of you volunteer to help us connect to them?"

While the discussion picks up and volunteers raise their hands, Darla and Mable quietly stand up and leave. They miss the rest of the meeting, and do not sign their names on the volunteer sign-up sheet that sits on a table beside the door. Later, when I interview Lisa, the youth organizer leading the workshop, she tells me that she spends most evenings each week after her shift at her organizing job trying to mobilize more African American students to become active in the struggle for student voice in education reform policy discussions. Although she herself and other organizers at her nonprofit have identified Black-Brown unity as a necessary bedrock for their broader educational justice campaigns, she has to do this organizing work "off the clock" because the rest of her organizing work is scripted out by the demands of the campaign she is working on, and the conditions of the campaign grant that funds it. She says with a sigh,

> I think a lot of funders have become more focused on quantitative impact, and so we have a lot of deliverables in terms of how many members we have, how many people we can mobilize. So there's always that stress, the organizer has to always be recruiting. But that leaves very little time to actually develop leaders, because you're always so busy building base and growing your base. And doing the reports, and all of that.

She is tired, and is about to give up. She wants her nights back. The campaign is intense and takes up all her emotional energy. When I ask her what she remembers about this brainstorming workshop she led, and whether she remembered the two Black women in the room who quietly walked out, she pauses to think, and then nods her head and gives a half-smile. "Oh yeah. I remember. You know, I think those women were actually from the teachers union. Sometimes they send folks to show up and just keep an eye on what we're doing." Although this was her understanding, Lisa was mistaken. Darla and Mable are not representatives of the teachers union. While the push-out of veteran teachers is one critique that non-institutionalized Black community activists have of the impact of school reform on their communities, Darla, Mable, and many other Black activists advance plenty of criticisms of teachers too. They do not regularly attend union-sponsored events or meetings, nor do they necessarily talk about the teachers union as an unconditional ally. Certainly, they do not view the teachers union as an unequivocal ally in the fight against neoliberal reform and gentrification, nor an ally to their larger struggle for Black community cohesion. They do not make a special effort to include representatives of the teachers union in their community meetings.

This moment of mistaken identity is revealing for two major reasons. First, it demonstrates the ways discrete nonprofit campaigns, often funded by entities that want specific outcomes such as changed policies or other quantitative deliverables, are constrained when it comes to building Black-Brown alliances for racial justice initiatives.[14] Lisa tries to do this work "off the clock" because she knows it is vital to the campaign, but since she has so many other deliverables she has to worry about, this critical coalition work is pushed to the margins of her organizing. Because Black-Brown coalitions are not necessarily a campaign mandate and are not easily fundable, Lisa and her colleagues are less able to forge connections to these Black community members who live just across the river and are mobilizing around similar racial and educational justice issues. Furthermore, political scientists Adolf Reed Jr. and Cedric Johnson reiterate throughout their work that coalitions based on racial interests alone do not necessarily come together seamlessly against a unitary enemy of White supremacy, because coalition politics are characterized by divergent class interests even as they are marked by presumably shared racial interests.[15] As an educational justice issue, the school-to-prison pipeline holds the potential to bring together Black and Brown communities and build Black and Brown unity, since Black and Brown youth are disproportionately impacted by police in schools and punitive discipline policies.[16] But a campaign that organizes around this—without also aligning with those same communities of color against neighborhood school closures, charter school expansions, and even broader mechanics of urban development and gentrification—leaves racialized working-class interests invisible and marginalized. Discrete nonprofit campaigns with accountability structures dictated by funders and constrained by quantitative deliverables are less likely to incorporate these multi-class interests into their racial justice campaigns.

Second, Black community members advance a critique of schooling that foregrounds the racial injustices of educational inequities and discipline policies, especially those that are cultivated in newly reformed school environments (chapter 3). This is why Darla and Mable attended the meeting, and why they were interested in potentially aligning their work with this nonprofit campaign. However, this moment also illustrates the difficulty of nonprofit campaigns to mobilize larger community constituencies around educational justice because of their alliances with contentious reformers. Although their own coalition philosophy is "no permanent enemies, no permanent allies," this philosophy does not make sense to low-income activists of color who view elite reformers and the movement they represent as fundamentally toxic to educational justice for low-income students of color. One Chicano community activist who had participated in some of these organizations a decade ago but has since moved away from these organizations in order to join the neighborhood activists, critically analyzes what he views as the downside of these nonprofit tactics to strategically partner with the reform movement:

> I think they [nonprofits] are speaking for the community, or they are claiming to speak for the community, but they have not listened to the community on this issue. But I understand why. They have been doing this work for so long. They have been trying to reform the education system. And they have moved the needle so little. In fact you might argue that from the time they started to today, things have gotten worse. So I understand.
>
> But organizers should understand that there are long-term implications. The short victories, while important, and saving that one student is important, has a cost to all the other students. When a charter school can save these one hundred kids, how many get a worse school because of that? How many get a school with less involved parents, with less

motivated students, with less resources, with worse teachers? You have to ask that question.

In his criticism, this activist underscores what he sees as the flaw of the "no permanent enemies, no permanent allies" approach. This approach is framed by the temporal boundaries of the formally funded campaign (allies and enemies are forged and then dismantled according to each campaign's goal) and resonates with the neoliberal mandate of urgency (chapter 2). Although community nonprofits view these campaigns as potent ways to make systemic and lasting change, this critic argues that the campaigns sacrifice the long-term success of *all* students in the quest to immediately save *some* students from educational disaster. In this trade-off, potentially broader coalitions are sacrificed in order to move specific agendas forward. This sacrificing of broader coalitions is notable, since many social movement scholars argue that SMOs, like the youth nonprofits featured in this chapter, are particularly well suited to build coalitions because they have greater administrative resources to sustain coalition ties and can coordinate resource distribution throughout a social movement network.[17] However, when funding sources so heavily dictate the direction and scope of an SMO's discrete organizational campaign, the accompanying ethic of "no permanent enemies, no permanent allies" can undercut the potential of the formalized SMO to sustain broader social movement coalitions. Indeed, as demonstrated by feminist scholar Sandra Morgen in her study of a feminist health clinic's quest for funding, an SMO's dependency on funding can erode its political autonomy.[18]

Some neighborhood activists who critique these community organization-reformer alliances express pain about the trade-off, likening it to a split within a family. As one longtime Latina activist put it,

It's like your children: they grow up and you hope they'll take the values you give them and do something with them. And then they go off-track and you're going, "Oh, my God! Who is this person?" These groups have taken some positions that have been a little odd to me. I don't know if you know, but they supported Students First. We all said, "How can you do this?"

And I know how hard funding can be. But when an ally becomes so restrictive that we can't deal with it, we know as a community we're gonna say no. It takes a lot of work, but it's very clear where we stand. We make them [reform elites] uncomfortable, but that's not my worry. That's theirs!

Although these community-based SMOs maintain a philosophy of "no permanent enemies, no permanent allies" in order to allow flexibility to build coalitions and move select campaigns forward, this adage seems to function more as an interpretive framework and rationale, rather than an accurate description of their coalition networks. On the one hand, they are courted for more permanent partnerships with elite education reformers who increasingly need them in order to legitimize contentious reforms. On the other hand, their periodic alliances with reformers inadvertently alienate other potential community allies who view these partnerships as colluding with the reform movement, and who then lose faith in the integrity of these funded campaigns. The creeping permanence of reformer partnerships and the increasing split between racial justice movements inside and outside the nonprofit context converge to limit the potential for community nonprofits to successfully bring racial *and* economic justice to the forefront of neoliberal school reform.

Conclusion

There is great potential for community groups and low-income youth of color to achieve special status and gain an important voice in education reform and policy making. As they are the very objects of reformer efforts, their challenges to and partnerships with reformers hold the power to bring explicitly politicized social justice issues—namely, racial justice—to the forefront of education reform. Since they are the only players in the school reform landscape with firsthand experience of how it feels to be on the receiving end of unjust educational policies day after day, young people's voices and experiences translate into a kind of expertise and authority in school reform debates, one that becomes recognized and respected by elite reformers. Just as various market-oriented educational entrepreneurs are welcomed into the fold of the neoliberal reform movement, so are select community activists like these youth of color, who have long been neglected in education policy making.

However, activists in nonprofit contexts like these (versus the activist youth in the underfunded or unfunded community collectives that protest neighborhood school closures) find themselves having to shift from being respected outside agitators to becoming valuable reformer allies and partners, which can at times compromise the spirit and message of their racial justice critiques. School reform elites begin as targets and soon become partners the longer that youth are "at the table" participating in education reform conversations. As one youth organizer explained, "We're having a challenge because [specific reformer partner] is sometimes our enemy and sometimes they're our ally at the same time on different campaigns." This ambivalent relationship with elite reformers makes it increasingly difficult for youth to call out reformers on what they perceive to be neglect of community (and specifically youth) demands for racial justice.

What kind of legitimacy and credibility does a partnership with racial justice nonprofits—especially those with youth activist contingents—lend to neoliberal school reforms? Clearly, not all youth and community voice is valuable in this landscape; reformers regularly delegitimize and render invisible youth walkouts and protests connected to larger community collectives that try to salvage neighborhood schools in rapidly gentrifying areas. Given the community outrage over contentious neoliberal reforms, reformers often use civil rights rhetoric and seek alliances with community organizations in order to bring a much-needed legitimacy to the implementation of controversial reforms. In some ways, these community organization-reformer partnerships may actually allow reformers to project a public image of themselves as connected to racial justice groups, open to community critique, and doing right by the very youth they are claiming to save from underperforming schools. Even as they enter into these partnerships, they pursue larger reforms that exacerbate other racial and economic injustices and exclude other communities of color from school reform processes. The struggle of community-based nonprofits to walk the thin line of "no permanent enemies, no permanent allies," and the limited successes that this philosophy brings, is one window through which to view how the neoliberal context of both education reform and the nonprofit industrial complex work in tandem to both facilitate and distort racial justice initiatives as they fight their way into education policy.

Conclusion

As the various movement mobilizations in Denver demonstrate, the resistance to neoliberal education reform is diverse. Resistance to this reform includes mobilizing around instituting more just forms of school choice (e.g., through new inclusive transportation systems) or subverting official systems of school choice altogether (by creating network- and neighborhood-based information sharing rather than relying on district information). It includes the resistance to charterization and the racialized push-out of low-income students of color in the quest to increase the market profile of particular schools. It also involves the resistance to school closures, as well as the fight for comprehensive, inclusive neighborhood schools that are more than just centers for children's learning, but are also vital public institutions and local community anchors.

This vast tapestry of reform resistance reaches beyond the labor organizing of the teachers most commonly featured in the media, who are also on the cutting edge of resistance to market-based education reform. Denver's collection of movements range from the Black and Latinx neighborhood activists who are struggling to regain control of their schools, parks, homes, and businesses in a rapidly gentrifying neighborhood, to the White neighborhood activists who reject school choice and the prospect of sending their children to learn in a neighborhood different from where they live, work, and play. The resistance to neoliberal reform spans the offices of nonprofit organizations—some of which have roots in Denver's 1960s and 1970s era of civil rights organizing and Chicano student activism—and the non-institutionalized movement spaces of neighborhood libraries, recreation centers, and McDonald's playrooms that transform into launching points for community self-determination and social movement action.

Neoliberal reform itself does not passively land on urban centers like Denver from above through mysterious, amorphous, and anonymous processes. To the contrary, the reform movement has actual movers attached to it.[1] They are corporate executives, wealthy philanthropic foundations, and hedge fund managers, to be sure. But as my study shows, they are also elite *local* activists. They are Teach for America alums, congresspeople and senators, journalists, and members of local think tanks and foundations. They are local business leaders. They actively transform neoliberal ideologies into movement rhetoric. They attempt to mobilize voters and taxpayers. And importantly, they do this by engaging in nascent coalition building with specific community partners. Neoliberal education reform relies on an ethic of multiculturalism, an active effort on the part of reformers and reform organizations to translate market-based reform ideologies into virtuous, multiracial civil rights goals.[2] I argue that local elite, pro-reform activists engage in this translation not just by transforming rhetoric, but also by actively seeking out partnerships with specific racial justice organizations and activists around targeted education initiatives. This helps to explain why reformers and some community organizations align with each other in specific moments around specific initiatives. This makes the reform movement even more insidious and difficult to decipher, as it does not indiscriminately reject *all* grassroots social and racial justice initiatives. Through local pro-reform activists, the neoliberal reform movement maintains touch points with authentic racial justice movement goals from below.

In the service of translating market ideologies into civil rights initiatives, the process of neoliberal reform entails a limited mechanism for community inclusion, and therefore opens up a space for grassroots justice movements to gain a foothold in local neoliberal policy processes. The subsequent victories of grassroots movements cannot be understated. However, this same process of community inclusion entails an even more profound process of community exclusion. In seeking out valuable community partners, pro-reform advocates develop paradigms for distinguishing worthy allies from unworthy foes, and therefore worthy social justice goals from unworthy goals. Perhaps not surprisingly, reformers rely on movement institutionalization as a proxy for making this distinction between worthy community allies and unworthy community activists. Those movements that are institutionalized in nonprofit organizations are tied to foundation funding, and operate through targeted campaigns that are more likely to find moments of alliance with elite pro-reform activists than are loosely networked, neighborhood-based movements that lack institutional space, funding, and dedicated staff resources.

Institutionalization is only one indicator of reformer inclusion or exclusion, however. It is no accident that those class-based movements fighting dispossession, urban revitalization, and displacement tend not to have the nonprofit institutional resources enjoyed by other community-based organizations.[3] Not only do reformers reject alliances with these working-class networks, they also engage in the active marginalization and disparagement of these activists and the visions they represent. In this way, the reform movement facilitates dispossession even as it incorporates piecemeal racial justice elements into local reform policies and practices.

Reformers' willingness to align (or not) with grassroots movements does not determine the whole story of how school reform manifests in a given city, however. The grassroots movements themselves also determine the direction of school reform. My goal in this book has not been to simply outline which movements are most successful in impacting education reform policy and which are least successful. Rather, my goal has been to outline the ways classism, racism(s), and movement institutionalization together shape the possibilities for coalition points *between* movements, as well as the disconnections between them. In studying how various movements organize to claim the heart and promise of public education, I have learned that there are strange bedfellows that successfully move specific policies forward. There are also missed opportunities to form important movement coalitions. These missed opportunities can translate into social movement failure and demobilization. The ways movements come together or break apart in part determine the reach of elite neoliberal reform. As these chapters demonstrate, elite White reformers and poor people of color are often on opposite sides of the struggle over public institutions like schools, especially as these institutions are central to different communities' claims to the city.

But if reformers and dispossessed poor people of color are on opposite sides of this struggle, there are also movements that fall on either side, or in between, and they too battle for their vision of schooling and for place and space in the city. Where these movements fall in alliance with these two poles also determines the direction of reform and resistance in cities like Denver. Below, I will spotlight the progressive potential of the surprising movement coalitions that have formed around school reform and educational justice, and will explain how these coalitions create conditions for nesting racial justice initiatives within neoliberal agendas. In mapping movement convergences, I will also underscore the continuity of White middle-class bias in movements that appear on the surface to conflict with each other, in order to demonstrate how the reformist belief that White middle-class resources can save urban schools runs throughout reformer and White-led neighborhood schools movements alike. The continuity of White middle-class bias across different movement sectors undercuts the progressive potential that antiracist campaigns bring to education reform politics.

I will also outline the implications of lost coalitions on reform outcomes. In this discussion, I will spotlight why distinct neighborhood schools movements that seem to share an anti-market ideology fail to coalesce into a larger multiracial movement against the charterization of the public school system and exclusionary systems of school choice. I will discuss why racial justice movements fail to coalesce across institutionalized and non-institutionalized contexts, and the implications of this lost opportunity for racial justice coalitions to more effectively take on the systematic racialized classism of neoliberal school reform. Finally, I will end this chapter by culling the lessons learned from movement victories and shortcomings in order to guide movements toward more effective coalition building. It is only through multiracial, multi-class, multi-issue, and multi-organizational coalition building that various movements can turn back the neoliberal tide and reclaim schools as community-anchored and equitable institutions.

Points of Convergence: Progressive Potential

In their book *A Match on Dry Grass*, the education scholars Mark Warren and Karen Mapp highlight grassroots educational justice movements across the United States that successfully partner with school reformers on key issues. According to Warren and Mapp, it is these grassroots movements that infuse social justice into a larger reform process that has otherwise operated as a top-down "expert-driven and technical enterprise."[4] Indeed, as their case studies show, grassroots movements successfully push social and racial justice initiatives to the forefront of local education reform processes in their cities, and help to institute new models of collaborative decision making in schools. These efforts also increase parent participation in schools, and build vital school-community relationships. Because they are institutionalized movements with committed spaces to meet, stable sources of funding, and staff support, and often they are linked to national networks (the authors name the PICO network as one such example), they also have the potential to make national change. Certainly, the institutionalized nonprofit context carries with it the promise of organizing, launching, and sustaining long-term campaigns that have the capacity to produce palpable and lasting educational change. This is one way that grassroots organizing disrupts the systemic racism rooted in elite neoliberal market-based school reform. Like reformers, some community-based organizations, especially those steeped in the 1960s and 1970s-era progressive movements for racial justice in education, see this historical moment as a promising one for changing education from the ground up. Many of these organizations represent decades-old efforts to mobilize against racist education, and have been fighting long before the reform movement landed in their city. The rhetoric of multiculturalism and civil rights deployed by the reform movement—even if deployed by elites, and even if, as critics claim, it is disingenuous—signals a political opportunity for grassroots movements to usher in a new incarnation of these older struggles. In many ways, this new political opportunity underscores how relatively *closed* the political opportunities in school systems like DPS have been, as they have long been plagued by racial disparities. The importance of this political moment for grassroots organizing to gain a foothold in education policy should not be understated. While it is important to continually criticize the reform movement's proclivity for railroading over community needs, as Pauline Lipman, Thomas Pedroni, and Kristen Buras have shown in their ethnographic studies, we must also not falsely romanticize the pre-reform capacity of the public school system to engage community critique and mobilization.[5] School systems have long been hostile to racial justice community organizing.

Some of the reason for this new political opportunity for specific nonprofit organizations to agitate for racial justice in education, ironically, lies in three major facets of neoliberal reform that dovetail with grassroots organizing. The first, as mentioned above, is what Wayne Au calls "meritocracy 2.0," or the degree to which neoliberal reform adopts a rhetoric of multiculturalism, equity, and civil rights.[6] Although Au emphasizes the extent to which this progressive rhetoric is used deceptively to advance market-based, meritocratic reforms, this racial justice rhetoric aligns with the authentic calls for racial justice from grassroots activists representing low-income communities of color. As a key organizer in one of these community organizations points out in chapter 5, activists running grassroots campaigns don't reject a potential campaign ally simply because that ally does not necessarily share the organization's larger worldview. In the Alinsky model, seasoned organizers running justice campaigns determine who the power holders are, and attempt to move power by compelling these power holders to align with specific nonprofit campaign goals.

As some youth activist scholars have pointed out, youth nonprofits and the structural supports they provide bolster the political power of youth of color in particular. Although Barbara Miner, Janelle Scott, Wayne Au, and other critics of the neoliberal education reform movement's use of civil rights rhetoric rightly see this rhetoric as a disingenuous cloak for the marketization and privatization of education, the racial rhetoric of reformers positions youth of color as the ultimate objects of saving.[7] I argue that although unintentional, this objectification of youth of color in the "meritocracy 2.0" of neoliberal reform actually creates a small window of political opportunity that youth of color can exploit through their development as activists in institutionalized nonprofit organizations. As Black and Latinx youth activists quoted in chapter 5 point out, their voices carry a particular weight in school reform policy discussions, since overwhelmingly the policy discussions rhetorically put them at the center. If neoliberal policy is cloaked in civil rights discourse, certainly the major objects of racial justice become the individual, disadvantaged kids that well-meaning but paternalistic reformers are claiming to save from "broken" neighborhoods and "self-interested" teachers.[8] When youth themselves interject their voices into policy debates and discussions directly with reformers, they gain a modicum of moral high ground. Overwhelmingly, the nonprofit context facilitates young people's political education, voice, and connections to powerful policy makers and reformers, who are predominantly White.[9] In this sense, there are facets of neoliberalism that actually strengthen *some* youth voices in school reform debates. These include neoliberal civil rights rhetoric, which overwhelmingly positions low-income Black and Brown youth as the objects of reformer saving, and the nonprofit movement organizational context that gives youth the staff support, space, and mentorship to speak directly to elites.

At the same time, reformer alliances with some youth-centered organizations help to publicly position reformers as siding *with*, instead of *against*, youth of color, which bolsters their image of doing right by the very youth they are claiming to save. This public alliance, crystallized in photo opportunities with Black and Latinx youth, seems to be mutually beneficial, even if only momentarily. It allows these nonprofit organizations to frame their work as effective and powerful. Since they demand a seat at the table with reform elites, they are positioned not just to speak directly to power, but also to be *heard*. This alliance allows reformers to frame their movement as cooperative with diverse city residents and responsive to community demands. The public makeover of reformer movement image via these moments of publicized alliance becomes important for the reformer movement as well, especially as community distrust grows in the wake of failed school reform experiments around the city. Neither a clear one-sided movement victory for grassroots activists nor a one-sided movement victory for the reform movement, these partnerships partially facilitated by a shared rhetoric of racial equity still translate into a complex mutual relationship that advances both market-based education reform *and* racial justice. These strange bedfellows may help to explain why Denver's brand of neoliberal school reform, as in other cities like it, is shot through with threads of progressive social change.

In addition to "meritocracy 2.0," two other facets of neoliberal reform that unexpectedly open up a space for social justice organizing from below are the core ethics of "urgency" and "accountability." As critics have pointed out, these have been used to curtail the participation of movement groups in education reform processes.[10] However, in the case of Denver and other cities where local reformers work to build nascent coalitions with area social justice groups, these core values of neoliberal school reform also resonate with grassroots struggles that have been raging long before neoliberalism became the guiding philosophy of education policy. Although reformers' indignant demands for accountability and urgency could very well have been appropriated from authentic grassroots community campaigns for educational justice, they still stand as values that community-based movement organizations also share. As activists housed in nonprofits explain, if the shared goal is to hold school districts accountable to promises of equity and closing the achievement gap, then the alliance with reformers is a worthy one. Educational justice activists, especially those who have been agitating for decades, also grow tired of the slow, bureaucratic pace of change across a school district. If they are participants in the process, then an urgent timeline for radical educational change is also desirable. I saw this in action in community forums that put school district officials and reformers in the hot seat. Community organizations, in front of the media and their constituents, and on their own organizational territory, assertively remind district officials and policy makers that they are organized and they are watching. They expect substantive social change quickly. This community power—the power to hold schools accountable for educational failure—also dovetails with reformers' notions of what real community power *should* be. Rather than acting as architects or co-creators of education policy, reformers believe that respectable community organizations act as external forces to the reform process—agitating when reform fails to move swiftly and efficiently, and raising hell to make sure reform is not stymied by the worst parts of educational bureaucracy. In the reformer imagination, the demonized stakeholders who defend the "status quo" rather than advocate much-needed change are the teachers unions and their presumably allied low-income neighborhood schools advocates.

In these partnerships and processes, reformers and nonprofit movement activists see community power differently. Community organizations view themselves as organized watchdogs, directing urgent change in the school system by agitating from the ground up. Reformers view these community organizations as fundamentally *cooperative* with and ancillary to market-based reform, echoing reformers' calls for a radical and urgent overhaul of the American school system. Despite these vast differences in perspective regarding the proper role of community-based organizations in school reform, urgency and accountability become shared paradigms through which reformers and grassroots organizations come together around specific educational justice goals.

It is not accidental that these convergences between grassroots organizations and the elite reform movement hinge on the institutionalization or nonprofitization of the justice movements from below. In the case of Denver, there is not one instance in which reformers could name a valuable alliance with a grassroots group that is not a formal nonprofit. In fact, in their careful parsing out of valuable allies versus foes, reformers regularly disparage and dismiss non-institutionalized neighborhood-based groups as misinformed, misguided, and blindly loyal to their failing neighborhood schools. This begs the question of how institutionalized and non-institutionalized grassroots movements operate differently in their coalition strategies and their social change tactics. What is it about the institutionalized social movement organization that makes it especially amenable to partnership with elite reformers?

In Denver, a striking similarity runs throughout community-based nonprofit struggles for educational justice and transformation. The dictum "no permanent enemies, no permanent allies" operates as a guiding philosophy for the launch of various campaigns like ending the school-to-jail track; expanding the promise of school choice through new transportation policies; or increasing student voice in teacher evaluation procedures. The "no permanent enemies, no permanent allies" approach, a strategy rooted in Alinsky's post-Depression community organizing, has become a principle that syncs well with the neoliberal moment of movement institutionalization. In this movement context, social justice struggles are segmented into fundable and distinct campaigns as governments cut their social spending. These campaigns are supported by foundation grants, or are enmeshed in national movement organizational networks. Often, this funding comes with strings attached—the requirement of "deliverables" or quantitative benchmarks for campaign success. As I have argued elsewhere, and as Soo Ah Kwon has underscored in her study of the neoliberalization of the youth nonprofit, the transformation of qualitative social justice goals into quantifiable benchmarks of "success" can sometimes repress youth political power and therefore movement power.[11] As Kwon argues, it is this nonprofitization of youth activism that acts as a mechanism to *manage* youth of color rather than empower them to directly challenge structural inequalities, and masks state divestment from public resources like schools. This divestment fundamentally characterizes the neoliberal era.[12] Furthermore, as John Arena argues, nonprofitization also moves marginalized and minoritized communities toward single-issue and identity politics, and away from the kind of class-based, multi-issue, and multiracial politics that could launch a more successful movement resistance against neoliberal capitalist accumulation.[13]

Movement institutionalization, and the segmenting of movement goals into distinct justice campaigns, affords institutionalized movement organizations the latitude to foreground guiding movement principles like "no permanent enemies, no permanent allies." As these nonprofit activists note in chapter 5, this means that one "enemy" or target in one campaign (for example, a campaign to institute in-state college tuition for undocumented students) could very well be an ally for another campaign (for example, a campaign to support a regional transportation system to better realize the promised liberty of school choice). While this can be confusing for nonprofit community activists to navigate (as one organizational ally can be in another instance that same organization's target), it gives their organizations the freedom and ability to leverage elite resources in the service of what they see as homegrown, community-generated educational equity goals. This has enabled some community nonprofits to make piecemeal change within the reformist agenda, forcing authentic racial justice goals into neoliberal processes. Even more powerfully, since these organizations sometimes have connections to national organizations, networks, and funded campaigns, they are able to coordinate racial justice campaigns that hold the potential to make local impact while extending nationally. Far from simply being dupes of the reformer movement, these institutionalized movements—through their campaigns and careful analysis of ever-shifting allies and enemies—are able to gain entry into elite education policy making and usher in important grassroots victories. In another section of this conclusion, however, I will detail the *cost* of these victories both to the nonprofit organizers themselves and to the other collectives of low-income people of color who organize outside the formal nonprofit context, and who are ultimately left behind in these negotiations.

Points of Convergence: White Middle-Class Hegemony across Opposing Movement Contexts

Elite reform networks and nonprofit grassroots movement organizations find moments of partnership along lines of key stated values, even if these values, especially on the reformer side, operate as opportunistic rhetorical devices and are momentary. These values include "civil rights," "urgency," and "accountability." However, there are other convergences between seemingly disparate movements in the landscape of school reform politics. There is a relationship between the elite reformer movement and the overwhelmingly White neighborhood activist networks that fight for control over their neighborhood schools. Although these different groups clash around some core tenets of neoliberal school reform—namely, the marketization of schooling and the accompanying systems of school choice—they share key underlying values that allow for movement convergence and limited movement victories for White middle-class newly settled residents.

Chapter 2, which features the voices of the reformers themselves, reveals that these advocates view themselves as civil rights heroes who are qualified—even *more* qualified than teachers, students, or other neighborhood stakeholders—to radically redesign schools and launch new reform experiments in low-income neighborhoods. From where do these presumed qualifications come? For reformers, who have a long history of consuming "quality" education (even if this education was private schooling), one qualification is having "good" experiences of schooling in order to know what good schooling is. When reformers charge that low-income neighborhood schools activists fall victim to misguided "happy talk" or knee-jerk nostalgia for their neighborhood schools, they imply that low-income neighborhood residents have no model for quality education to reference in their visions of educational justice. In contrast, elite reformers, who do not live in the neighborhoods in which they institute new school experiments, and who do not send their children to these experimental schools (nor would they ever, as they openly admit), trust their colleagues' visions of what education reform should be. In their worldview, reformers hold all the cultural and economic capital, and poor Black and Latinx children and their families hold none. Reformers therefore congratulate themselves for recognizing their own privilege and their willingness to "give" some of their cultural capital to less privileged "others." Indeed, they insist on giving their privileged perspective over and against the stated visions that communities themselves put forward, "for their own good."

This paternalistic perspective is problematic for many reasons. First, it relies on a deficit model of the communities that public schools serve. When reformers argue that they are more privileged and are therefore *obligated* to share their privileged perspectives on and prescriptions for public schooling, elite and exclusionary reform becomes a "gift" of sorts to less privileged people.[14] This benevolent vision allows reformers to ignore or minimize their role in community dispossession. Second, when reformers congratulate themselves on recognizing their privilege and cultural capital, and on being willing to *share* their privilege (e.g., instituting dress codes like polo shirts and khakis in reformed schools that mimic the environment of corporate workplaces), rarely do they investigate the root inequalities that determine *why* they are privileged in the first place. What makes them privileged? As critics like Linda Darling-Hammond have claimed, school reform rhetoric about school "failure," "accountability," "equity," and "achievement gaps" obfuscates the root historical causes of contemporary educational injustices.[15] The role of state divestment, the late twentieth-century backlash against desegregation and the resulting resegregation of schools, the growing wealth gap, tax revolts, and other political developments in recent decades that have deepened inequality along racial and class lines are all rendered invisible in reformer rhetoric about educational inequality.

On the other hand, the White gentry who revolt against school choice, refuse to drive their children across town for a "better" education, and rally for access to comprehensive neighborhood schools appear to hold progressive promise for fighting the White-dominated, neoliberal tide in public education. Their refusal to view schools as products, and their embrace of collectivist orientations to their neighborhood schools seem to indicate a White neighborhood movement that is ready to link arms with Black and Latinx activists who are also fighting to reclaim their neighborhood schools from the market. Like many Black and Latinx neighborhood schools activists, they too are deeply distrustful of the neoliberal reformer movement. Some of these White middle-class activists are especially distrustful of the corporate reformer model because they see the flaws and corruption up close in their own corporate work-places. This is one reason many of them leave these workplaces to pursue individual consulting work or other forms of self-employment.

Chapter 4 features the voices of parents who refuse to see their children as "special" and therefore worthy of the best educational products on the market. They take risks to commit to their neighborhood schools in ways that the reform movement does not anticipate, thwarting the re-former expectation that White affluent urban newcomers will welcome "islands of excellence" in a "crappy urban district" and will exercise their financial and spatial mobility to get their children into the best schools the system has to offer. Their collectivism runs directly counter to the deep-seated neoliberal value of individual choice and mobility in the quest for educational excellence. As they move into more affordable and central low-income neighborhoods with recent histories of rezoned, re-segregated, and underfunded schools now labeled "failing" or "in crisis," they are also subject to reformers' mandates for school turnarounds, clo-sures, and educational experimentation. For a moment, the gentry also becomes subject to the kind of radical school reforms most often expe-rienced by low-income Black and Latinx communities.

However, what undergirds their refusal of market-based choice and their risk to commit their children to "failing" neighborhood schools is strikingly similar to the racial and class privilege that is part and parcel of White elite reformers' sense of benevolence and heroism. The White gentry who value the cultural flavor of the Black and Latinx neighbor-hoods and the ideal of culturally diverse neighborhood schools believe that schools should be first and foremost *community anchors* instead of valuable educational *products*. They believe this precisely because of their faith in their own families and households to supplement the cul-tural and social capital necessary for future success. White and relatively affluent neighborhood schools activists take these collectivist risks to rally for their neighborhood schools because they know they can access private tutoring if they need it and professional networks of knowledge workers to which they can connect their children when the time comes for job hunting or college selection.[16] They also take these risks because ultimately, despite their commitment to the neighborhood school as the lifeblood of their neighborhoods, they have faith that since they are giv-ing up their privilege by rejecting school choice, they can always fall back on that privilege should the neighborhood school somehow fail their children. Their ability to drive far distances and the employment and temporal flexibility that knowledge-work affords enable these activists to feel secure should their mobilizing efforts for strong and accessible neighborhood schools fail to compel elite reformers.

More profoundly, however, the movement of the White gentry to reject school choice and embrace diverse, multicultural neighborhood schools also rests on two core assumptions held by these educational activists. The first is that their commitment to the city's public schools, as affluent middle-class urban residents, is a *valuable asset* to the city's economic growth and *should actively be promoted* by school reform. And they are not wrong in their perception of their worth in the larger goal of capital accumulation. The reform movement, with a focus on "revitalizing" urban education, has long been interested in wooing back the leagues of White families that fled urban districts a generation before under court-ordered desegregation. Their investment in public schools—and the potential resources this investment brings—not only promises to enrich the school system; it is also *the* key to urban revitalization.[17] If the schools look appealing to the creative class, those creative knowledge workers will pour their resources and innovation into cities, and will help to transform urban centers like Denver—and certainly like New York and Chicago—into increasingly recognized anchors for business, globalization, and capital accumulation.[18]

The second assumption held by these White neighborhood schools activists is that their cultural, social, and financial capital will improve neighborhood schools for *everyone*. Although the activists featured in chapter 4 had different ways of framing their assets—most often in terms of "proficiency"—they all took for granted that their participation in and commitment to neighborhood schools would transform "failing" schools into high-quality and even highly rated institutions. Therefore, the reluctance of their Latinx immigrant neighbors to join them in their fight to reclaim their schools from elite reformers baffled them. Why would a low-income neighborhood resident of color refuse to link arms with a neighborhood mobilization that could transform their children's school into a shining example of a well-resourced, diverse, welcoming, culturally inclusive community institution? In White neighborhood schools activists' worldview, everyone wins when the new gentry commits to the neighborhood school and to the larger fight to protect these schools from reform experimentation.

Like the reformers whom they criticize so harshly, the White gentry *also* view themselves as heroic in the struggle to deliver educational equity to those who have long been denied it. They see their test score proficiency—the centerpiece of standardized testing and the basis for the sorting of schools into "good" or "substandard" educational products in urgent need of eliminating or revamping—as undeniable gifts to the less privileged families who live just around the corner from them. And like the reformers, these neighborhood activists render invisible the very sources of their privilege. This is especially true in their narratives of gentrification. Rather than seeing themselves as unfairly benefitting from their low-income neighbors' dispossession, or seeing themselves as active contributors to the very gentrification process that threatens to erase the "cool" of their new neighborhoods, they frame gentrification as a passive process that is inevitable and mysteriously removed from their own agency. While they might lament the changes gentrification brings to a neighborhood that was at first desirable precisely because it represented the antithesis to the more racially homogeneous and "culture-less" suburbs, they also actively resist seeing their own role in contributing to these changes. In both cases of the elite reformers and the White neighborhood schools activists who mobilize to counter reformers, the belief in their own heroism, cultural capital, and resources means that elite reformers and White neighborhood activists both frame their mobilizing as a "gift" they are giving to low-income people of color. They both express surprise when the recipients of this supposed gift fail to join their movement. This allows them to wage battles for public education that fail to meaningfully include the very people of color they claim to be fighting for.

The gentry's movement for strong neighborhood schools that was featured in chapter 4 eventually fell apart. Racial and class capital enabled these activists to retreat from activism, and the mechanisms for school choice and other resources these activists had at their disposal enabled them to exit from their neighborhood school as soon as it became clear that the reformist district was not yielding to their organizing pressure. For a moment, they experienced an exclusion from school reform processes, and a devaluation of the possible assets they could bring to the school system. Their movement failed to draw more of the Latinx families connected to their school, which also contributed to their demobilization.

However, it must be noted that part of the fuel for their organizing in the first place was the inspiration they received from the previous movement successes of similar struggles for comprehensive and accessible neighborhood schools. There had been other community mobilizations around specific schools in the same sector of the city, where architects, lawyers, city planners, and other professionals leveraged their social networks and skills to work in tandem with the reformist school district to proactively reshape a "failing" neighborhood middle school. These previous successes, which were more proactive than reactive, also point to the potential for White middle-class neighborhood schools activists to successfully harness reform efforts to their own ends. These activists who identify themselves as neighborhood schools champions rather than "reformers" enjoy periodic success in mobilizing resources and localized support around visions for specific neighborhood schools. This is most typical in gaps between when a given neighborhood school is deemed "failing" by the district and when the district institutes specific turnaround strategies that it mandates from the top down. To wedge themselves into this critical gap, neighborhood movement activists need to be already well resourced and networked with each other in order to get the ear of reformers. In the case of previous battles for other elementary and middle schools in the neighborhood, well-connected affluent residents mobilized quickly in this critical gap in order to advance their own visions of quality, accessible, and diverse neighborhood schools. Importantly, they also had the kind of cultural capital that reformers respected from the get-go, including their own histories of presumably trustworthy and "good" education (versus the presumably "untrustworthy" educational histories that guide the preferences of low-income Black and Latinx neighborhood schools activists).

These White activists also utilize the same rhetoric of multiculturalism and educational equity that reformers use. In these specific cases of movement success, reformers and the reform-oriented district relent to the community pressure launched *before* school turnaround or closure, and even grow to support the community fight for neighborhood schools. In the case of McDonwell Elementary School, however, families mobilized *in reaction* to a chain of events that were already in motion to radically turn around their school. These events included the district's firing a large portion of the school's teachers; hiring a new principal without community input or transparency; and suddenly changing the curricular focus of the school, again, without community input.

In this sense, although they are non-institutionalized (e.g., they do not have stable sources of funding, they do not have formal 501(c) 3 status, and they don't necessarily have formal organizational spaces and staff), there are moments when non-institutionalized neighborhood movements are able to convince reformers that their buy-in to a given school is *valuable*, and will result in that school's success. If the reform movement aims to integrate more affluent families into a school district that has for decades served a majority low-income student population, this represents one political opportunity for a gentry-led neighborhood schools movement to push back on market-based prescriptions for school reform. These movements have the chance to manifest the kinds of quality neighborhood schools they dream of, in the very hearts of the neighborhoods in which they live, so that they can live, work, and educate their children in the same geographical space.

This confluence of living, schooling, and working in the same neighborhood, however, deepens the gentry's connection to the neighborhood and intensifies their sense of ownership over it. In essence, White affluent mobilizations around specific neighborhood schools successfully resist neoliberal marketization while deepening the White settler colonialism that is also endemic to neoliberal urban revitalization. As Chase Billingham writes,

> It is not necessarily the intrusion of the market into the public domain that leads to educational stratification in cities, but rather the operation of exclusionary social closure mechanisms championed by affluent urban residents and implemented by municipalities eager to use public schools as an amenity designed to attract and retain prosperous families.[19]

The gentry's focus on their own test score "proficiency" as an undeniable gift to Black and Latinx "others" in their neighborhood and the key to school stability and autonomy ironically transforms into a market mechanism itself.[20] As quantitative ratings and scores increase at these schools, the institutions earn a reputation for excellence in a larger land-scape of school choice. They become desirable market products precisely because of their reputation for being islands of protection against the vagaries of district reforms. As a result, more White families are drawn to the neighborhood, home prices shoot up, and new settler families flock to the school. Soon, the school no longer serves a critical mass of low-income families of color.

However, as the failure of community activism around McDon-well Elementary demonstrates, elite reformers do not always trust the gentry's neighborhood schools movements. This is particularly true if they are mobilized in reaction to mandated and reformer-designed turnaround, and if they fail to demonstrate that they have buy-in from communities of color. Reformers can easily dismiss their protests as the uninformed rantings of non-institutionalized, disconnected, and self-interested activists, and can frame their own continued plans for reform as serving the needs of the low-income students of color who are largely shut out of these loosely organized neighborhood movements. One elite reformer at a local reform organization explained her take on these White middle-class movements for neighborhood schools in this city sector, and admitted why these loosely organized movements lose credibility and traction:

> I'm really frustrated by the fact that I feel like there are some isolated voices that are very vocal and they create the tone and the perception of what this community wants. And I'm not convinced they're talking about what a lot of people want. Some people may not like the process for district decision making around charters, but they might agree with the outcome and want to send their kid there. They don't care if it's a charter, magnet school, innovation school, or who knows what. They just want a good school that works.
>
> I feel like we never have constructive conversations where we can come to the table and say, "I think this, I think this, let's talk that through and find a common ground and then create an agenda or let's do some things around that common agenda." I feel like that never happens, be-cause there hasn't been the leadership to make that happen. I think that's it. I don't think it's ill will on the part of these different voices. There's just been no one either committed to or able to create that leadership.

To a certain extent, the polarization in Denver and the lack of cohesion serves the district well, because they can make whatever decisions
they want and can point to those voices and simply say, "You all aren't on
the same page."

Movement disorganization and non-institutionalization, even when
led by "valuable" and resourced White settler residents, can be dismissed by reformers as lacking leadership and vision, cooperation and
strategy, willingness to compromise, and most importantly the buy-in
from neighboring communities of color. The institutionalization of
movements—such as that of established nonprofit community-based
organizations—can help to protect from this kind of reformer dismissal
and delegitimization.

Points of Divergence: The Impact of Lost Coalitions

Lost Coalitions: The Fight for Neighborhood Schools

Many critics of neoliberal school reform worry that the reform movement has destroyed the promise of public schooling to be the great
equalizer in the United States. Education historian and analyst Diane
Ravitch argues that the "billionaire boys club" has marketized the
school system by destroying the potential for traditional, comprehensive neighborhood schools to thrive and to more equitably serve the
communities around them.[21] As I have demonstrated in this book, there
is a broad resistance to school choice, charterization, school closures,
and co-locations, and what these signal in terms of the weakening of
the public neighborhood school model. In fact, reformers themselves
lament that there is always more public support for traditional neighborhood schools than there is for charters, and insist that community
organizing *in support* of charter schools should be a top priority of the
reform movement.

I ended chapter 3 with the perspective of Bruce, the head of a progressive statewide organization who sympathizes with the plight of dispossessed Latinx and Black city residents mobilizing against school reform
experimentation and the closure of their local schools. Fundamentally,
these networks of activists fight to reclaim their local schools from
what they view as elite, White supremacist reform. Although ideologi-

cally aligned with this fight, Bruce is reluctant to commit his nonprofit organization's resources to the fight against reform, since he perceives that the fight would be too stacked against him. In Denver, as in other reform hot spots, local foundations and mainstream media have been overwhelmingly pro-reform. However, he predicts that the movement to reclaim neighborhood schools will gain traction as more communities feel the impact of reform experimentation. Bruce feels that White, relatively advantaged urban neighborhood residents will one day be mobilized to fight the reform movement, since they will also bear the brunt of haphazard and radical reform in their communities. He argues that once they get into the fight, they will be able to move the resistance even further, given their financial, social, and voting power. At that moment, progressive nonprofit organizers like Bruce will consider taking on the fight and giving it an organizational home.

Is Bruce right? Is there a tipping point at which the casualties of school reform look more White and affluent, and this common thread is enough to forge a truly multi-class and multiracial resistance that stands a chance of winning community control of neighborhood schools? Indeed, in gentrifying areas, the very White middle-class newcomers whom urban planners and school reform districts are trying to woo back to the city end up being caught in the storm of rapid school redesigns, turnarounds, and closures. As in the case of low-income Black and Latinx neighborhood residents, these quick, exclusionary reforms feel more like betrayal and haphazard experimentation. In some cases, reform experiments spur enough collective indignation to produce organized action. As sociologists Thomas Beamish and Amy Luebbers assert, a shared sense of place is an important asset in cross-movement coalitions: "Attention to the role of place-experience shifts analysis away from a solely discursive account and towards the nexus of both lived experience and the social and cultural currents that embed activists and movements."[22]

Bruce is right to imagine that since they share the same lived experience of place and the same embattled community institutions as their neighbors, White gentrifiers are therefore positioned similarly to low-income communities of color vis-à-vis school reform, but I argue that a number of factors impede the formation of such a powerful neighborhood schools coalition and override this shared experience of place. The first is that in this sector of Denver, the White gentry organize their battles around particular schools—*their* schools—while their low-income counterparts across the river organize both locally in their neighborhoods and *beyond* their neighborhoods. As in the case of the Democrats for Educational Justice (DEJ), largely led by women of color, neighborhood schools movements morph into campaigns for voter power, and connect to other racial justice efforts like criminal justice reform, access to healthcare, and economic justice issues. The White gentry can more easily make school choice work for them, whether this means driving their children to a different neighborhood for their education; homeschooling their children; moving to a different (and perhaps better-performing) suburban district; or opting out of the public system entirely and sending their children to private school. Their movements, like the mobilization to reclaim Mc-Donwell Elementary, tend to be short-lived. School choice as a policy and the social and cultural capital of White neighborhood activists conspire to facilitate these activists' demobilization. School choice also unmoors these advantaged activists from their shared lived experience of place, which undercuts one potential resource for coalescing across race, ethnic, and class positionality differences.

The second factor that impedes multiracial and multi-class organizing around reclaiming neighborhood schools is that these White neighborhood activists are buoyed by their belief in the ultimate goodness of their own resources, privilege, and *value* to their low-income counterparts of color and to the city at large. They refuse to recognize their own contributions to gentrification, displacement, and dispossession. This renders their ability to draw critical Black and Latinx voices to their fight for neighborhood schools difficult. The less able they are to engage in difficult discussions around racial tensions and gentrification, the less able they are to build trusting partnerships with the low-income communities of color who are also disadvantaged by neoliberal reform. This means the more credibility they lose in the eyes of reformers and the reform-oriented district. In order to discredit their efforts, the reform movement easily dismisses these activists as disorganized and not representative of a given neighborhood community. Reformers also dismiss these activists as self-interested and working *against* diversity, educational equity, and inclusiveness, which further bolsters reformers' claims to the moral high ground of racial equity.

Importantly, the racial and class divide between these neighborhood movements to reclaim the local school demonstrates the degree to which the cores of these movements are vastly different, even if market-based reform remains the shared target and thus a potential point of movement convergence. In the case of the low-income activists in the African American Parent Project (AAPP), the Community Education Collective (CEC), and Democrats for Educational Justice (DEJ), their organizing is fundamentally against a broader community fragmentation, displacement, and dispossession. Their fight for neighborhood schools cannot be abstracted from their fight to keep their homes, community businesses, and public parks in a city that is becoming more expensive to live in, more hostile to low-income communities of color, and more intent on remaking neighborhoods into desirable places for more affluent people to settle.

Contrast this with the anti-reform movements of White middle-class newcomers who also fight for their neighborhood schools. Their mobilizing actually serves as an extension of their desire to intensify their ownership and connectedness to their newly settled neighborhoods. Despite their good intentions, their seemingly radical surrender of privilege and entitlement to "islands of excellence" within a given city school portfolio, and their stated commitment to neighborhood diversity, these activists do not see gentrification and displacement as an urgent problem that needs to be addressed. On the contrary, these neighborhood newcomers feel an entitlement to their neighborhood's public institutions. This root difference between these two types of neighborhood schools movements means that the resistance to school reform marketization and the community fight for neighborhood schools are far-reaching but profoundly fragmented along racial and class lines. This fragmentation further enables the elite reformer movement to gain traction and maintain local hegemony.

Lost Coalitions: The Fight for Racial and Economic Justice

Another lost opportunity for movement coalition lies in the struggles waged by communities of color inside and outside formal movement organizations. Since they share a similar open critique of White supremacy in education policy, it would seem that movement networks largely led by Latinx and Black community activists would find points of convergence across institutionalized and non-institutionalized contexts. I witnessed one of these key moments, in which Black neighborhood schools activists attended a nonprofit organization's strategic organizing session to halt the school-to-prison pipeline in Denver Public Schools, since these neighborhood school activists also have strong criticisms of the racial disparity in school discipline systems and see up close the unfair treatment of their own children in DPS schools. This moment, however, was short-lived. In just under an hour, these neighborhood schools activists excused themselves from the meeting and did not return to participate in any of the organization's campaigns. This was one of the very few instances of overlap I witnessed in the course of my multi-year research, and even this moment was remarkably fleeting.

In Denver, there is a stark divide between institutionalized and non-institutionalized racial justice movements. This divide is reflected in the issues that the organizations take on and the alliances they build. For non-institutionalized Black and Latinx neighborhood schools activists, the resistance against school reform is fundamentally nested in their larger critiques of urban revitalization and development. Their fight against school reform is anchored in their experiences of community displacement and dispossession. By and large, their opposition to urban development in their backyards is unpopular and unpalatable to local political representatives, local mainstream media, and local foundations. They network, consciousness-raise, and hell-raise in their interpersonal interactions with each other, with reformers, with White neighborhood newcomers, with local school leaders, and at the ballot box.

In contrast, the activists in community-based nonprofits transform their grassroots campaigns for racial justice into initiatives that are fundable and winnable through progressive local, regional, and national foundations. They coordinate with reformers in ongoing discussions on shared goals of accountability, urgency, and equity. As they gain a seat at the negotiating table, they push reformers to foreground authentic racial justice initiatives in their policy reforms. They harness media to spotlight their capacity to hold elite political representatives and reformers accountable to their promises to fix the school system. By continually negotiating and pushing, they compel reformers to make substantive change rather than to continually engage in empty rhetoric.

Nonprofit activists' delicate dance with reformers shifts from campaign to campaign. It does not represent a knee-jerk, permanent partnership. Rather, it is a reflection of a very careful, deliberate, and strategic process. But from the outside, it appears to their non-institutionalized counterparts like an organizational "selling out" and a fundamental betrayal. For these neighborhood schools activists, there are very clear enemies: key foundations that continually fund school reform experiments; specific political representatives who carry the torch for school reform and predatory urban development; elite reformers in the school district; specific school board members who openly identify as reformers; and other untrustworthy players in city school reform politics. Furthermore, in practice some of these non-permanent alliances tend to take on a quasi-permanence the longer that community nonprofits are at the table. As community organizations gain power and standing, they also become valuable to reformers as community partners. This is both a blessing and a curse. On one hand, it allows nonprofits to continue to drive educational justice forward, but on the other hand it means that from time to time, community partners have to temper their messages as they engage with reformers and the larger public.

Ultimately, nonprofit activists push forward agendas that hold the promise of disrupting the White supremacy of the elite school reform movement and making substantial changes to education policy. They can and should be credited for forcing reformers to realize their rhetorical promises of equity. At the same time, these organizations are tacitly willing to overlook reformers' exclusionary, class-based practices with other low-income populations of color like those featured in chapter 3. Their formal social justice campaigns mostly sidestep the issues of gentrification and urban displacement in order to partner on other potentially viable and urgent educational justice goals. In her analysis of LGBTQ and immigrant rights coalitions that cultivate a collective civil rights identity, political scientist and legal scholar Erin Adam points out how these rights-based coalitions contain a powerful paradox that makes them both inclusive and exclusive at the same time:

> On the one hand, coalitions sometimes can form across movements, contributing to new partnerships, fostering lasting unity across organizations that represent people who hold seemingly disparate identities,

and facilitating rights campaign "wins." On the other hand, these newly formed coalitions often reinforce existing hierarchical exclusions through the continued marginalization of those issues that uproot conventional power dynamics the most.[23]

The relative inability of racial justice activists to partner across institutionalized and non-institutionalized movement contexts limits the potential for racial justice campaigns to more powerfully conquer neoliberal racist reforms and engage in fights that arguably "uproot conventional power dynamics the most." These fights would be represented by educational justice campaigns that explicitly oppose gentrification, dispossession, and displacement. Although community nonprofits have undeniably won progressive and important changes in school reform designs, the split between racial justice movements is a consequence of the ways institutionalization itself has shaped movement organizing in recent decades. The nonprofitization of racial justice, and specifically of *youth* organizing, adds specific funding and political constraints.[24] Institutionalization can transform multi-issue struggles into discrete campaigns that are fundable and winnable, and are therefore able to more effectively move policy forward.

Nonprofits win their victories, however, by sacrificing the broader racial justice agendas of low-income and working-class people of color. In his critique of Saul Alinsky's continued influence on contemporary progressive political organizing, writer and organizer Aaron Petcoff argues that the apolitical pragmatism of the "no permanent enemies, no permanent allies" approach, which champions the maintenance of a professional class of organizers who work for single-issue, winnable campaigns, "has shut the door to more democratic and transformational forms of working-class mobilization."[25] Nonprofitization and movement institutionalization, in this sense, can produce racial justice mobilizations that contain both regressive and progressive elements.[26] In this sense, nonprofits—even those that are well meaning and even explicitly antiracist—can facilitate broader neoliberal agendas like settler colonialism, even as they actively confront other inequities in education reform (e.g., the school-to-prison pipeline, food insecurity in schools, and inequitable transportation systems that deny families adequate educational choices). Certainly, the nonprofit community activists featured in chapter 5 do not express opposition toward those communities fighting against gentrification, dispossession, and displacement. In fact, many of their organizations' members also discuss these as important issues facing communities of color in their backstage discussions. Unfortunately, these discussions rarely make it into their formal organizational campaigns.[27]

Bruce, the director of the statewide progressive nonprofit who is featured at the end of chapter 3, serves as a compelling example of the difficult position in which racial justice organizers find themselves in a landscape dominated by the neoliberal reform movement. Bruce knows that if he takes on the fight to oppose school reform—especially if this is framed as a fight against a larger elite project of gentrification—he will end up alienating his organization's existing funders who also take a pro-education reform stance.

Unlike the two anti-reform neighborhood schools movements featured in chapters 3 and 4, which are marked by deep ideological differences around the relative value of White middle-class resources and the larger racialized forces of gentrification, the racial justice movements featured in chapters 3 and 5 are *not* marked by such deep ideological differences. Instead, they are marked by profoundly different organizational contexts and strategies to take on the elite reform movement. Up against a powerful White elite, nonprofit racial justice activists must secure as many political and economic resources as possible in order to launch campaigns that result in political victories for students of color and their families in the DPS system. In carefully crafting their strategies and culling their resources, they must sometimes jettison other grassroots political agendas that will fail to gain resources and political traction, and might even endanger their careful relationships with policy makers, the media, and school district officials. In order to *move* power, they must engage *with* power.

This means that the struggle over public schooling becomes an ongoing conversation and negotiation between elite reformers and a small handful of community organizations that are resourced, but simply unable to adequately represent the full scope of racial justice issues in education reform or all of the marginalized constituencies in the city. As a result, institutionalized grassroots community mobilizing actually *narrows* as it pursues concrete educational change. Johnson's analysis of how the mass protests against police brutality in Baltimore and Chicago in 2015 were eventually quelled is instructive: "The dissipation of popular energy by nonprofits, and the opportunistic maneuvers of both black and white political elites of various stripes had the combined effect of deflecting mass pressure and preserving the status quo."[28] Even as we recognize and laud movement victories in education reform, we must ask which and *whose* grassroots agendas are sacrificed in this process of this narrowing.[29] As in the case of the split between neighborhood schools movements that express similar critiques of school choice, charterization, and the corporate reform movement, the split between institutionalized and non-institutionalized racial justice movements actually *enables* the continued hegemony of the neoliberal reform movement in cities like Denver, despite the city's broad array of grassroots resistance movements. It also stymies cross-racial coalition building between low-income Black and Latinx communities, much to the dismay of the actual activists on either side of the nonprofit/non-institutionalized divide. Critical education scholars Sonya Douglass Horsford, Enrique Alemán Jr., and Phillip A. Smith argue that although the experiences of "being raced" relative to Whiteness do not automatically forge a connection between Black and Brown people, these distinct experiences and their legacies *could* converge into a potent political race coalition. This coalition would include a shared political agenda, the recognition of a shared fate, and the development of a Black and Brown fight "for educational justice that can serve as a lever for building community power," particularly in the face of neoliberal education reform.[30] However, the split between institutionalized and non-institutionalized resistance, at least in the Denver case, poses yet one more barrier to realizing such a Black-Brown alliance.

How Community Movements Reclaim Education, and Where They Fall Short

The periodic convergence of reformers and grassroots activists demonstrates the reach and potential for community movements to harness neoliberal reform to their own ends. In the case of Denver, there are two community-based, grassroots efforts that stand out as at least *partially* successful. The first is the mobilization and strategic action of institutionalized movements for social justice, which operate by a guiding philosophy of "no permanent enemies, no permanent allies." This coalition philosophy adapts well to the neoliberal value of "agility" that also guides successful corporate ventures and ensures organizational survival.[31] But these movements also seize the political opportunities that neoliberal notions of multiculturalism present.[32] They dovetail with the elite reform movement around shared ethics of accountability and urgency, and they are able to exploit these convergences in key moments in order to push forward racial justice agendas like fair transportation, restorative justice and food justice in schools, and student voice in teacher evaluation processes. It is important to note here that these social movement victories from below are more often systemic; these wins produce educational change across whole city sectors, school districts, and states, and even hold the potential to contribute to national campaigns. *These movements work to counter some elements of the White supremacy of market-based reform.* However, they do not necessarily counter choice processes, school closures, or charterization, which also contribute to racial injustice in school reform.

The second grassroots effort to counter neoliberal reform that is periodically able to reclaim schools as community institutions is the school-by-school mobilization of largely White affluent neighborhood activists. Many of these activists defy reformer expectations by refusing to participate in choice processes, and instead make a radical and "risky" commitment to their low-rated neighborhood schools, but their collectivist orientation to saving their neighborhood schools from reform experimentation pivots on a shared belief with reformers and urban planners that they are *inherently* worthy to the school, the neighborhood, and the city.[33] Viewing themselves as assets to their schools—instead of as contributors to the displacement and dispossession of their neighbors—these activists leverage their affluence, "proficiency," and cultural and social capital in the service of redesigning schools from the ground up. Despite their commitment to diversity, they share with reformers a sense that educational improvement hinges on the participation of the White affluent gentry in the public school system.

Because of this key convergence, some neighborhood mobilizations around specific schools are able to gain traction depending on how quickly they can mobilize around "failing" schools before the reform-oriented districts take radical action. If they are able to hold together a multiracial coalition, then they stand to gain even more traction. Over the course of this research, I witnessed these kinds of small-scale neighborhood school mobilizations successfully compel the district to agree to their vision of open and accessible dual-language education; to delay the closure of a middle school; and to delay a co-location of a charter school within a neighborhood high school. Although these movements also experience defeat and demobilize, they still are able to make the kind of grassroots impact on neoliberal policy that their low-income Black and Latinx neighborhood schools activists across the river are seldom able to make. This is not a reflection of their unique savvy or wise strategic choices. Rather, I argue that the successes of non-institutionalized movements of White affluent neighborhood newcomers to reclaim education have everything to do with their racial and class capital. These movements are small-scale and school-by-school, and are therefore less systemic in comparison to those launched by institutionalized racial justice movements. *They work to counter the marketization of reform,* including choice processes, school closures, and charterization. However, they do not always succeed in countering the White supremacy of neoliberal school reform. With their claims to the neighborhood schools, they often deepen their ownership of local public spaces and institutions in ways that further displace low-income residents of color through gentrification.[34] In so doing, these movements can actually *accelerate* racial dispossession. They also reinforce—rather than disrupt—the value reformers give to the White gentry in their larger project to revitalize schools and cities.

These lessons about local educational justice organizing not only draw attention to patterns of movement convergence and divergence, but also highlight what these coalitions, or failed coalitions, demonstrate about the potential for grassroots movements to resist neoliberal policy. To what extent can grassroots movements counter neoliberal agendas, especially in regard to public education? Which elements of neoliberalism are effectively thwarted as a result of movement mobilizing from below, and which elements of neoliberalism are more durable in the larger project of the new urbanism? In chapter 1, I break down what is usually referred to as the "neoliberal education reform" agenda by identifying its constituent elements, especially those that inspire community resistance. These major elements include standardized testing and accountability; the expansion of charter schools; school choice; urban gentrification and dispossession (including settler colonialism); and the appropriation of racial justice and civil rights rhetoric.

In the end, reformer and nonprofit racial justice alignment succeeds in bringing more equity to school choice processes (especially through grassroots demands for transportation systems), more student voice to school reform processes, and in some cases, changing disciplinary cultures of both traditional neighborhood and charter schools.[35] When institutionalized movements and reformers converge, institutionalized movements also challenge reformers' appropriation of racial justice rhetoric. These racial justice organizations compel reformers to support initiatives that put actual substance behind this rhetoric. These are significant wins. Similarly, the gentry's resistance to school choice and embrace of their neighborhood schools, even as these converge with reformers' valuation of White middle-class newcomers to the school district, hold the potential to slow down school reform experimentation and resist new systems of market choice.

However, these movements neither counter nor stall the settler colonialism associated with urban school reform. Neither the nonprofit organizational attempts nor the gentry's mobilizations successfully take on displacement and gentrification as central issues. For varied reasons, whether strategic and tactical (e.g., an anti-reform stance is too risky to take on for a funded nonprofit) or ideological (e.g., the belief that gentrification is a passive, inevitable, and even constructive process), *the local grassroots movements that move the needle in urban education policy end up facilitating—either through benign neglect or active participation—reform's central role in urban dispossession.* The White affluent neighborhood schools activists accelerate urban dispossession by laying claim to their neighborhood schools while failing to bridge the larger cultural, racial, and class divides in their neighborhoods and reckon with their active role in the displacement of their low-income neighbors of color. The racial justice nonprofit activists push the neoliberal envelope to accommodate authentic racial justice initiatives. But in doing so, they inadvertently enable the reform movement to continue to seek community buy-in, credibility, and the appearance of community partnership, even as their elite movement continues to displace low-income communities of color. As Adolf Reed Jr. notes, the institutionalization of racial justice mobilization—a key mechanism of urban neoliberalism over the last half century—has contributed to a public perception that nonprofitization is the *only* legitimate expression for racial justice politics: "Insofar as the NGOs and their elites carry the historical sediment of adversarial, protest politics, their integration into the new regime further ratifies its common sense and protocols as the only thinkable politics, as the totality of what politics *is*."[36] Despite the political intentions, commitments, and orientations of nonprofit activists themselves, the hegemony of the nonprofit model contributes to the isolation, marginalization, and invisibility of the low-income activists of color like those who form the AAPP, the CEC, and DEJ who fight against school closures, exclusionary charters, and other school experiments in their neighborhoods. This also isolates and renders invisible the activism of low-income Black city residents in particular, who for the most part are estranged from Black middle-class solidarity, political representation, and nonprofit infrastructure.[37]

The most *durable* dimension of urban neoliberal education reform in this political climate—or in other words, the most entrenched element that is unmoved by grassroots educational justice organizing—is the continued displacement of low-income people of color from urban neighborhoods and the capture of their neighborhood wealth. It is the settler colonialism associated with neoliberalism, as expressed through school reform politics, that is the most resistant to challenges from the grassroots.

Critical education scholars like Pauline Lipman, Kristen Buras, and Thomas Pedroni have detailed school reform's violence on Black communities in particular in cities like Chicago, New Orleans, and Detroit. However, the chapters in this book demonstrate the role that grassroots movements play in resisting or colluding with elite reformers who specifically take aim at Black and Latinx community resources in order to remake school systems and further enrich the city's elite. Although grassroots organizing can and should continue to challenge neoliberal reform, these chapters demonstrate that the neoliberal war on low-income communities of color is also mediated by the complex relationships that local movements have with elites and with each other. In fact, in a national landscape polarized by elite reformers on one hand, and teachers unions and dispossessed Black and Brown people on the other, local grassroots movements fighting for self-determination and the right to shape public education have the capacity and the potential to tip the balance in either direction.

Reed surmises that the deck is stacked against low-income opponents of neoliberal privatization, given "the class, ideological, and organizational forces aligned on the other side."[38] My aim is not to deny the extent to which reformers hold disproportionate financial and political power over any other group featured in this book, or to deny the social and political forces that contribute to the upward redistribution of wealth. Rather, my aim is to demonstrate how the elite reform movement is supported by and relies upon public support, public opinion, and even a modicum of public participation. It is in this vital space where grassroots movements—whether housed in formal nonprofits or more loosely and informally networked—can make their mark and wield their power.

Lessons from the Trenches: How to Build Local Movements That Win

As sociologist Paul Almeida demonstrates, successful movements against neoliberal privatization rely on a broad coalition of diverse movement groups and interests, and often come on the heels of previous failed efforts launched by comparatively narrower coalitions.[39] There are two major lessons I draw from this examination of the two partially successful movement networks in this book, the racial justice nonprofit organizations and the movement of White affluent newcomers who value diversity and sacrifice some privilege to commit to their neighborhood schools. These lessons might point the way to what could be the next iteration of resistance to neoliberal urban school reform, one that could be launched by a much broader and more diverse coalition.

Fundamentally, White neighborhood schools activists who mobilize for control over local schools need to broaden their reach and expand their movements in order to include other issues. If they truly want broad coalitions around building strong, accessible, and diverse neighborhood schools, they should reach out to dispossessed communities and fight for neighborhood schools in tandem with community-owned businesses and other community-owned spaces. They can ensure that they also have instituted equitable processes for the oversight of neighborhood associations and parks. If they seek Latinx and Black participation in their movements for comprehensive neighborhood schools, then they can align with those communities around allied issues of immigrant protection and justice, food security, affordable housing, and more just policing, for example. These leagues of progressive urban Whites would also need to support communities of color in organizing for justice *beyond* schooling, before they expect communities of color to join their fight for specific neighborhood schools. It is not enough to hold a collectivist attitude about the neighborhood school. To sustain the battle for integrated, diverse, accessible, and local public schools, White newcomers will need to be active on multiple fronts in order to actualize the kind of authentic multiracial and multicultural neighborhood justice that they ostensibly seek, and that the elite reform movement rhetorically champions but rarely fosters.

Is this tenable? In order to transform into these kinds of activists, the White gentry would need to come to terms with their own role in gentrification and their own unearned privilege.[40] Their collectivist ethic would have to change significantly, from viewing their commitment to their neighborhood schools as an undeniable "gift" to their less privileged counterparts, to understanding their active participation in dispossession. They would need to recognize their role in settler colonialism, and that they are rooting their lives into an existing community with needs, concerns, histories, and goals that may or may not differ from their own. This consciousness-raising shift must be nested in a larger counter-gentrification movement. These activists would need to enact their solidarity "in ways that have the potential to decolonize their relationships through their very practice," as the iconic "Raging Grannies" activists have done in order to forge solidarities with indigenous people's movements in Canada.[41] While not all of the activists featured in chapter 4 would be willing to make such a transformation and commit to such a multi-issue, multiracial movement, some of their key organizers might. Indeed, in successful coalitions that are able to bridge vast class and race divides, such privileged organizers can and do act as powerful movement allies and coalition partners when they demonstrate a personal and ideological commitment to movement bridging.[42] It is these bridge builders in particular who make movement cause affirmation—or the commitment to protect and center the perspectives and experiences of those members of the coalition who are the *most* marginalized—possible.[43]

More to the point, their movement success would *depend* on such a transformation and commitment to bridge building across social divides. Reformers and reform-oriented districts can easily dismiss such movements, when convenient, if these movements fail to mobilize across racial and class lines and demonstrate broader community support. They must build the substantive multiracial alliances that hold the power to counter reformers' paternalistic multicultural rhetoric. This is a tall order, as this transformation must counter the deeply entrenched White supremacy of urban school and housing politics.

Similarly, community-based, racial justice nonprofit organizations need to place gentrification at the heart of their racial justice struggles. They need to take more risks to partner with locally networked, non-institutionalized movement groups. The "no permanent enemies, no permanent allies" ethic may help to launch winnable campaigns, but these organizations cannot expect the support and alliance from marginalized populations if they also partner with entities that have actively advocated the erasure, displacement, and dispossession of these communities of color. Is this tenable? Can nonprofits afford to do this? They risk alienating powerful allies, funding sources, and stability. But their risk taking could translate into broader resonance with urban communities and more deeply impactful wins. Importantly, it could also culminate in stronger Black-Latinx grassroots alliances. This, too, is a tall order. This transformation must counter the deeply entrenched politics of contemporary movement institutionalization, necessitating a new model for community organizing and movement funding. As political scientist Michael Heaney and sociologist Fabio Rojas point out, social movement organizations (SMOs) have the ability to create multifaceted collective identities. Indeed, these authors argue that in the case of antiwar mobilization, for example, the more successful SMOs hybridize their identities in order to resonate with disparate audiences and mobilize participants into multi-movement coalitions. In fact, because these hybrid organizations have the capacity to sustain inter-organizational networks that can evolve over time, they are vital to the growth of new movements into the future.[44] For the institutionalized movement organizations featured in this chapter, transformation will require the construction of more enduring hybridized identities, and a shift away from the shorter-term, funded campaign-driven "no permanent enemies, no permanent allies" approach.

Because the Denver Classroom Teachers Association's turn toward progressive labor activism is only in its infancy, teacher mobilizations in Denver are not the focus of this book. But the lessons for teachers unions moving forward would be the same as those for White urban neighborhood school activists and those carrying out racial justice campaigns from the home bases of community nonprofits. As Lipman has argued, the Chicago teachers' strikes harnessed power largely because the progressive wing of the Chicago teachers union partnered with local, community-based racial justice groups to launch an offensive against what they explicitly recognized as White supremacist school reform, which includes the broader displacement of communities of color.[45] The Los Angeles teachers union approached the bargaining table in the same way, laying the groundwork for labor-community coalitions over a period of years and expanding their bargaining to encompass broader community issues like immigrant rights and housing justice. These issues inevitably shape teachers' working conditions and children's experiences of schooling.[46] Teachers cannot go at it alone. These labor organizations must also adopt broader movement goals in order to more effectively harness resistance to school reform, which is lived beyond the school walls by the families with whom teachers work.

What will it take for these transformations to take place, and for these vital coalitions to form? These transformations would require the movements for educational justice to more effectively coalesce with antiracist movements for urban sustainability. Throughout her work, sociologist and political activist Frances Fox Piven has underscored the concept of "interdependent power" to describe power relations between the haves and have-nots. She uses this term to explain the historical moments in which those with less social and economic power effectively mobilize and win concessions from those who are more powerful. In this view, dependency runs both ways: employers need workers, universities and schools need students and teachers, and in a capitalist economy even the wealthy need debtors. Piven describes interdependent power this way: "power sometimes wielded by subordinate groups does not arise from wealth or control of the militia or the army. Rather, their power is rooted in the occasional ability of people at the bottom end of economic or political or social relationships to refuse, to strike, to withdraw or threaten to withdraw from systems of institutionalized cooperation."[47] This means that in the rush to revitalize cities, the elite are also dependent on those they dispossess for their access to community institutions and real estate.

There is a burgeoning anti-gentrification movement brewing in cities like Denver and elsewhere that are quickly becoming unlivable as a result of the last several decades of urban revitalization and settler colonialism. This movement is beginning to realize its "interdependent power" in relation to community dispossession and urban revitalization. In Denver, as in other cities, community land trusts are just beginning to gain traction as a way to stall displacement and dispossession, and to maintain neighborhood stability as well as racial and economic diversity.[48] There are also other community resistances to gentrification that are led by young millennials of color who are disproportionately shouldering the burden of the country's growing urban divide between rich and poor.[49] Their opposition manifests in protests like those launched against Ink Coffee's ill-conceived advertising slogan, which read, "Happily gentrifying the neighborhood since 2014" on a sandwich board in Denver in 2017. These spontaneous protests have made national news.[50] As Johnson writes, "We need a new progressive urban politics not in older modes of racial justice per se, but in the variegated, but common experiences of dispossession and exploitation that define city life for millions of residents."[51] It remains to be seen how this growing movement will further realize its power. Movements and movement coalitions that are able to span decentralized and hierarchical organizational forms are more likely to increase the scope of tactics the movement or coalition can use to make political and social change.[52] In order to maximize their impact on neoliberal school reform and bring about more comprehensive antiracist and equitable social change, the various educational justice movements featured in this book will have to reckon with this growing movement for self-determination, land, and urban stability. They will have to find ways to resonate with its advocates. It is this ideal movement convergence that holds the potential for returning schools to diverse community control, and for tipping the balance of power away from the neoliberal elite and to those who have been wronged by urban education policy for too long.

ACKNOWLEDGMENTS

From the beginning of this research to the publishing of this book, this journey has been a long one. I want to acknowledge all the people who made this research possible and have sustained me through this journey. First, a huge debt of gratitude goes to the activists and reform advocates featured in this book, who gave generously of their time to talk with me, shared their political perspectives on educational crises, and allowed me to enter their territory in order to study as best I could, from their vantage point, what educational justice can and *should* be. Although I advance various critiques of some of these activists and advocates and the larger movements they represent, I am humbled by the many long hours, days, months, and years that these activists and advocates have put into trying to create equitable education reform in Denver and across Colorado.

Special thanks goes to Ilene Kalish, my editor at New York University Press, as well as the anonymous reviewers of my chapters and full manuscript. They gave the necessary guidance that helped me to sharpen my analysis and broaden the arguments in this book. This work would not have been the same without their input. Ilene Kalish continued to believe in me and in this project, and tolerated what turned out to be a much longer timeline for the delivery of this book.

I have been blessed to have wonderful colleagues at the University of Denver and elsewhere who have given me valuable feedback as I began to analyze data and write from this project. Nancy Wadsworth, Lisa Pasko, Scott Phillips, Jared Del Rosso, Lisa Martinez, Tate Steidley, Nancy Reichman, Jeffrey Lin, and Barbara Sutton have all provided me with helpful feedback on my work in progress. In the course of writing this book, life took an unexpected turn when my husband and father to our two children died in a tragic accident. I am thankful to Lisa Martinez, Lynn Schofield-Clark, Antonia Banducci, Santhosh Chandrashekar, Beth Suter, Jared Del Rosso, Tate Steidley, and Casey Stockstill—the wonderful members of my various writing groups—who encouraged me to keep going, keep writing, and keep the project alive throughout this extraordinarily difficult transition. I really could not have finished the book without their encouragement. A major thanks goes to Jennifer Reich, who read my chapter on reformers and gave me extensive and thoughtful feedback. She undoubtedly helped me to put forward a much clearer analysis of these privileged players in school reform.

Other friends and family helped me to keep my perspective, humor, and sanity as I completed this book project. LeThi Cussen, Kate Willink, Kris Boesch, Naomi Weber, and Jenn James in particular provided their love, friendship, and laughter when I needed it most. Thanks to Melissa Harris, Todd Clough, Erin Ganser, Drew Lockman, and Heather and Pete Ramirez for giving so much support to my children and me as we made our way into a new life. My siblings (and their spouses) Josh and Eve Gordon, Rebecca Gordon and Michael Propper, Davey Gordon and Susan Siegel, Ilise and Glen Meyers, Steven and Bethany Gordon, and Marcia and Steve Wunsch all supported me in various ways throughout the writing of this book and I love them immensely. We lost my brother-in-law Steve Wunsch in 2019, and will forever hold his light in our memories. Thanks to my mother, Marcia Gordon, who has always believed in me. Many thanks to Jason McKain's family: Steve McKain, Jane McKain, Thad McKain, Adam McKain, Ruthann McTyre, and Elaine Heron, who have also loved and supported us throughout the years it took to research and write this book.

My biggest thanks go to Andy Proctor, Lael McKain, and Oliver McKain, my loving "herd." Andy gave his unflagging support, love, humor, and care. I could not have reached the finish line without his love. My amazing children, Lael and Oliver McKain, motivate me every day to be a better person, and buoy me every day with their empathy, brilliance, creativity, and humor. They are the greatest gifts in my life.

METHODOLOGICAL APPENDIX

Researching Urban School Reform and Community Movements

Origins of the Study

At the turn of the millennium, I conducted comparative ethnographic research on teenage activists in Portland and Oakland, which resulted in my first book, *We Fight to Win: Inequalities and the Politics of Youth Activism* (Rutgers University Press). In both of my participant-observation sites, White middle-class teens and low-income Latinx and Black teens were organizing around two simultaneous issues: the burgeoning war in Iraq and military spending, and the defunding of public education. Indeed, both groups of teens worked to politically link these issues together. They were outraged that landmark budget cuts to public education were taking place just when the country was gearing up to pour more public funding into what appeared to be an unjust war with no clear end. The book analyzes their different strategies, wins, and defeats in relation to intersecting forces of race, class, gender, and age inequalities during 2002–2004. At the end of that research, I knew there were political and social phenomena—especially in regard to education reform—that were shaping the conditions of young activists' lives and the possibilities for their organizing. I also knew that I did not fully understand these phenomena well enough to analyze them, and so they never made their way into my first book. Looking back, though, I know that these phenomena crystallized into particular moments in my field research that have stayed with me to this day, even though I did not recount them in the book.

For example, I remember that in Oakland, some of the activist teens I knew were attending a large public high school when a fellow student had been murdered in their neighborhood. Their large high school had just been transformed into three small schools. Even though students attending the high school were now parsed out into three small institutions, they still shared the same campus, the same facilities, and the same neighborhood. They still knew each other from previous years of shared schooling, and their identities and sense of community spanned the manufactured dividing lines between each of the small schools that now occupied the giant high school campus.[1] On the day of the funeral, one principal of the newly instituted small school where the murdered student attended allowed fellow students in that small school to leave for the afternoon to attend the funeral of their friend. But the principals of the other two small schools—small institutions that shared the same physical spaces of the larger school and neighborhood—would not allow their students to attend. A handful of teen activists, already grieving, were outraged that they were forced to either skip school to attend the funeral or miss it altogether. This was my first glimpse into the ways newly reformed small schools, carved out of formerly large comprehensive neighborhood schools, failed to adjust to the realities of the community ties that bind students to each other across their neighborhoods and to the school itself. Although the teen activists in Oakland discussed the jarring transition of their comprehensive high school as it transformed into a small schools model, their experiences and their criticisms of school reform never translated into action. There did not seem to be a place in their formal social movement campaigns to oppose the quick reform experiments that were taking over their school system. Rather, their energies focused on improving public education opportunities for low-income kids of color, and trying to end the school-to-prison pipeline and the criminalization of Black and Brown students. The critiques of school district and state-level reforms, although constant, remained backstage and in the margins of their formal organizing campaigns.

I moved to Denver from Portland, Oregon, in 2006 to begin work at the University of Denver. After researching youth activist campaigns in the area, I found a coalition of students opposing the recent closure and redesign of Central High (discussed at length in chapters 1, 2, and 3 of this book). This was the school located in the center of Denver's historically Black community. The students were demanding that justice be done for the other students they feared were lost in the transition during the closure. They were concerned that the school district would not do enough to track the students who would be left without a neighborhood school in the wake of the closure. Despite student and community protests, the reforms—buttressed by national foundation money—proceeded anyway, and resulted in a small schools experiment that lasted just a year before it ended. I began to wonder why it was I was seeing the same shift to small schools in Denver that I witnessed in Oakland a few years earlier. I also began to wonder about the impact of these reforms, which seemed to be dictated by forces outside the impacted communities and which appeared to be immune to their concerns.

With these questions in the back of my mind, I joined my colleague Nancy Wadsworth in political science at the University of Denver in a small public good project to investigate what kinds of community supports a reformed school like Central needs to thrive. Especially in the wake of the failed small schools experiment, it seemed as though increasing community supports would be vital to the success of the next round of reforms at Central. Nancy, who had been researching racial reconciliation politics in religious communities for years, saw this as an opportunity to examine possibilities for racial alliance and healing around issues of neighborhood schooling. Over 2007–2008 we conducted interviews with Central's school staff, community liaisons, and other stakeholders both inside and outside the school. It was during this project that I came into contact with community organizers from the AAPP (African American Parent Project), the CEC (Community Education Collective), and DEJ (Democrats for Educational Justice). Their criticisms echoed and extended the criticisms of the high school student activists who protested the Central High closure and redesign. As we encountered more and more of these voices critical of Central High's reforms, my major research questions shifted. Although Nancy and I wanted to discover how community and neighborhood residents could help the newly reformed school succeed, we also came to question the rightness of the reforms themselves. What *was* the process of reforming the school? Who carried it out? Which groups did the process include, and which did it exclude? Through what major processes did it include and exclude? What was the impact of the reform on the community? Why did there exist a river of anger at the school district and the so-called reformers who descended on Denver to allegedly orchestrate these controversial reforms? What was the response of the reformers to this community outrage? How much could the "community" really participate in shaping these reforms, and who counted as the "community"? Who were these mysterious reformers anyway, and where did they come from?

Integrating Critical Participatory Action Research with Black Neighborhood Schools Activists

After our initial public good project unearthed more questions than answers, I decided to pursue these questions in a separate ethnographic research project that ended up lasting for five years: from 2008 to 2013. At first, my focus was on informal community networks of mostly Black and Latinx activists. I wanted to understand what school reform and educational justice looked like from their perspective, and what impact their resistance made on school reform policy in Denver. This segment of the research integrated elements of critical participatory action research (CPAR) with the AAPP in particular. After sitting in on many meetings and building relationships with these parents, AAPP participants and I developed an in-depth interview guide together that sought to elucidate Black parents' perspectives on school reform; their experiences with school choice and charter schools; and their experiences in trying to interject their voices into community debates. We also wanted to access other Black parents' visions for educational justice, and identify goals for educational change.

AAPP coordinators wanted the interviews themselves to be moments for critical interventions and consciousness raising. They were concerned about the parents they knew who were tangentially related to the AAPP and had Black children in the schools who were not thriving. The AAPP wanted to take stock of the ways Black parents negotiated their children's negative experiences of schooling, and wanted to encourage Black parents to take a more critical perspective on the marketing promises of new charter or innovation schools in their neighborhoods, as well as the school district at large. AAPP organizers envisioned that the interviewer could go beyond simply collecting information about Black parents' experiences with public schooling. They could also urge parents to trust their own eyes and ears, as well as their children's own accounts of schooling, in order to make better educational decisions and advocate for their children's success *despite* school reform and not because of it. I trained AAPP members to conduct qualitative interviews, and collectively we completed interviews with AAPP participants and other members of the Black community. In line with their informal methods of movement organizing and what one of their members characterized as their "little process" of information sharing and consciousness raising (see chapter 3), the interview methodology became one more vehicle for the AAPP to share information, raise awareness, counter reform spin, and support community advocacy. I conducted thirty-one interviews with core AAPP organizers and members of DEJ and the CEC. AAPP members conducted an additional ten interviews with other Black parents in the neighborhood. Although my in-depth interview process resembled more "traditional" research and did not seek to raise consciousness or share political information (since I myself am not a member of the AAPP, DEJ, or the CEC), for AAPP interviewers, the research itself became an extension of their face-to-face organizing.

AAPP organizers and I also jointly facilitated three focus groups with AAPP participants and other community members. These focus group conversations, which typically involved fifteen to twenty community members at a time, explored Black residents' perceptions of and experiences with various elements of education reform, including community forums, charter schools, and school choice processes; schooling and discipline policies; and visions for educational justice. These group discussions echoed themes in the in-depth interviews, and served as another powerful avenue for community information sharing and consciousness raising. The focus groups also allowed participants to collectively analyze and validate their own frustrating experiences with their children's schooling and with school reform processes in general, and opened up an opportunity for community members to be more candid about systemic racial and class oppression than they might have been in individual interviews with me, a White researcher who did not live in their neighborhood or share the fabric of their everyday lives. As the late criminologist Esther Madriz noted, focus group methodology—in contrast to one-on-one, in-depth interviewing—is especially appropriate for studying the lived experiences and narratives of low-income women of color. In forums where women of color can come together, they are more able to reveal complex layers of racial, class, and gender inequality as well as patterns of collective resistance and agency. Importantly, the focus group format can shift power in the research process from the interviewer to the collective experiences of the group. Participants are more able to center their own concerns and direct the flow of discussion.[2] This is especially important in cases when the interviewer is White and middle-class, as I am. Furthermore, focus groups allow the genesis of what critical race scholars Daniel Solorzano and Tara Yosso term "counter-stories."[3] Using this method in addition to in-depth interviews was important, given the social distance along racial and class lines between myself and community members, as well as the CPAR priorities of this particular line of research.

Throughout this research I was funded by an internal University of Denver grant, which provided me with just enough money to support summer data collection, pay for the transcription of interviews, and provide incentives for interviewees to participate in this study. Although researchers are often at a disadvantage without large research grants to fund their work, I found that the lack of any other funding was actually an asset in this particular study, and a way to gain trust with these community members. When Nancy Wadsworth and I first encountered the activists of the AAPP, the CEC, and DEJ, they were initially suspicious that our study was funded by any number of pro-reform foundations in Denver that have supported various school reform experiments and urban development. In a landscape dominated by pro-reform funding, the fact that only university money supported this research helped to build rapport. Besides wanting to use the interviews for consciousness raising, information sharing, and movement building, AAPP members also wished to leverage my research funds to build the kind of movement infrastructure that sustains nonprofit organizations. Unfortunately, these were things I was less able to provide with my relatively small research grant. These non-institutionalized community activists needed funding assistance to publish newsletters, since local news outlets were overwhelmingly pro-reform and not likely to feature critical voices counter to urban revitalization and school reform projects. They wanted funding to sustain more stable places to meet. They wanted funding to provide food and other incentives for a broader array of neighborhood residents to participate in their meetings. Unfortunately the flip side to my small research grant was that I could not meet the larger needs of these non-institutionalized movement networks to launch a more formidable resistance against the powerful and well-funded reform movement that they knew was aligned against their interests.

Researching the "Reformers" in Relation to Black and Latinx Community Activists

During my initial short project with Nancy Wadsworth, and subsequently learning about the experiences of marginalized Black and Latinx residents subject to school reform experimentation in gentrifying neighborhoods, I began to identify some key architects of local and statewide reform policy. These reformers were eager to sit down with me for an interview. Through snowball sampling, I interviewed a total of twenty self-identified reformers. Despite the fact that these reformers were harshly criticized in Black community members' narratives about school reform exclusion, they struck me as kind and genuinely caring in their one-on-one interviews with me. They were diverse in terms of their institutional bases: they worked inside the school district and outside the district; they were members of educational associations in both the city and the state; they were politicians and journalists; they were foundation representatives and independent consultants. Many of them had a special zeal for reform, and viewed this as some of the most important civil rights work they had ever done.

I believe that because I am also White and middle-class, these reformers revealed things to me they might not have revealed to Black or Latinx researchers.[4] The ease with which they admitted that they would never send their own children to the same militaristic charter schools that they publicly championed for poor Black and Latinx kids, for example, struck me as an admission that they would not so easily make to an interviewer who was not White. On one hand, they were generous with their time in explaining to me their worldview and their role within the larger reform movement and moment. They were convinced that they were doing the right thing to address social inequality. On the other hand, they continually engaged in an uncritical doublespeak regarding what is best for their own advantaged children versus what is best for "other" children. There was also a thread of hypocrisy that ran throughout their insistence on "saving" Black and Brown communities even as they refused and disparaged input from these same communities in school reform decisions. In all, these were difficult extremes to navigate. The competing narratives required me to untangle the threads of their heroism, their relative insulation from community critique, and their good intentions. In this sense, I had to critically assess their good intentions—their civil rights speak—as a potent discourse that allows neoliberal reforms to advance and keep these reformers relatively insulated from the outrage of the mostly working-class and poor people of color on the margins of school reform policy.[5]

The other outcome AAPP coordinators wanted, besides a community-building and intervention-focused interview process with parents in the neighborhood, was a face-to-face meeting with some of the reformers at local foundations, media outlets, and even inside the school district. Because they felt continually rebuffed by reformers who would rarely accept invitations to talk with them, they thought that perhaps I could broker a meeting in which we would present our findings from interviews with reformers and Black community members, and hold a discussion between the two camps. Indeed, I did broker such a meeting. I was quite nervous to bring these two strands of my research together, since I knew that despite what might be expected of an "objective" researcher, my sympathies were much more in line with the community members in the AAPP and the other non-institutionalized groups in Denver featured in chapter 3. Famous for his groundbreaking work on elites, anthropologist George Marcus reflects on the messiness of this kind of multi-sited research enterprise: "In conducting multi-sited research, one finds oneself with all sorts of cross-cutting and contradictory personal commitments."[6] Indeed, these contradictory commitments are reflected in my research design: I did not conduct critical participatory action research with reformers, for example, nor any other groups featured in this study.[7] My research presentation culled the reformer narratives about civil rights and contrasted those with the perspectives of Black community members themselves, a juxtaposition that ultimately made for a much more critical view of the reformer movement than of the community movement represented by the AAPP. Because reformers willingly gave of their time for in-depth interviews, I thought that they might also accept my invitation to this discussion. When it came time for the research presentation, however, most reformers we invited did not show. It was disappointing that so many reformers could not or would not find the time to attend such a community discussion, even when I hosted it on seemingly neutral territory at my university. Although reformers were eager to speak with me and generous with their time, they were reluctant to engage in deeper discussions with Black community members. This was consistent with Black residents' alienation from school reform processes in general. In this study, I alone was unable to use my academic, racial, and class privilege to alter this pattern. This is often why robust critical participatory action research projects involve multiple researchers, multiple disciplinary perspectives, and multiple stakeholders. These larger projects also measure their impact along dimensions that extend beyond the production of scholarship. These dimensions include community impact and community education, as well as impact on policy.[8] Although my work with the AAPP in particular contained elements of CPAR, it was not a full CPAR project in this regard.

Researching Nonprofit Social Justice Organizations

At first, my project centered on the vast divergence between elite White reformers on one hand and low-income African American and Latinx activists on the other. My questions focused on the polarization of these two networks that both claim the mantle of civil rights. I began to see the movement of local reformers as fundamentally hostile to community organizing from below. However, I soon noticed through in-depth interviewing and participant-observation that reformers felt great respect for a handful of social justice nonprofits in the city. Even as they denigrated the perspectives of the activists in the AAPP, the CEC, and DEJ, they applauded the approach of specific racial justice community organizations that periodically partnered with reformers on key initiatives in education policy. I asked every interviewee, no matter which movement or movement group they represented, to map out which people or groups they believe hold "power" in school reform decisions. Inevitably, reformers would mention the same universe of key legislators, foundations, media outlets, and specific political figures who carried the torch for reform. But in a second tier they would place organized social movement nonprofits as important forces that keep reformers accountable to their promises of racial and educational equity. As I began to attend reformer forums and community meetings about school and broader neighborhood revitalization, I noticed the presence of these nonprofits. Although reformers could not name a single African American organization with which they periodically aligned, they spoke highly of the other nonprofits in their world, some of which have roots in the Chicano movement in Denver and/or the growing immigrant rights movement in the city.

Because of this realization, my research questions changed. Why do reformers partner with some racial justice organizations but not others? What are their criteria for community inclusion and exclusion as they build alliances? Why do they need these community partners? What do these reformer-community partnerships lend to the reform cause, and what do they win for community organizations' campaigns for racial equity in education? It was at this point that my study began to question why some community collectives are able to influence neoliberal reform, but others are not. I could not find this kind of nuanced discussion in existing critiques of the ways the elite reform movement railroads over disadvantaged and dispossessed communities. Who wins and who loses in the community struggle over school reform? What explains why certain groups prevail over others? Are these tactical? Or are these related to larger racial and class inequalities?

I sought out these organizations and their activists for interviews and exposure to their organizing meetings, protests, and community forums. In all, I conducted ethnographic research with three social justice non-profits that were often named as "powerful" by reform advocates, and that happened to also have significant youth activist contingents. Although reformers spoke of these organizations favorably, these social movement organizations' key organizers were much less likely to name reformers as consistent allies in their long-term project of challenging systemic racial inequity. In all, I conducted nineteen interviews with organizers and rank-and-file activists from these groups. These interviewees were mostly agnostic on the reform question. They justified alliances with reformers as periodic, strategic, and functional for specific educational justice campaigns. Pairing participant-observation with in-depth interview research allowed me to discover disconnects between what organizers said (e.g., "no permanent enemies, no permanent allies" as a guiding dictum) and what they actually experienced in the course of moving their social justice campaigns forward. For example, the complicated reality of partnering with elites and trying to hold them accountable at the same time, and of staying at the table with powerful reformers and feeling pressured to tame their critiques in order to keep their status as players in urban school reform became impossible tightropes to walk. It also allowed me to understand why these paid organizers wanted to build more Black-Brown unity around shared goals like reducing the school-to-prison pipeline or instituting new models of school transportation, yet couldn't seem to carve out the time around their campaign mandates to actually reach out to Black communities to do this vital bridge work. I also witnessed their backstage conversations about school closures and gentrification. Indeed, these were the same issues discussed by low-income Black and Latinx community members featured in chapter 3. But I also noticed the ways these conversations disappeared before they could make their way into their organizations' formal campaigns.

In viewing their racial justice work in action, I also saw them clash with some of the White neighborhood schools activists who organized to save their local schools from reform. In many cases, these nonprofit organizations championed certain reforms at schools located in gentrifying neighborhoods, and in doing so, found themselves aligned with reformers in opposition to these mostly White networks of neighborhood schools activists. I began to wonder about the strange bedfellows this clash made of nonprofit social justice activists and elite reformers. I also began to wonder about the White neighborhood schools activists who opposed district reforms. What similarities did these neighborhood schools activists have to the Black anti-reform neighborhood schools activists housed in the non-institutionalized groups like the AAPP, the CEC, and DEJ? Did these neighborhood schools activists align across a shared anti-reform stance, and was this enough to bridge a profound racial and class divide between these similarly non-institutionalized networks? On which points could their movements converge, and why didn't they converge more often?

Researching Affluent Neighborhood Schools Activists

My research with the McDonwell schools activists sought to answer these questions. This strand of the research hit closer to home. There were racial, class, and geographical differences between me and the Black neighborhood schools activists, but McDonwell Elementary was actually my neighborhood school, and these neighborhood activists mostly looked like me (White, middle-class) and lived near me. At the time, my own twin children were just old enough to enter the earliest early childhood education programs in the city, and our family had participated in the choice process for the very first time. As a parent and a researcher trying to decipher the complicated school choice process, I listed McDonwell Elementary as one of my top choices based on its promise of a traditional, comprehensive neighborhood school model. After the choice deadline passed, I was also one of the neighborhood parents dismayed by the school's sudden shift to a more focused expeditionary learning model. The expeditionary learning itself was not the target of community ire. Rather, it was the abrupt shift from the comprehensive neighborhood school model that McDonwell had long represented, and that had been promoted as a viable choice just a few weeks earlier, to the new and seemingly random expeditionary focus of this redesigned school. It seemed to some prospective families, like mine, as a confusing bait and switch.

For the existing McDonwell families, however, the sudden shift in the focus of the school was accompanied by a much more disturbing shift in administration and staff. This shift included the district's unilateral institution of a new principal, and the firing of most of the school's teachers. Only a fraction of existing teachers were selected to continue working at the school through the redesign. My uncertainty about my children's public school future dovetailed with my research on the community mobilization at this particular school, and I began to attend their community forums, protests, and meetings. I was open about my identity as both a parent and a researcher. Certainly, my race and class status, the fact that I could also claim this neighborhood as my "home," and my status as a parent in the neighborhood who had listed the school as a possible choice for my own children all worked together to facilitate my entrée into this group of activists. As their movement wore on, I approached several of the organizers for interviews. Through their stories and organizing knowledge, I learned of previous community mobilizations in the same sector of the city that had resulted in a few limited wins at specific schools. These previous wins inspired neighborhood activists to fight the reforms at McDonwell. I sought out those activists in previous neighborhood efforts as well. I then witnessed the McDonwell community activists try to reach out to other similar activists in the neighborhood also fighting against district reforms at nearby schools in the area. In this way, I began to learn how these White neighborhood activists attempted to stitch together their struggles across the neighborhood and link their small-scale, school-by-school fights in order to more effectively counter DPS reforms. In total, I conducted eighteen in-depth interviews with the neighborhood schools activists in this area of the city. Four of these interviews were with Latinx neighborhood schools advocates who either stuck with the White-dominated neighborhood schools movement or left this network of activists in frustration. For those Latinx neighborhood activists who remained in the network, their presence was indicative of the possibilities that this resistance *could* bridge racial tensions in the neighborhood and counter top-down neoliberal reforms. But the exodus of the other Latinx activists indicated that the potential for cross-racial alliance throughout the movement was undercut by other tensions. The remaining fourteen interviews were conducted with White activists in the neighborhood.

Throughout their struggle, members of the McDonwell school contingent continually searched for multiracial alliances in their movement to save their neighborhood school, but the search for diversity within their movement continually eluded them. Their movement fell apart before they had a chance to meaningfully address the persistent lack of diversity in their struggle. Had I not already studied the neighborhood schools mobilizations of Black and Latinx people across the river, I would have likely viewed the McDonwell school community movement through a much different lens. This is largely the strength of comparative ethnography. In this study, I discovered these different activist camps by "following the conflict" in order to branch out to different sites and activist lifeworlds within the same city.[9] Because of my comparative focus, I could move beyond analyzing what was in front of my eyes to also analyzing what was missing—the coalitions, discourses, strategies, and tactics that might have made for stronger multi-issue movements but were thwarted along the way. Because a comparative perspective allowed me to see the disjuncture and missing links between movements, I was better positioned to study the movements in terms of their relative capacity to coalesce, and not just as singular forces taking on neoliberal school reform piecemeal.

As surprising as the movements that seemed to align on some issues but rarely coalesced were the movements that seemed to clash but unexpectedly joined forces. In this comparative ethnography, I ended up using sociologist Michael Burawoy's extended case method approach.[10] Instead of seeking to discover patterns across cases from the ground up in order to generate new theory, as grounded theory would suggest, I began to center the anomalies I noticed in my data. I used these as distinct analytical anchors that I then traced back to the larger geographical and historical forces that might be shaping the particularities of the data. It is these macro forces that powerfully animate social conditions, but are rarely accessible or observable through participant-observation research. As Burawoy notes, we have the chance to revise broader social theory through extended case method's focus on what runs counter to our expectations. By starting with the anomaly or the surprise in the field, we can move from the particular to the more general, even though ethnographic research is not, technically, generalizable. This means that even though this research is firmly anchored in Denver, Colorado, and is not necessarily generalizable to other cities undergoing similar processes, analyzing local anomalies might help us to modify existing theory to better account for the broader historical forces that span specific locations and give rise to these anomalies.

In this study, the anomalies were many: the surprising outreach done by reformers to activists in community-based social movement organizations; the moments when racial justice groups willingly aligned with elite White reformers on specific initiatives; the resistance to school choice on the part of the very affluent gentry who are supposed to benefit from such a stacked system of choice; and the relative inability of racial justice activists to join forces across the non-institutionalized/institutionalized divide. My hope is that by studying each of these surprising phenomena as opportunities to understand how movements relate to each other and not just to elites, I have elucidated some of the features of this historical moment of neoliberalism. This historical moment shapes not only public policy, but also the conditions under which people organize to make social change and actually *shape* this policy from the ground up. This moment is marked by deep racial and class inequalities that run throughout elite policy making and the very processes of mobilization and movement building. Given these deep racial and class inequalities, this study has also highlighted which elements of neoliberal education policy are more "moveable" through certain kinds of community organizing, and which are more resistant to community pressure. By identifying the reasons why various activists so often fail to coalesce across social and institutional divides to more effectively take control of the public institutions ostensibly meant to serve them, we can identify clearer possibilities for creating more sustainable and powerful coalitions around educational, racial, and urban justice issues into the future.

NOTES

1 See Campbell, "Why Are Achievement Gaps So Wide."

2 The report, issued by the National Commission on Excellence in Education in 1983, argued that substandard education—rather than corporate consolidation and deindustrialization, for example—was *the* cause of national economic decline in an increasingly globalizing world. In *Radical Possibilities*, Anyon provides a powerful critique of this framing, and persuasively argues that any education reform not connected to broader social and economic justice is destined to fail.

3 For an excellent examination of inequalities within intra-movement networks such as in LGBTQ and immigrant rights organizing, see Adam, "Intersectional Coalitions."

4 Barker, "Class Struggle and Social Movements," 48.

5 Layton, "Poll."

6 For examples of this type of media coverage, see Dillon, "A School Chief Takes on Tenure," a 2008 *New York Times* article on national reform icon Michelle Rhee.

7 Gutstein and Lipman, "Rebirth of the Chicago Teachers Union."

8 One community-driven response to school reform that received widespread news coverage was the Dyett hunger strike in Chicago. Some of this coverage explicitly framed the hunger strike as a racial justice issue. See, for example, Strauss, "Why Hunger Strikers Are Risking Their Health."

9 See, for example, Press, "It's Time to Acknowledge."

10 In "Capital of Education Reform," an opinion piece in *U.S. News & World Report* about Michelle Rhee's legacy as a major catalyst for a national movement for education reform, Sara Mead concludes, "The education reform movement must broaden its political base if it is to continue to drive progress. That's an important lesson. But it's equally important to learn from the ways reform strategies have worked in Washington, D.C. The results here show that it's possible to improve results for historically underserved kids and dysfunctional districts. It would be a shame if that gets lost amid the adult politics." Rhee herself started a national political lobbying organization called StudentsFirst, which aimed to influence policy makers on various school reform agendas, including the abolishment of teacher tenure. The organization's name evokes the repeated moral claim that the reform movement is safeguarding children's interests against those of self-interested adults.

11 Indeed, Lipman, "Landscape of Education 'Reform'" argues that the Chicago teachers union strike would not have been as strong or as successful without the backing of local racial justice community organizations.

12 Lipman, "Landscape of Education 'Reform.'"

13 Warren and Mapp, *Match on Dry Grass*.

14 Throughout the book I refer to reformers as "reform advocates" instead of "reform activists" to better clarify the distinction between these political actors and the community activists they encounter. Importantly, not all reform advocates identify themselves as "activists," but they strongly self-identify as "reformers."

15 See Warren and Mapp, *Match on Dry Grass* for an overview of powerful examples of parent and student community organizing across several major cities that can provide direction for a socially just and inclusive vision of school reform. Lipman, "Landscape of Education 'Reform'" details the community-labor antiracist coalition that sustained one of the most notable teachers' strikes in recent years in Chicago. Kirshner, *Youth Activism* documents the ways student activism for educational justice reinvigorates democracy and serves as a powerful educational environment that cultivates positive youth development and political power.

16 For example, see Apple, *Educating the "Right" Way*; Au, *Unequal by Design*; and Saltman, *Gift of Education*.

17 As Van Dyke and McCammon argue in their introduction to *Strategic Alliances*, coalitions are more vital than ever to social movement success in a globalized era. Globalization brings common threats and political opportunities for movements to coalesce across national borders and across political issues. Almeida, "Sequencing of Success" demonstrates that coalitions with more breadth and diversity stand a greater chance of defeating neoliberal privatization initiatives than do social struggles launched by more narrow coalitions.

18 Omi and Winant, *Racial Formation*.

CHAPTER 1. THE NATIONAL CONTEXT

1 By the target year, no state in the nation had reached 100 percent proficiency.

2 Hursh, "Assessing No Child Left Behind."

3 Au, "Meritocracy 2.0."

4 For more insight into why school reform has become a centerpiece of urban gentrification and revitalization projects, see Pedroni, "Urban Shrinkage"; Dumas, "'Losing an Arm'"; Lipman, *High Stakes Education*; Lipman, "From Accountability to Privatization"; and Lipman, "Landscape of Education 'Reform.'"

5 Lipman, *High Stakes Education*; Lipman, "From Accountability to Privatization"; and Lipman, "Landscape of Education 'Reform.'"

6 Hursh, "Assessing No Child Left Behind."

7 Apple, *Educating the "Right" Way*.

8 Ronald Reagan argued that desegregation orders discriminated against White students, and in the 1980s he eliminated federal desegregation funds and advocated

for the end to hundreds of school-desegregation court orders. This set the stage for NCLB nearly two decades later. See Hannah-Jones, "Choosing a School."

9 Allen, "Globalization of White Supremacy," for example, argues that nation-states are themselves relics of a White supremacist, European colonial history.

10 Hursh, "Assessing No Child Left Behind."

11 See Nikole Hannah-Jones, "How the Systemic Segregation of Schools Is Maintained by 'Individual Choices,'" interview, National Public Radio, January 16, 2017.

12 Harvey, *Brief History of Neoliberalism*.

13 Hursh, "Exacerbating Inequality."

14 Hursh, "Exacerbating Inequality"; and Au, *Unequal by Design*.

15 Au, *Unequal by Design*.

16 For a classic study on the class bias of standardized testing, see Bowles and Gintis, *Schooling in Capitalist America*. On cultural capital, see Yosso, "Whose Culture Has Capital?"

17 See Au, *Unequal by Design* for a history of standardized testing in the United States. As Au notes, this testing originated in the military in the early twentieth century and was designed to differentiate workers for various job duties. Standardized testing has always been a nationalist project, and was imported into education in 1920. NCLB overtly positioned high-stakes testing as a nationalist project, one that could advance the status of the United States in a globalizing world.

18 Ravitch, *Death and Life*.

19 See Au, *Unequal by Design*; Burch, *Hidden Markets*; and Saltman, *Gift of Education*.

20 See Bowles and Gintis, *Schooling in Capitalist America*; Au, *Unequal by Design*; and Ravitch, *Death and Life* for more on how standardized testing reflects broader race and class inequalities.

21 As Lipman has underscored throughout her research, school closures tied to neoliberalism's accountability standards have disproportionately impacted Black neighborhoods in Chicago, leaving entire neighborhoods without a neighborhood school.

22 Ravitch, *Death and Life*.

23 Sondel, "Raising Citizens" argues that Teach for America, in concert with "no excuses" charter schools, overwhelmingly focus on teaching students "personal responsibility"—a cherished neoliberal value and narrow notion of citizenship—as a route to individual mobility and higher education attainment. This stands in sharp contrast with Valenzuela's findings that caring relationships between teachers and students facilitate educational persistence and success, especially for Mexican American youth. Valenzuela, *Subtractive Schooling*.

24 Tuck and Gorlewski, "Racist Ordering," 201.

25 Buras, *Charter Schools*.

26 Klein, *Shock Doctrine*.

27 See Klein's coverage of disaster capitalism in the wake of Hurricane Maria in Puerto Rico, *Battle for Paradise*. As in the case of New Orleans, Klein notes that one of the first acts of privatization and dispossession in the wake of the storm was to push through radical legislation that would charterize Puerto Rico's school system. See also Bonilla, Brusi, and Bannan, "6 Months after Maria."

28 Buras, *Charter Schools*.

29 Fabricant and Fine, *Charter Schools*.

30 Au, *Unequal by Design*.

31 Fabricant and Fine, *Charter Schools*.

32 Lipman, "Landscape of Education 'Reform'" notes that between 2012 and 2014, African American students in the Chicago public school system were significantly less likely to have access to music, art, or Advanced Placement classes due to the concentration of charter schools in their communities.

33 See Stahl, *Ethnography of a Neoliberal School*.

34 See Lack, "No Excuses." Golan, "Paradox of Success," for example, argues that even though "no excuses" charter schools show some success in narrowing the achievement gap as measured on standardized test scores, they also limit higher-level skills like "creativity, entrepreneurship, and problem-solving." This charter model also produces increased stress, lower motivation, and strained student relationships with teachers.

35 For powerful critiques of how broken window policing is imported into charter school cultures serving low-income students of color, see Whitman, *Sweating the Small Stuff*; Stahl, *Ethnography of a Neoliberal School*; and Golan, "Paradox of Success."

36 See Welner, "Dirty Dozen" for a list of common mechanisms charter schools use to selectively engineer their student populations, whether through restrictive admission policies or student push-out.

37 Stahl, *Ethnography of a Neoliberal School*.

38 See Frankenberg, Siegel-Hawley, and Wang, "Choice without Equity"; and Rotberg, "Charter Schools."

39 Brown and Makris, "Different Type of Charter School," 95.

40 See Bulkley and Henig, "Local Politics."

41 See Coughlan, "Divergent Trends"; and Renzulli and Evans, "School Choice."

42 See Coughlan, "Divergent Trends"; and Saporito and Sohoni, "Mapping Educational Inequality."

43 Lipman, *New Political Economy*.

44 As Finnegan, "Economics of Empire" argued, the free trade agenda, as in the case of the free trade neoliberalism imposed on postcolonial Latin American countries like Bolivia, is simply an ideology that accelerates capital accumulation through extreme corporate capitalism. Despite the ideology, the "free" in "free trade" does not in fact free those who were already impoverished by colonialism. It stands in sharp contrast to the actual loopholes and advantages for corporate elites built into the "free trade" deals forcibly imposed by global hegemons like the

International Monetary Fund. In this same way, neoliberal policy that relies on the discourse of "freedom" in regard to school choice often works to consolidate educational advantage and property value for White city settlers.

45 See Cucchiara, *Marketing Schools*; and Lipman, "Contesting the City."

46 See Billingham, "Parental Choice"; and Hannah-Jones, "Choosing a School."

47 Ball and Vincent, "'I Heard It.'"

48 See Diamond and Gomez, "African-American Parents' Education Orientations."

49 Einhorn, "Extreme Sacrifice."

50 Saltman, *Gift of Education*.

51 Lipman, *New Political Economy*.

52 Lipman, "Contesting the City."

53 As Klein notes in *Shock Doctrine*, Milton Friedman's brand of fundamentalist capitalism argued that pure market reforms are so unpopular that they can only be pushed through in the wake of a crisis, "real or perceived" when the public is disoriented.

54 Lipman, "Landscape of Education 'Reform.'"

55 Harvey, *Brief History of Neoliberalism*.

56 Detroit's emergency manager stands as a potent symbol of the recent turn toward disaster capitalism, where crisis is invoked in order to push through unpopular reforms and bypass democratic processes. In the case of Detroit beginning in 2009, democratically elected school board and city representatives were stripped of their power to represent low-income communities across Detroit, and voters were stripped of their power to influence the direction of local politics both inside and outside the school system. Emergency managers have also given rise to the Flint water crisis and other unpopular financial reforms across Michigan. See Bosman and Davey, "Anger in Michigan."

57 Pedroni, "Urban Shrinkage."

58 See Sassen, *Global City*.

59 See Florida, *Rise of the Creative Class Revisited* on the notion of the "creative class"; and Friedman, *World Is Flat* for a description of the global growth in knowledge workers.

60 See, for example, Bello, *Capitalism's Last Stand?*; and Shiva, *Staying Alive* for critiques of neoliberal capitalist globalization as neocolonialism.

61 See Tuck and Gorlewski, "Racist Ordering."

62 See Harvey, "Neoliberalism as Creative Destruction" for his notion of creative destruction as it applies to neoliberalism.

63 Pedroni, "Urban Shrinkage."

64 In my own interviews with local reformers (described in chapter 2), they use terms like "disarray" and "ruins" to describe low-income communities and the households that comprise these communities. See also Lipman, "Landscape of Education 'Reform.'"

65 See Anyon, *Ghetto Schooling*; and Good, "Histories That Root Us."

66 Lipman, *High Stakes Education*.

67 For examples, see Lipman, "Landscape of Education 'Reform'"; and Dumas, "'Losing an Arm.'"

68 Good, "Histories That Root Us," 862.

69 See Hursh, "Exacerbating Inequality."

70 Au, "Meritocracy 2.0."

71 Scott, "Rosa Parks Moment?," 14.

72 Clay, "'Despite the Odds.'"

73 Scott, "Rosa Parks Moment?," 12.

74 See Buras, *Charter Schools*; and Lipman, *New Political Economy*.

75 See Berrey's critical analysis of corporate diversity rhetoric in *Enigma of Diversity*.

76 Berrey, *Enigma of Diversity*, 8–9.

77 See Quiroz, "Marketing Diversity." "New urbanism" refers to an urban development model that emphasizes mixed-income housing, walkability and ecological sustainability, and easy connections between work, home, and schooling. This movement arose in the early 1980s as the antithesis to urban sprawl and car-dependent urban development. Although in theory it supports diversity in housing and neighborhood population, in practice it has contributed to the Whitening and gentrification of urban spaces.

78 Quiroz, "Marketing Diversity," 77.

79 Reed, "Post-1965 Trajectory," 266.

80 Johnson, "Panthers Can't Save Us," 68.

81 See Johnson, "Half-Life of the Black Urban Regime"; and Johnson, "Panthers Can't Save Us."

82 See Scott, "Rosa Parks Moment?"

83 See Pizmony-Levy and Saraisky, *Who Opts Out*.

84 Au, "Meritocracy 2.0."

85 For in-depth coverage of New York's opt-out movement at this time, see *Democracy Now*'s story "Test Mutiny: Thousands of New York Parents Revolt against Standardized Exams," aired April 17, 2015.

86 Lipman, "Landscape of Education 'Reform.'"

87 See Klein, *Shock Doctrine*; and Pedroni, "Urban Shrinkage."

88 See Osborne, "Mile-High City Leads the Way" for praise for Denver's approach to school reform and charter expansion in *U.S. News & World Report*; and Wingert, "Best and Worst Cities" for *Newsweek* coverage of Denver as one of the highest-ranking cities for education reform.

89 But several community groups, especially those rooted in the low-income Black and Latinx communities that experience the highest rates of school closure, are pressuring the district to make the one-year moratorium permanent.

90 See Oakes, *Keeping Track* for more on tracking in public schools.

91 See, for example, Shiller, "Marketing Small Schools" for a critique of the small schools experiments in New York. She argues that the neoliberal small schools movement in the city translated into poorer choices and poorer education (narrowed by curricula designed to teach to the test) for low-income youth.

92 For more on philanthropies and their role in neoliberal school reform, see Salt-
    man, *Gift of Education*.
93 All names of schools, organizations, and activists in this book are identified by
    pseudonyms. The landmark reform at Central High is described in more detail in
    chapters 2 and 3.
94 See the pro-reform organization A+ Colorado's 2014 report for more on innova-
    tion schools' mixed results, www.aplusdenver.org.
95 Johnson, "Half-Life of the Black Urban Regime," 253.
96 For example, the conservative American Enterprise Institute ranked Denver in
    the top five US cities (along with reform hot spots like New Orleans, New York
    City, and Washington, DC) for educational entrepreneurs in 2010. The report
    cited the passage of Senate Bill 191, the concentration of charter schools in the
    district, a well-networked pro-reform philanthropic community, and a reform-
    friendly major newspaper (the *Denver Post*) in the making of Denver as a national
    model of school reform. The Brookings Institution ranked Denver's school district
    number 1 for school choice in the nation in 2016.
97 See Advancement Project/Civil Rights Project, *Opportunities Suspended*; and
    Skiba et al., "Race Is Not Neutral" for a more in-depth examination of the school-
    to-prison pipeline.
98 Strauss, "Dark Money."
99 For more reporting on the historic DPS board flip, see Asmar, "Why the Denver
    School Board 'Flipped.'"
100 See Asmar, "Why the Denver School Board 'Flipped.'"
101 Jaffe, "Radical Organizing."
102 Blanc, "Denver Teachers Strike Back."
103 See Florida, *Rise of the Creative Class Revisited*.

CHAPTER 2. THE REFORMERS

1   See Saltman, *Gift of Education*.
2   Lipman, "From Accountability to Privatization."
3   See Saltman, *Gift of Education*.
4   See Miner, "Keeping Public Schools Public"; Scott, "Market-Driven Education
    Reform"; and Anderson and Dixson, "Down by the Riverside."
5   Anderson and Dixson, "Down by the Riverside."
6   For example, see Anderson and Dixson, "Down by the Riverside."
7   Scott, "Market-Driven Education Reform."
8   Quiroz, "Marketing Diversity," 77.
9   See Kundu and Noguera, "Why America's Infatuation with 'Grit'" for a searing
    critique of the overuse of "grit" in education policy discussions.
10 See Whitman, *Sweating the Small Stuff*; Buras, *Charter Schools*; and Dixson, Buras,
    and Jeffers, "Color of Reform."
11 Dixson, Buras, and Jeffers, "Color of Reform," 289.
12 See Klein, *Shock Doctrine*.

13 See Klein, *Shock Doctrine*; and Saltman, "Schooling in Disaster Capitalism."
14 On interest convergence, see Bell, "*Brown v. Board of Education.*"
15 Suspitsyna, "Accountability in American Education," 570.
16 Suspitsyna, "Accountability in American Education," 578.
17 Scott, "Market-Driven Education Reform," 594.
18 See Whitman, *Sweating the Small Stuff*; and Scott, "Market-Driven Education Reform."
19 It is this same uncritical reliance on racial and class privilege that is replete throughout the movement for neighborhood schools that is led by the White middle-class neighborhood schools activists detailed in chapter 4.
20 Reed, *Stirrings in the Jug*, 121–22.
21 For more detailed reporting on the resegregation of public schooling, see Frankenberg, Lee, and Orfield, *Multiracial Society*; and Orfield and Lee, *Historic Reversals*.
22 See Frankenberg, Lee, and Orfield, *Multiracial Society*; and Lipman, "Cultural Politics."
23 Posey-Maddox, *When Middle-Class Parents Choose*.
24 Smiley and Fakunle, "From 'Brute' to 'Thug,'" 350.
25 See Yosso, "Whose Culture Has Capital?"
26 See Whitman, *Sweating the Small Stuff*.
27 On the school-to-prison pipeline, see Advancement Project/Civil Rights Project, *Opportunities Suspended*; and Skiba et al., "Race Is Not Neutral."
28 For example, see Fine, *Framing Dropouts*.
29 See Anderson and Dixson, "Down by the Riverside."
30 Wilson and Kelling, "Police and Neighborhood Safety."
31 For an example, see Lack, "No Excuses."
32 Yang, "Rites to Reform," 146.
33 Saltman, *Gift of Education*.
34 For example, see Lipman, "From Accountability to Privatization."

CHAPTER 3. THE DISPOSSESSED

1 As described in chapter 2, Central High's closing by the district was the first signal that neoliberal reform had arrived in Denver. Backed by a prominent national foundation, DPS closed the school despite community protest, and reopened the school as three small schools. The foundation-funded experiment lasted only a year, but it kick-started a succession of destabilizing experiments at Central High that would persist for another decade.
2 See Lipman, "Cultural Politics"; Lipman, "Contesting the City"; Lipman and Haines, "From Accountability to Privatization"; and Pedroni, "Urban Shrinkage."
3 Kozol, *Savage Inequalities*.
4 For a critical analysis of this anti-union and anti-teacher media framing of school reform, see Goldstein, "Imaging the Frame."

5 See Lawyers Committee for Civil Rights et al., "Framework for Providing All Students an Opportunity to Learn through Reauthorization of the Elementary and Secondary Education Act," July 2010, https://lawyerscommittee.org.

6 Pedroni, "Urban Shrinkage."

7 Lipman and Haines, "From Accountability to Privatization."

8 Stephen, *Women and Social Movements*.

9 Spence, "Neoliberal Turn," 145.

10 Arena, *Driven from New Orleans*.

11 See Reed, "Post-1965 Trajectory"; Johnson, "Half-Life of the Black Urban Regime"; and Johnson, "Panthers Can't Save Us."

12 Reed, "Post-1965 Trajectory," 268.

13 Johnson, "Panthers Can't Save Us."

14 Johnson, "Half-Life of the Black Urban Regime," 250.

15 See, for example, Abarca, "Snapshot of Education Reform."

16 For example, see Lipman and Haines, "From Accountability to Privatization"; and Miraftab, "Public-Private Partnerships."

17 Miraftab, "Public-Private Partnerships," 89.

18 See Scott, "School Choice."

19 Scott, "Market-Driven Education Reform."

20 Spence, "Neoliberal Turn," 144–45.

21 Diamond and Gomez, "African-American Parents' Education Orientations."

22 See Shiller, "Marketing Small Schools."

23 See Sondel, "Raising Citizens."

24 See Sleeter, "Equity, Democracy, and Neoliberal Assaults"; Au, "Teaching under the New Taylorism"; and Shiller, "Marketing Small Schools."

25 Au, "Teaching under the New Taylorism."

26 Sleeter, "Equity, Democracy, and Neoliberal Assaults."

27 See Sleeter, "Equity, Democracy, and Neoliberal Assaults"; and Shiller, "Marketing Small Schools."

28 Valenzuela, *Subtractive Schooling*.

29 Sondel, "Raising Citizens."

30 Diamond and Gomez, "African-American Parents' Education Orientations."

31 Dumas, "'Losing an Arm'" argues that schooling has long been a source of suffering for Black students and their families. He defines suffering as a "constant travelling between historical memory and current predicament, that there is a psychic link between the tragedy of antebellum African bondage and post–civil rights (indeed, 'post-racial') black suffering in schools. . . . Black educators, children and families are never quite sure when they will be taken (back) to this place of trauma, nor can they fully determine when, or if the pain will end" (3).

32 Pedroni, "Urban Shrinkage."

33 For example, see Ferguson, *Bad Boys*; Noguera, "Schools, Prisons, and Social Implications"; and Fenning and Rose, "Overrepresentation."

34 Ferguson, *Bad Boys*.

35 Yosso, "Whose Culture Has Capital?"
36 Tuck and Gorlewski, "Racist Ordering"; Valenzuela, *Subtractive Schooling*.
37 Bonilla-Silva, *Racism without Racists*.
38 DeMoss and Vaughn, "Reflections on Theory."
39 Diamond and Gomez, "African-American Parents' Education Orientations."
40 See, for example, Sleeter, "Equity, Democracy, and Neoliberal Assaults"; and Shiller, "Marketing Small Schools."
41 Klein, *Shock Doctrine*.
42 Haney López, *Dog Whistle Politics*.
43 See Brecher, Costello, and Smith, *Globalization from Below*.
44 Meltzer, "How Education Reform Became a Wedge Issue."
45 See Reckhow, Henig, and Jacobsen, "'Outsiders with Deep Pockets.'"
46 See Robnett, *How Long*; Johnson, "Half-Life of the Black Urban Regime"; Johnson, "Panthers Can't Save Us"; Reed, *Stirrings in the Jug*; and Reed, "Post-1965 Trajectory."
47 See Brown, "Long before Sinking Roy Moore's Candidacy."
48 See Miner, "Keeping Public Schools Public"; and Spence, "Neoliberal Turn."
49 Spence, "Neoliberal Turn."
50 Saltman, *Gift of Education*.
51 McAdam, *Political Process*.
52 Arena, *Driven from New Orleans*.
53 McAdam, *Political Process*.
54 INCITE!, *Revolution Will Not Be Funded*.
55 Arena, *Driven from New Orleans*.
56 Staggenborg, "Consequences of Professionalization."
57 Arena, *Driven from New Orleans*, xxviii.

CHAPTER 4. FRAGILE ALLIANCES

 1 See Saporito, "Private Choices."
 2 See, for example, Coughlan, "Divergent Trends"; and Renzulli and Evans, "School Choice"; also see Saporito and Sohoni, "Mapping Educational Inequality."
 3 Ball and Vincent, "'I Heard It.'"
 4 Reay and Lucey, "Limits of 'Choice.'"
 5 The term "creative class" was popularized by Richard Florida in *Rise of the Creative Class*, where he argued that this growing class of workers includes the "super-creative core" (innovative workers who discover complex problems and generate solutions for new commercial products and services) and the "creative professionals" (highly educated knowledge workers), as well as creative artists and entertainers. He predicted that the creative class would be the major engine of economic growth in cities across the globe, and mapped out recommendations for cities to grow by attracting this class of workers. Critics of Florida's promotion of the creative class as a desirable engine for urban development point to the broader racial and economic inequality and

displacement that so often accompany the growth of the creative class in urban centers.

6 Butler, "Living in the Bubble," 2484.

7 Cucchiara and Horvat, "Perils and Promises."

8 Kimelberg and Billingham, "Attitudes towards Diversity."

9 Billingham, "Parental Choice."

10 Posey-Maddox, *When Middle-Class Parents Choose*.

11 Importantly, in describing her schooling experience as "boring" because it lacked diversity even though, she admits, "we had a lot of Asians," this neighborhood schools activist reproduces the problematic Black/White binary that dominates racial politics in the United States. As Alcoff argues, the Black/White binary as a dominant frame for understanding race is problematic for a number of reasons, but specifically because it marginalizes the experiences of Asian Americans and Latinx people. In negating these experiences, this dominant frame works to prevent the formation of effective coalitions between different racialized groups. Alcoff, "Latino/as, Asian Americans."

12 Cucchiara and Horvat, "Choosing Selves."

13 Dominant cultural capital can be described as inherited through family "habitus," a system of dispositions that direct action, perception, and thought. This habitus, which cultivates dominant cultural capital, predisposes advantaged children to be more successful in educational systems than less advantaged children. See Grenfell and James, *Bourdieu and Education*.

14 Tuck and Gorlewski, "Racist Ordering."

15 Valenzuela, *Subtractive Schooling*.

16 Cucchiara, *Marketing Schools*.

17 See Billingham, "Parental Choice"; and Posey-Maddox, *When Middle-Class Parents Choose*.

18 See Cucchiara and Horvat, "Perils and Promises."

19 Beamish and Luebbers, "Alliance Building."

CHAPTER 5. NO PERMANENT ENEMIES, NO PERMANENT ALLIES

1 Giroux, "Racial Injustice."

2 See Margonis and Parker, "Choice."

3 See, for example, Flanagan and Faison, *Youth Civic Development*; Ginwright, Noguera, and Cammarota, *Beyond Resistance!*; and Youniss et al., "Youth Civic Engagement."

4 McAdam, *Political Process*.

5 Piven and Cloward, *Poor People's Movements*.

6 Staggenborg, "Consequences of Professionalization."

7 Fisher, *Activism Inc.*.

8 INCITE!, *The Revolution Will Not Be Funded*.

9 Building on Foucault, Kwon characterizes "affirmative governmentality" as a product of the neoliberal turn toward self-responsibility and self-governance. In

a historical moment when youth of color face criminalization and incarceration, funders have increasingly embraced the youth nonprofit as a critical intervention that can save youth from themselves and their environments through community engagement. Kwon argues that positive youth development, a goal of philanthropic giving, aims to empower youth through self-improvement and community improvement. But institutionalizing this into the funded nonprofit structure actually blunts young activists' power to meaningfully challenge the very structural inequalities responsible for their marginalization, and instead becomes a tool for social control.

10 Kwon, *Uncivil Youth*, 72.
11 Lipman and Haines, "From Accountability to Privatization," 496.
12 On the concept of "backstage" speech, see Goffman, *Presentation of Self*.
13 See Eliasoph, *Avoiding Politics*.
14 Kwon, *Uncivil Youth*.
15 See Reed, "Post-1965 Trajectory"; and Johnson, "Panthers Can't Save Us."
16 See Noguera, "Schools, Prisons, and Social Implications"; and Skiba et al., "Race Is Not Neutral."
17 See, for example, McAdam, Tarrow, and Tilly, *Dynamics of Contention*; and Borland, "Social Movement Organizations."
18 Morgen, "Dynamics of Cooptation."

CONCLUSION

1 See, for example, Au, *Unequal by Design*; Lipman, *High Stakes Education*; Lipman, "From Accountability to Privatization"; Lipman, "Contesting the City"; Ravitch, *Death and Life*; and Saltman, *Gift of Education*.
2 See Au, "Teaching under the New Taylorism"; and Quiroz, "Marketing Diversity."
3 See Arena, *Driven from New Orleans*.
4 Warren and Mapp, *Match on Dry Grass*, 250–51.
5 See Lipman, "Cultural Politics"; Lipman, "Contesting the City"; Pedroni, "Urban Shrinkage"; and Buras, *Charter Schools*.
6 Au, "Meritocracy 2.0."
7 See Miner, "Keeping Public Schools Public"; Scott, "Rosa Parks Moment?"; and Au, "Meritocracy 2.0."
8 See Whitman, *Sweating the Small Stuff*; and Buras, *Charter Schools*.
9 Gordon, "Breaking Through and Burning Out."
10 See Klein, *Shock Doctrine*; Saltman, "Schooling in Disaster Capitalism"; and Suspitsyna, "Accountability in American Education."
11 Gordon, "Breaking Through and Burning Out"; Kwon, *Uncivil Youth*.
12 See Klein, *Shock Doctrine*.
13 Arena, *Driven from New Orleans*.
14 Saltman, *Gift of Education*.
15 Darling-Hammond, *Flat World* emphasizes deepening structural inequalities like school resegregation and a lack of access to quality curricula and qualified educa-

tors that lead to a marked "opportunity gap" for low-income students of color. She argues that this opportunity gap manifests as an achievement gap. This structural explanation stands in sharp contrast to the kind of "culture of poverty" thesis so often invoked to explain the cultural determinants of the achievement gap.

16 Friedman, *World Is Flat*.
17 See Cucchiara, *Marketing Schools*; Lipman, "Landscape of Education 'Reform'"; Lipman, *New Political Economy*; and Lipman, "Contesting the City."
18 Sassen, *Global City*; Lipman, *New Political Economy*; Lipman, "Contesting the City."
19 Billingham, "Parental Choice," 697.
20 Cucchiara, *Marketing Schools*.
21 Ravitch, *Death and Life*.
22 Beamish and Luebbers, "Alliance Building," 652.
23 Adam, "Intersectional Coalitions," 134.
24 Kwon, *Uncivil Youth*.
25 Petcoff, "Problem with Saul Alinsky."
26 See Barker, "Class Struggle and Social Movements."
27 In his study of local insurgent groups' efforts to secure international patronage, Clifford Bob's insights are instructive for understanding how coalition politics can compel distortions in movement messages. He argues that the disparity in need between locally disadvantaged groups and influential NGOs that partner with a select few of these creates an asymmetrical power relationship: "As a result, movements must alter key characteristics to meet the expectations of patrons." Bob, *Marketing of Rebellion*, 5.
28 Johnson, "Panthers Can't Save Us," 79.
29 Warren and Mapp, *Match on Dry Grass*.
30 See Horsford, Alemán, and Smith, "Our Separate Struggles," 234.
31 See Gillies, "Agile Bodies" for an overview of neoliberalism's value of "agility." In a globalized era, "agility" is now a prized goal of individuals and companies for not only adapting to quickly changing conditions, but for thriving in this competitive environment. Gillies offers a critique of how agility, as a market value, has been imported from the corporate sector into educational institutions' strategies for competition and survival. Gillies argues that agility links well to Foucault's notion of governmentality, which elucidates a process of governance that extends into the interior of the self, and transforms individuals—or in this case organizations—into tools of the market. Although Gillies discusses the movement of corporate agility into education, I would argue that this corporate agility has also moved into the survival strategies of formalized social movement organizations.
32 See Au, "Meritocracy 2.0"; Berrey, *Enigma of Diversity*; Scott, "Rosa Parks Moment?"; and Quiroz, "Marketing Diversity."
33 Cucchiara, *Marketing Schools*.
34 Billingham, "Parental Choice."
35 Warren and Mapp, *Match on Dry Grass*.

36 Reed, *Stirrings in the Jug*, 120.
37 See Arena, *Driven from New Orleans*; Johnson, "Half-Life of the Black Urban Regime"; Johnson, "Panthers Can't Save Us"; Reed, *Stirrings in the Jug*; Reed, "Post-1965 Trajectory"; and Spence, "Neoliberal Turn."
38 Reed, "Post-1965 Trajectory," 268.
39 Almeida, "Sequencing of Success."
40 McIntosh, "White Privilege."
41 Chazan, "Settler Solidarities."
42 See Rose, *Coalitions across the Class Divide* for an examination of how critical individuals, or "bridge builders," were able to forge connections across the class divides between peace, environmental, and labor movements.
43 Beamish and Luebbers, "Alliance Building."
44 Heaney and Rojas, "Hybrid Activism."
45 Lipman, "Landscape of Education 'Reform.'"
46 Jaffe, "Radical Organizing."
47 Piven, "Interdependent Power," 226.
48 Choi, Van Zandt, and Matarrita-Cascante, "Can Community Land Trusts Slow Gentrification?"
49 Romano and Franke-Ruta, "New Generation."
50 For example, see Turkewitz, "Denver Café."
51 Johnson, "Half-Life of the Black Urban Regime," 253.
52 Taylor and Van Dyke, "'Get Up, Stand Up.'"

METHODOLOGICAL APPENDIX

1 Shiller, "Marketing Small Schools."
2 See Madriz, "Focus Groups."
3 For Solorzano and Yosso, "counter-storytelling" is consistent with a broader critical race methodology. Counter-stories are a method for "telling the stories of those people whose experiences are not often told (i.e. those who are on the margins of society). The counter-story is also a tool for exposing, analyzing, and challenging the majoritarian stories of racial privilege. Counter-stories can shatter complacency, shatter the dominant discourse on race, and further the struggle for racial reform." Solorzano and Yosso, "Critical Race Methodology," 32.
4 See Dunbar, Rodriguez, and Parker, "Race, Subjectivity."
5 My critique of education reformers' good intentions parallels Gorski's critique of intercultural education, which represents another White-dominated movement in education. See Gorski, "Good Intentions Are Not Enough." Gorski characterizes most forms of intercultural education as well intended but ultimately unable to challenge unequal relations of power and privilege, in part because they are steeped in deficit perspectives of disadvantaged communities. In this same way, reformers' good intentions and civil rights advocacy ultimately fail to address the kinds of structural inequalities that produce educational disadvantage in the first place, especially with reformers' focus on deficit theory in discussing the

problems faced by low-income youth of color and their communities. See Gorski for more on his criticism of well-intended cultural competency projects that are steeped in deficit perspectives, and how to fix these in order to create a more just, "decolonized" movement for intercultural education.

6   Marcus, "Ethnography in/of the World System," 113.

7   The choice to align with the AAPP in a critical participatory action research project, however, reflects the core tenets of CPAR as an epistemology. CPAR seeks to leverage research specifically in support of altering social inequalities. As Torre et al. write, "Joining social movements and public science, critical PAR projects document the grossly uneven structural distributions of opportunities, resources and dignity; trouble ideological categories projected onto communities (delinquent, at risk, damaged, innocent, victim); and contest how science has been recruited to legitimate dominant policies and practices." Torre et al., "Critical Participatory Action Research," 2.

8   Excellent examples of CPAR research include the projects associated with the Public Science Project at the City University of New York (see Fine, *Just Research in Contentious Times*), and Ben Kirshner's work on youth activism and educational justice, *Youth Activism*, among many others.

9   Marcus, "Ethnography in/of the World System."

10 Burawoy et al., *Ethnography Unbound*.

BIBLIOGRAPHY

Abarca, Marco Antonio. "A Snapshot of Education Reform: Latino Students in DPS." *Denver Post*, September 12, 2013.

Adam, Erin M. "Intersectional Coalitions: The Paradoxes of Rights-Based Movement Building in LGBTQ and Immigrant Communities." *Law and Society Review* 51, no. 1 (2017): 132–67.

Advancement Project/Civil Rights Project. *Opportunities Suspended: The Devastating Consequences of Zero Tolerance and School Discipline*. Cambridge, MA: Civil Rights Project, 2000.

Alcoff, Linda Martin. "Latino/as, Asian Americans, and the Black-White Binary." *Journal of Ethics: An International Philosophical Review* 7, no. 1 (2003): 5–27.

Allen, Ricky Lee. "The Globalization of White Supremacy: Toward a Critical Discourse on the Racialization of the World." *Educational Theory* 51, no. 4 (2001): 467–86.

Almeida, Paul. "The Sequencing of Success: Organizing Templates and Neoliberal Policy Outcomes." *Mobilization* 13 (2008): 165–87.

Anderson, Celia, and Adrienne Dixson. "Down by the Riverside: A CRT Perspective on Education Reform in Two River Cities." *Urban Education* 51, no. 4 (2016): 363–89.

Anyon, Jean. *Ghetto Schooling: A Political Economy of Urban Education Reform*. New York: Teachers College Press, 1997.

———. *Radical Possibilities: Public Policies, Urban Education, and a New Social Movement*. New York: Routledge, 2014.

Apple, Michael. *Educating the "Right" Way: Markets, Standards, God, and Inequality*. New York: Routledge, 2006.

Arena, John. *Driven from New Orleans: How Nonprofits Betray Public Housing and Promote Privatization*. Minneapolis: University of Minnesota Press, 2012.

Asmar, Melanie. "Why the Denver School Board 'Flipped' and What Might Happen Next." *Chalkbeat*, November 7, 2019.

Au, Wayne. "Meritocracy 2.0: High-Stakes Standardized Testing as a Racial Project of Neoliberal Multiculturalism." *Educational Policy* 30, no. 1 (2016): 39–62.

———. "Teaching under the New Taylorism: High-Stakes Testing and the Standardization of the 21st Century Curriculum." *Journal of Curriculum Studies* 43, no. 1 (2011): 25–45.

———. *Unequal by Design: High-Stakes Testing and the Standardization of Inequality*. New York: Routledge, 2009.

Ball, Stephen J. *Class Strategies and the Education Market: The Middle Classes and Social Advantage*. New York: RoutledgeFalmer, 2003.

Ball, Stephen, and Carol Vincent. "'I Heard It on the Grapevine': 'Hot' Knowledge and School Choice." *British Journal of Sociology of Education* 19, no. 3 (1998): 377–400.

Barker, Colin. "Class Struggle and Social Movements." In *Marxism and Social Movements*, edited by Colin Barker, Laurence Cox, John Krinsky, and Alf Gunvald Nilsen, 41–61. Chicago: Haymarket, 2014.

Beamish, Thomas, and Amy Luebbers. "Alliance Building across Social Movements: Bridging Difference in a Peace and Justice Coalition." *Social Problems* 56 (2009): 647–76.

Bell, Derrick. "*Brown v. Board of Education* and the Interest-Convergence Dilemma." *Harvard Law Review* 93, no. 3 (1980): 518–33.

Bello, Walden. *Capitalism's Last Stand? Deglobalization in the Age of Austerity*. London: Zed, 2013.

Berrey, Ellen. *The Enigma of Diversity: The Language of Race and the Limits of Racial Justice*. Chicago: University of Chicago Press, 2015.

Billingham, Chase. "Parental Choice, Neighborhood Schools, and the Market Metaphor in Urban Education Reform." *Urban Studies* 52, no. 4 (2015): 685–701.

Blanc, Eric. "Denver Teachers Strike Back." *Jacobin*, February 11, 2019.

Bob, Clifford. *The Marketing of Rebellion: Insurgents, Media, and International Activism*. New York: Cambridge University Press, 2005.

Bonilla, Yarimar, Rima Brusi, and Natasha Lycia Ora Bannan. "6 Months after Maria, Puerto Ricans Face a New Threat—Education Reform." *Nation*, March 21, 2018.

Bonilla-Silva, Eduardo. *Racism without Racists: Color-Blind Racism and the Persistence of Racial Inequality in America*. New York: Rowman and Littlefield, 2013.

Borland, Elizabeth. "Social Movement Organizations and Coalitions: Comparisons from the Women's Movement in Buenos Aires, Argentina." In *Research in Social Movements, Conflicts and Change*, edited by Patrick G. Coy, 83–112. Bingley: Emerald Group, 2008.

Bosman, Julie, and Monica Davey. "Anger in Michigan over Appointing Emergency Managers." *New York Times*, January 22, 2016.

Bowles, Samuel, and Herbert Gintis. *Schooling in Capitalist America: Educational Reform and the Contradictions of Economic Life*. New York: Basic Books, 1976.

Brecher, Jeremy, Tim Costello, and Brendan Smith. *Globalization from Below: The Power of Solidarity*. Cambridge: South End, 2000.

Brown, DeNeen. "Long before Sinking Roy Moore's Candidacy, Black Women in Alabama Were a Force for Change." *Washington Post*, December 16, 2017.

Brown, Elizabeth, and Molly Vollman Makris. "A Different Type of Charter School: In Prestige Charters, a Rise in Cachet Equals a Decline in Access." *Journal of Education Policy* 33, no. 1 (2018): 85–117.

Bulkley, Katrina, and Jeffrey Henig. "Local Politics and Portfolio Management Models: National Reform Ideas and Local Control." *Peabody Journal of Education* 90, no. 1 (2015): 53–83.

Buras, Kristen. *Charter Schools, Race, and Urban Space: Where the Market Meets Grassroots Resistance.* New York: Routledge, 2014.

Burawoy, Michael, Alice Burton, Ann Arnett Ferguson, Kathryn Fox, Joshua Gamson, Nadine Gartrell, Leslie Hurst, Charles Kurzman, Leslie Salzinger, Josepha Schiffman, and Shiori Ui. *Ethnography Unbound: Power and Resistance in the Modern Metropolis.* Berkeley: University of California Press, 1991.

Burch, Patricia. *Hidden Markets: The New Education Privatization.* New York: Routledge, 2009.

Butler, Tim. "Living in the Bubble: Gentrification and Its 'Others' in North London." *Urban Studies* 40, no. 12 (2003): 2469–86.

Campbell, Spencer. "Why Are Achievement Gaps So Wide at Denver Public Schools?" *5280 Magazine,* November 2018.

Chazan, May. "Settler Solidarities as Praxis: Understanding 'Granny Activism' beyond the Highly-Visible." *Social Movement Studies* 15, no. 5 (2016): 457–70.

Choi, Myungshik, Shannon Van Zandt, and David Matarrita-Cascante. "Can Community Land Trusts Slow Gentrification?" *Journal of Urban Affairs* 40, no. 3 (2018): 394–411.

Clay, Kevin. "'Despite the Odds': Unpacking the Politics of Black Resilience Neoliberalism." *American Educational Research Journal* 56, no. 1 (2018): 75–110.

Coughlan, Ryan. "Divergent Trends in Neighborhood and School Segregation in the Age of School Choice." *Peabody Journal of Education* 93, no. 4 (2018): 349–66.

Cucchiara, Maia. *Marketing Schools, Marketing Cities: Who Wins and Who Loses When Schools Become Urban Amenities.* Chicago: University of Chicago Press, 2013.

Cucchiara, Maia, and Erin Horvat. "Choosing Selves: The Salience of Parental Identity in the School Choice Process." *Journal of Education Policy* 29, no. 4 (2013): 486–509.

———. "Perils and Promises: Middle-Class Parental Involvement in Urban Schools." *American Educational Research Journal* 46, no. 4 (2009): 974–1004.

Darling-Hammond, Linda. *The Flat World and Education: How America's Commitment to Equity Will Determine Our Future.* New York: Teachers College Press, 2010.

DeMoss, Susan, and Courtney Vaughn. "Reflections on Theory and Practice in Parent Involvement from a Phenomenographical Perspective." *School Community Journal* 10 (Spring–Summer 2000): 45–59.

Diamond, John B., and Kimberley Gomez. "African-American Parents' Education Orientations: The Importance of Social Class and Parents' Perceptions of Schools." *Education and Urban Society* 36, no. 4 (2004): 383–427.

Dillon, Sam. "A School Chief Takes on Tenure, Stirring a Fight." *New York Times,* November 12, 2008.

Dixson, Adrienne, Kristen Buras, and Elizabeth Jeffers. "The Color of Reform: Race, Education Reform, and Charter Schools in Post-Katrina New Orleans." *Qualitative Inquiry* 21, no. 3 (2015): 288–99.

Dumas, Michael. "'Losing an Arm': Schooling as a Site of Black Suffering." *Race Ethnicity and Education* 1, no. 1 (2014): 1–29.

Dunbar, Christopher, Dalia Rodriguez, and Laurence Parker. "Race, Subjectivity, and the Interview Process." In *Handbook of Interview Research: Context and Method*, edited by Jaber F. Gubrium and James A. Holstein, 279–98. Thousand Oaks, CA: Sage, 2001.

Einhorn, Erin. "The Extreme Sacrifice Detroit Parents Make to Access Better Schools." *Atlantic*, April 11, 2016.

Eliasoph, Nina. *Avoiding Politics: How Americans Produce Apathy in Everyday Life*. Cambridge: Cambridge University Press, 1998.

Fabricant, Michael, and Michelle Fine. *Charter Schools and the Corporate Makeover of Public Education: What's at Stake?* New York: Teachers College Press, 2012.

Fenning, Pamela, and Jennifer Rose. "Overrepresentation of African American Students in Exclusionary Discipline: The Role of School Policy." *Urban Education* 42, no. 6 (2007): 536–59.

Ferguson, Ann Arnett. *Bad Boys: Public Schools in the Making of Black Masculinity*. Ann Arbor: University of Michigan Press, 2001.

Fine, Michelle. *Framing Dropouts: Notes on the Politics of an Urban High School*. New York: State University of New York Press, 1991.

———. *Just Research in Contentious Times: Widening the Methodological Imagination*. New York: Teachers College Press, 2018.

Finnegan, William. "The Economics of Empire: Notes on the Washington Consensus." *Harper's Magazine*, May 2003.

Fisher, Dana. *Activism Inc.: How the Outsourcing of Grassroots Campaigns Is Strangling Progressive Politics in America*. Stanford: Stanford University Press, 2006.

Flanagan, Constance, and Nakesha Faison. *Youth Civic Development: Implications of Research for Social Policy and Programs*. Ann Arbor, MI: Society for Research in Child Development, 2001.

Florida, Richard. *The Rise of the Creative Class: And How It's Transforming Work, Leisure, Community and Everyday Life*. New York: Perseus, 2002.

———. *The Rise of the Creative Class Revisited*. New York: Basic Books, 2014.

Frankenberg, Erica, Chungmei Lee, and Gary Orfield. *A Multiracial Society with Segregated Schools: Are We Losing the Dream?* Cambridge: Civil Rights Project, Harvard University, 2003.

Frankenberg, Erica, Genevieve Siegel-Hawley, and Jia Wang. "Choice without Equity: Charter School Segregation and the Need for Civil Rights Standards." Los Angeles: Civil Rights Project/Proyecto Derechos Civiles, UCLA, 2010.

Friedman, Thomas. *The World Is Flat: A Brief History of the Twenty-First Century*. New York: Farrar, Straus and Giroux, 2007.

Gillies, Donald. "Agile Bodies: A New Imperative in Neoliberal Governance." *Journal of Education Policy* 26, no. 2 (2011): 207–23.

Ginwright, Shawn, Pedro Noguera, and Julio Cammarota, eds. *Beyond Resistance! Youth Activism and Community Change*. New York: Routledge, 2006.

Giroux, Henry. "Racial Injustice and Disposable Youth in the Age of Zero Tolerance." *Qualitative Studies in Education* 16, no. 4 (2003): 553–65.

Goffman, Erving. *The Presentation of Self in Everyday Life*. New York: Doubleday, 1959.

Golan, Joanne. "The Paradox of Success at a No-Excuses School." *Sociology of Education* 88, no. 2 (2015): 103–19.

Goldstein, Rebecca. "Imaging the Frame: Media Representations of Teachers, Their Unions, NCLB, and Education Reform." *Educational Policy* 25, no. 4 (2011): 543–76.

Good, Ryan. "Histories That Root Us: Neighborhood, Place and the Protest of School Closures in Philadelphia." *Urban Geography* 38, no. 6 (2014): 861–83.

Gordon, Hava. "Breaking Through and Burning Out: The Contradictory Effects of Young People's Participation in Institutionalized Movements." *Emerald Studies in Media and Communications* 14 (2017): 149–76.

Gorski, Paul. "Good Intentions Are Not Enough: A Decolonizing Intercultural Education." *Intercultural Education* 19, no. 6 (2008): 515–25.

Grenfell, Michael, and David James. *Bourdieu and Education: Acts of Practical Theory*. Bristol, PA: Falmer, 1998.

Gutstein, Eric, and Pauline Lipman. "The Rebirth of the Chicago Teachers Union and Possibilities for a Counter-Hegemonic Education Movement." *Monthly Review* 65, no. 2 (2013): 1–10.

Haney López, Ian. *Dog Whistle Politics: How Coded Racial Appeals Have Reinvented Racism and Wrecked the Middle Class*. New York: Oxford University Press, 2014.

Hannah-Jones, Nikole. "Choosing a School for My Daughter in a Segregated City." *New York Times Magazine*, June 9, 2016.

Harvey, David. *A Brief History of Neoliberalism*. Oxford: Oxford University Press, 2005.

———. "Neoliberalism as Creative Destruction." *Annals of the American Academy of Political and Social Science* 610, no. 1 (2007): 21–44.

Heaney, Michael, and Fabio Rojas. "Hybrid Activism: Social Movement Mobilization in a Multimovement Environment." *American Journal of Sociology* 119, no. 4 (2014): 1047–1103.

Horsford, Sonya Douglass, Enrique Alemán Jr., and Phillip A. Smith. "Our Separate Struggles Are Really One: Building Political Race Coalitions for Educational Justice." *Leadership and Policy in Schools* 18, no. 2 (2019): 226–36.

Hursh, David. "Assessing No Child Left Behind and the Rise of Neoliberal Education Policies." *American Educational Research Journal* 44, no. 3 (2007): 493–518.

———. "Exacerbating Inequality: The Failed Promise of the No Child Left Behind Act." *Race Ethnicity and Education* 10, no. 3 (2007): 295–308.

———. "Neo-Liberalism, Markets and Accountability: Transforming Education and Undermining Democracy in the United States and England." *Policy Futures in Education* 3, no. 1 (2005): 3–15.

INCITE!, ed. *The Revolution Will Not Be Funded: Beyond the Non-Profit Industrial Complex*. Durham: Duke University Press, 2017.

Jaffe, Sarah. "The Radical Organizing That Paved the Way for LA's Teachers' Strike." *Nation*, January 19, 2019.

Johnson, Cedric. "The Half-Life of the Black Urban Regime: Adolf Reed Jr. on Race, Capitalism, and Urban Governance." *Labor Studies Journal* 41, no. 3 (2016): 248–55.

———. "The Panthers Can't Save Us Now." *Catalyst* 1, no. 1 (2017): 57–85.

Kimelberg, Shelley, and Chase Billingham. "Attitudes towards Diversity and the School Choice Process: Middle-Class Parents in a Segregated Urban Public School District." *Urban Education* 48, no. 2 (2012): 198–231.

Kirshner, Ben. *Youth Activism in an Era of Education Inequality*. New York: New York University Press, 2015.

Klein, Naomi. *The Battle for Paradise: Puerto Rico Takes on the Disaster Capitalists*. Chicago: Haymarket, 2018.

———. *The Shock Doctrine: The Rise of Disaster Capitalism*. New York: Metropolitan Books, 2007.

Kozol, Jonathan. *Savage Inequalities: Children in America's Schools*. New York: Harper Perennial, 1992.

Kundu, Anindya, and Pedro Noguera. "Why America's Infatuation with 'Grit' Can't Solve Our Educational Dilemmas." *Virginia Policy Review* 11 (Summer 2014): 49–53.

Kwon, Soo Ah. *Uncivil Youth: Race, Activism, and Affirmative Governmentality*. Durham: Duke University Press, 2013.

Lack, Brian. "No Excuses: A Critique of the Knowledge Is Power Program (KIPP) within Charter Schools in the USA." *Journal for Critical Education Policy Studies* 7, no. 2 (2009): 126–53.

Layton, Lindsey. "Poll: Parents Don't Support Many Education Policy Changes." *Washington Post*, July 21, 2017.

Lipman, Pauline. "Contesting the City: Neoliberal Urbanism and the Cultural Politics of Education Reform in Chicago." *Discourse: Studies in the Cultural Politics of Education* 32, no. 2 (2011): 217–34.

———. "The Cultural Politics of Mixed-Income Schools and Housing: A Racialized Discourse of Displacement, Exclusion, and Control." *Anthropology and Education Quarterly* 40, no. 3 (2008): 215–36.

———. *High Stakes Education: Inequality, Globalization, and Urban School Reform*. New York: RoutledgeFalmer, 2004.

———. "The Landscape of Education 'Reform' in Chicago: Neoliberalism Meets a Grassroots Movement." *Education Policy Analysis Archives* 25, no. 54 (2017): 1–28.

———. *The New Political Economy of Urban Education: Neoliberalism, Race, and the Right to the City*. New York: Routledge, 2013.

Lipman, Pauline, and Nathan Haines. "From Accountability to Privatization and African American Exclusion: Chicago's 'Renaissance' 2010." *Educational Policy* 21, no. 3 (2007): 471–502.

Madriz, Esther. "Focus Groups in Feminist Research." In *Handbook of Qualitative Research*, 2nd ed., edited by Norman K. Denzin and Yvonna S. Lincoln, 835–50. Thousand Oaks, CA: Sage, 2001.

Marcus, George. "Ethnography in/of the World System: The Emergence of Multi-Sited Ethnography." *Annual Review of Anthropology* 24 (1995): 95–117.

Margonis, Frank, and Laurence Parker. "Choice, Privatization, and Unspoken Strategies of Containment." *Educational Policy* 9, no. 4 (1995): 375–403.

McAdam, Doug. *Political Process and the Development of Black Insurgency, 1930–1970.* 2nd ed. Chicago: University of Chicago Press, 1999.

McAdam, Doug, Sidney Tarrow, and Charles Tilly. *Dynamics of Contention.* Cambridge: Cambridge University Press, 2001.

McGray, Douglas. "Working with the Enemy." *New York Times,* January 16, 2005.

McIntosh, Peggy. "White Privilege and Male Privilege: A Personal Account of Coming to See Correspondences through Work in Women's Studies." In *Race, Class, and Gender: An Anthology,* edited by Margaret Andersen and Patricia Hill Collins, 70–81. Belmont: Wadsworth, 1992.

Mead, Sara. "The Capital of Education Reform: Put Politics Aside to Learn from the Successful Changes Michelle Rhee Brought to Washington DC Schools." *U.S. News & World Report,* April 30, 2017.

Meltzer, Erica. "How Education Reform Became a Wedge Issue among Colorado Democrats This Election Year." *Chalkbeat,* May 31, 2018.

Miner, Barbara. "Keeping Public Schools Public: Distorting the Civil Rights Legacy." *Rethinking Schools* 18, no. 3 (2004): 17–23.

Miraftab, Faranak. "Public-Private Partnerships: The Trojan Horse of Neoliberal Development?" *Journal of Planning Education and Research* 24 (2004): 89–101.

Morgen, Sandra. "The Dynamics of Cooptation in a Feminist Health Clinic." *Social Science and Medicine* 23, no. 2 (1986): 201–10.

Noguera, Pedro. "Schools, Prisons, and Social Implications of Punishment: Rethinking Disciplinary Practices." *Theory into Practice* 42, no. 4 (2003): 341–50.

Oakes, Jeannie. *Keeping Track: How Schools Structure Inequality.* 2nd ed. New Haven: Yale University Press, 2005.

Omi, Michael, and Howard Winant. *Racial Formation in the United States.* New York: Routledge, 2014.

Orfield, Gary, and Chungmei Lee. *Historic Reversals, Accelerating Resegregation, and the Need for New Integration Strategies.* Los Angeles: Civil Rights Project/Proyecto Derechos Civiles, UCLA, 2007.

Osborne, David. "The Mile-High City Leads the Way: Denver's Embrace of Charter Schools Should Serve as a Model for How to Bring School Systems into the 21st Century." *U.S. News & World Report,* May 12, 2016.

Pedroni, Thomas. "Urban Shrinkage as a Performance of Whiteness: Neoliberal Urban Restructuring, Education, and Racial Containment in the Post-Industrial, Global Niche City." *Discourse Studies in the Cultural Politics of Education* 32, no. 2 (2011): 203–13.

Petcoff, Aaron. "The Problem with Saul Alinsky." *Jacobin,* May 10, 2017.

Piven, Frances Fox. "Interdependent Power: Strategizing for the Occupy Movement." *Current Sociology* 62, no. 2 (2014): 223–31.

Piven, Frances Fox, and Richard A. Cloward. *Poor People's Movements: Why They Succeed, How They Fail.* New York: Vintage, 1979.

Pizmony-Levy, Oren, and Nancy Green Saraisky. *Who Opts Out and Why? Results from a National Survey on Opting Out of Standardized Tests.* New York: Teachers College, Columbia University, 2016.

Posey-Maddox, Linn. *When Middle-Class Parents Choose Urban Schools: Class, Race, and the Challenge of Equity in Public Education.* Chicago: University of Chicago Press, 2014.

Press, Alex. "It's Time to Acknowledge That Strikes Work." *Washington Post*, May 31, 2018.

Quiroz, Pamela A. "Marketing Diversity and the 'New' Politics of Desegregation: Overview of an Urban Education Ethnography." *Race Ethnicity and Education* 16, no. 1 (2012): 59–79.

Ravitch, Diane. *The Death and Life of the Great American School System: How Testing and Choice Are Undermining Education.* New York: Basic Books, 2016.

Reay, Diane, and Helen Lucey. "The Limits of 'Choice': Children and Inner City Schooling." *Sociology* 37, no. 1 (2003): 121–42.

Reckhow, Sarah, Jeffrey Henig, and Rebecca Jacobsen. "'Outsiders with Deep Pockets': The Nationalization of Local School Board Elections." *Urban Affairs Review* 53, no. 55 (2016): 783–811.

Reed, Adolf, Jr. "The Post-1965 Trajectory of Race, Class, and Urban Politics in the United States Reconsidered." *Labor Studies Journal* 41, no. 3 (2016): 260–91.

———. *Stirrings in the Jug: Black Politics in the Post-Segregation Era.* Minneapolis: University of Minnesota Press, 1999.

Renzulli, Linda, and Lorraine Evans. "School Choice, Charter Schools, and White Flight." *Social Problems* 52, no. 3 (2005): 398–418.

Rivzi, Fazal, and Bob Lingard. "Globalization and Education: Complexities and Contingencies." *Educational Theory* 50, no. 4 (2000): 419–26.

Robertson, Susan, and Hugh Lauder. "Restructuring the Education/Social Class Relation: A Class Choice?" In *Education Reform and the State: Twenty-Five Years of Politics, Policy, and Practice*, edited by Robert Phillips and John Furlong, 222–36. New York: RoutledgeFalmer, 2001.

Robnett, Belinda. *How Long, How Long? African-American Women in the Struggle for Civil Rights.* New York: Oxford University Press, 1997.

Romano, Andrew, and Garance Franke-Ruta. "A New Generation of Anti-Gentrification Radicals Are on the March in Los Angeles and around the Country." *HuffPost*, March 5, 2018.

Rose, Fred. *Coalitions across the Class Divide: Lessons from the Labor, Peace, and Environmental Movements.* Ithaca: Cornell University Press, 2000.

Rotberg, Iris. "Charter Schools and the Risk of Increased Segregation." *Phi Delta Kappan* 95, no. 5 (2014): 26–31.

Saltman, Kenneth J. *Collateral Damage: Corporatizing Public Schools—A Threat to Democracy.* Lanham: Rowman and Littlefield, 2000.

———. *The Gift of Education: Public Education and Venture Philanthropy.* New York: Palgrave Macmillan, 2010.

———. "Schooling in Disaster Capitalism: How the Political Right Is Using Disaster to Privatize Public Schooling." *Teacher Education Quarterly* 34, no. 2 (2007): 131–56.

Saporito, Salvatore. "Private Choices, Public Consequences: Magnet School Choice and Segregation by Race and Poverty." *Social Problems* 50, no. 2 (2003): 181–203.

Saporito, Salvatore, and Deenesh Sohoni. "Mapping Educational Inequality: Concentrations of Poverty among Poor and Minority Students in Public Schools." *Social Forces* 85 (2007): 1227–53.

Sassen, Saskia. *The Global City*. Princeton: Princeton University Press, 1991.

Scott, Janelle. "Market-Driven Education Reform and the Racial Politics of Advocacy." *Peabody Journal of Education* 86 (2011): 580–99.

———. "A Rosa Parks Moment? School Choice and the Marketization of Civil Rights." *Critical Studies in Education* 54, no. 1 (2012): 5–18.

———. "School Choice and the Empowerment Imperative." *Peabody Journal of Education* 88, no. 1 (2013): 60–73.

Shaker, Paul, and Elizabeth Heilman. "The New Common Sense of Education: Advocacy Research versus Academic Authority." *Teachers College Record* 106, no. 7 (2004): 1444–70.

Shiller, Jessica. "Marketing Small Schools in New York City: A Critique of Neoliberal School Reform." *Educational Studies* 47, no. 2 (2011): 160–73.

Shiva, Vandana. *Staying Alive: Women, Ecology, and Development*. Berkeley: North Atlantic Books, 2016.

Skiba, Russell J., Robert Horner, Choong-Geun Chung, M. Karega Rausch, Seth L. May, and Tary Tobin. "Race Is Not Neutral: A National Investigation of African American and Latino Disproportionality in School Discipline." *School Psychology Review* 40, no. 1 (2011): 85–107.

Sleeter, Christine. "Equity, Democracy, and Neoliberal Assaults on Teacher Education." *Teaching and Teacher Education* 24, no. 8 (2008): 1947–57.

Smiley, CalvinJohn, and David Fakunle. "From 'Brute' to 'Thug': The Demonization and Criminalization of Unarmed Black Male Victims in America." *Journal of Human Behavior in the Social Environment* 26 (2016): 350–66.

Solorzano, Daniel, and Tara Yosso. "Critical Race Methodology: Counter-Storytelling as an Analytical Framework for Education Research." *Qualitative Inquiry* 8, no. 1 (2002): 23–44.

Sondel, Beth. "Raising Citizens, or Raising Test Scores? Teach for America, 'No Excuses' Charters, and the Development of the Neoliberal Citizen." *Theory and Research in Social Education* 43, no. 3 (2015): 289–313.

Spence, Lester. "The Neoliberal Turn in Black Politics." *Souls* 14, nos. 3–4 (2012): 139–59.

Staggenborg, Suzanne. "The Consequences of Professionalization and Formalization in the Pro-Choice Movement." *American Sociological Review* 53, no. 4 (1988): 585–605.

Stahl, Garth. *Ethnography of a Neoliberal School*. New York: Routledge, 2017.

Stephen, Lynn. *Women and Social Movements in Latin America: Power from Below*. Austin: University of Texas Press, 1997.

Strauss, Valerie. "Dark Money Just Keeps on Coming in School Board Races." *Washington Post*, October 29, 2017.

———. "Why Hunger Strikers Are Risking Their Health to Save a Chicago Public High School." *Washington Post*, August 29, 2015.

Suspitsyna, Tatiana. "Accountability in American Education as a Rhetoric and a Technology of Governmentality." *Journal of Education Policy* 25, no. 5 (2010): 567–86.

Taylor, Verta, and Nella Van Dyke. "'Get Up, Stand Up': Tactical Repertoires of Social Movements." In *The Blackwell Companion to Social Movements*, edited by David A. Snow, Sarah A. Soule, and Hanspeter Kriesi, 262–93. Oxford: Blackwell, 2004.

Torre, Maria Elena, Michelle Fine, Brett Stout, and Madeline Fox. "Critical Participatory Action Research as Public Science." In *APA Handbook of Research Methods in Psychology*, edited by Harris Cooper and Paul Camic, 171–84. Washington, DC: American Psychological Association, 2012.

Tuck, Eve, and Julie Gorlewski. "Racist Ordering, Settler Colonialism, and EdTPA: A Participatory Policy Analysis." *Educational Policy* 30, no. 1 (2016): 197–217.

Turkewitz, Julie. "Denver Café 'Happily Gentrifying'? Neighbors Aren't So Happy." *New York Times*, November 27, 2017.

Valenzuela, Angela. *Subtractive Schooling: U.S.-Mexican Youth and the Politics of Caring*. Albany: State University of New York Press, 1999.

Van Dyke, Nella, and Holly J. McCammon. "Introduction: Social Movement Coalition Formation." In *Strategic Alliances: Coalition Building and Social Movements*, edited by Nella Van Dyke and Holly J. McCammon, xi–xxviii. Minneapolis: University of Minnesota Press, 2010.

Warren, Mark, and Karen Mapp. *A Match on Dry Grass: Community Organizing as a Catalyst for School Reform*. New York: Oxford University Press, 2011.

Weber, Rachel. "Extracting Value from the City: Neoliberalism and Urban Redevelopment." *Antipode* 34, no. 3 (2002): 519–40.

Welner, Kevin. "The Dirty Dozen: How Charter Schools Influence Student Enrollment." *Teachers College Record*, April 2013, www.tcrecord.org ID Number 17104.

Whitman, David. *Sweating the Small Stuff: Inner-City Schools and the New Paternalism*. Washington, DC: Thomas B. Fordham Institute Press, 2008.

Whyte, William F. "Advancing Scientific Knowledge through Participatory Action Research." *Sociological Forum* 4, no. 3 (1989): 367–85.

Wilson, James, and George Kelling. "The Police and Neighborhood Safety: Broken Windows." *Atlantic* 127 (1982): 29–38.

Wingert, Pat. "Best and Worst Cities for School Reform." *Newsweek*, August 24, 2010.

Yang, K. Wayne. "Rites to Reform: The Cultural Production of the Reformer in Urban Schools." *Anthropology and Education Quarterly* 41, no. 2 (2010): 144–60.

Yosso, Tara. "Whose Culture Has Capital? A Critical Race Theory Discussion of Community Cultural Wealth." *Race, Ethnicity and Education* 8, no. 1 (2005): 69–91.

Youniss, James, Susan Bales, Verona Christmas-Best, Marcelo Diversi, Milbrey McLaughlin, and Rainer Silbereisen. "Youth Civic Engagement in the Twenty-First Century." *Journal of Research on Adolescence* 12, no. 1 (2002): 121–48.

INDEX

AAPP. *See* African American Parent
    Project
academic achievement: in middle-class
    culture, 82; school uniforms and, 82–
    84; as social justice goal, 81
accountability, in education reform: as
    coalition value, 64–68; community
    groups' role in, 66–67; demonstration
    of, 67; as empowerment, 67; language
    of, 66–67; in managerialist paradigm,
    66; in neoliberalism, 66; in "no perma-
    nent enemies, no permanent allies"
    approach, 187–89; parents' role in,
    66–67; resegregation of schools and,
    73–74; Urban Parent Network and,
    188–89
accountability mechanisms, for schools:
    in neoliberal education reform, 39–40,
    213–15; under No Child Left Behind
    Act, 16, 18–22, 34; school choice and, 29
accumulation by dispossession, 22
achievement gaps: within Denver Public
    Schools system, race as factor in, 49;
    for low-income students, 81; racial
    justice and, 65–66; systemic racism as
    influence on, 80–81
activism: in Denver, history of, 207–8;
    gentrification and, 99; institutional-
    ized, 7, 189; school reform and, 2; of
    teachers, 1; triple shift of, 100; youth,
    187, 231. *See also* African American
    Parent Project; Community Education
    Collective; Democrats for Educational
    Justice; non-institutionalized activism

activists, for education reform: against
    neoliberal reforms, 5; privatization of
    schools for, 5; on school choice, resis-
    tance to, 5; against school reform, 5
Adam, Erin, 230–31
adequate yearly progress levels (AYP
    levels), under NCLB Act, 16, 21
affirmative governmentality, 187
African American communities: Black
    professional class in, 37; Black work-
    ing class in, 37; Central High (Den-
    ver) and, 43; in Chicago, displacement
    of, 40; city services in, shuttering of,
    31; closure of Central High and, long-
    term impacts of, 93–94; Community
    Education Collective and, 58; com-
    munity interests, conflicts over, 102;
    community mobilization within, 4; in
    critical participatory action research,
    248–51; cultural capital of, 78–79;
    Democrats for Educational Justice
    and, 135; displacement through
    neocolonialism, 32; dispossession of,
    91; divisions about education reform
    within, 101–2; education reform and,
    personal experiences of, 103–22;
    exclusion from education reform
    movement, 99, 103–9; experiences of
    education reform, 103–22; Family of
    Central organization and, 106; "hap-
    py talk" about school performance
    in, 116; lack of expertise in, 68–73;
    loss of power in, with charter schools,
    112–13; marginalization of, 99;

Ravitch, Diane, 20, 225
Reagan, Ronald, 18, 262n8
Reed, Adolf, Jr., 37, 74, 101–2, 201, 237–38
reform. *See* education reform; neoliberal education reform
reformer-community alliances, 92
reformers. *See* community activism and activists; community organizing; neoliberal education reform; youth activism and activists
resegregation of schools: accountability as coalition value in, 73–74; charter schools and, 76; in Denver, 1; in low-income neighborhoods, 73–79; remaking of school communities through, 73–79; through school choice, 27, 74–75, 144–45, 155; urgency as coalition value in, 73–74; White resistance and, 77
resistance movements: African Americans' role in, 137–38; against classism, 9; against neoliberalism, 9; against racism, 9. *See also* social movements
resistant capital, 120
The Revolution Will Not Be Funded, 186
Rhee, Michelle, 96–98, 261n10; on parents' resistance to reform movement, 97; reform agenda for, 109
Richards, Darren, 127
Ridgeview High School (Denver), 148–49; co-location of, 176–77
Rise of the Creative Class (Florida), 270n5
Rojas, Fabio, 240

Saltman, Kenneth, 30, 55
sanctions, under No Child Left Behind Act, 16
Sassen, Saskia, 31
Savage Inequalities (Kozol), 16, 27
school choice: accountability issues and, 29; activist resistance to, 5; advisors for, 110; for African American parents, 165; African American parents on, negative

assessment of, 111; antiracist individuality and, 34; after *Brown v. Board of Education*, 27; in civil rights agenda, 26, 28; community power negatively affected by, 112–13; consumerist model of, 124; criticisms of, 27, 109, 113; in Denver, availability of, 47; under DeVos, expansion of, 17; differentiated learning opportunities influenced by, 30; as dispossession, 109–13; duplicity of, 111; early childhood education programs, 110; economic class and, 189; educational equity through, 27; in education marketplace, 26, 89; for elite White reformers, as consumer decision, 95; as exclusionary, 110–11; governance types and, 26; growth of, 26; through "hot knowledge," 28; McDonwell Elementary School and, 165–66; in neoliberal education reform, 39–40, 109, 144; privilege and, 28; race as factor in, 29, 189; racial justice through, 27; as reflection of gentrification, 113; rejection of, 147–51; resegregation of schools as result of, 27, 74–75, 144–45, 155; standardized testing and, 28–29; White activists' rejection of, 156–61; after White flight, 27. *See also* charter schools; education markets
school closures: activist resistance to, 5; in African American communities, 21–22; in Chicago, 21; for neighborhood schools, protests over, 4; shuttering of city services and, 31. *See also* Central High
school communities, resegregation of, 73–79
school reform: activist resistance as result of, 2; community mobilization as result of, 2; as experiments, 1; in media, 3; under No Child Left Behind Act, 2. *See also* neighborhood schools
schools. *See* public schools

ABOUT THE AUTHOR

HAVA RACHEL GORDON is Associate Professor of Sociology at the University of Denver.

Made in United States
North Haven, CT
24 January 2023

31586121R00189